The Calculator Afloat

The Calculator Afloat

A MARINER'S GUIDE TO THE ELECTRONIC CALCULATOR

By Henry H. Shufeldt and Kenneth E. Newcomer

NAVAL INSTITUTE PRESS
Annapolis, Maryland

Library of Congress Cataloging in Publication Data

Shufeldt, H H   1898–
  The calculator afloat.

  Edition of 1972 published under title: Slide rule
for the mariner.
  Bibliography: p.
  Includes index.
  1. Calculating-machines.   2. Navigation—Problems,
exercises, etc.   I. Newcomer, Kenneth E., 1946–
joint author.   II. Title.
VK587.S48 1980   623.89′076   80-81091
ISBN   0-87021-116-1

Printed in the United States of America

Dedicated to the memory
of the founding members
of the Guild of the
Holy Trinity, a fraternity of
pilots and navigators founded
in England in 1514 during the
reign of Henry VIII.

"Of all the inventions and improvements the wit and industry of man has discovered and brought to perfection, none seems to be so universally urgent, profitable and necessary as the Art of Navigation."

John Locke
1632–1704

Contents

Foreword

This book, in effect, is a second edition of *Slide Rule for the Mariner*, published in 1972, which contained formulae for the rapid solution of many problems in navigation and other areas of concern to the mariner. Since then, a new and very powerful tool, the scientific calculator, capable of solving trigonometric problems involving sines, cosines, tangents, cotangents, and logs, has become available at a price comparable to that of a good slide rule. The calculator can solve the same problems, and more, with greater rapidity, and with far greater accuracy.

The Calculator Afloat contains the same formulae, in some cases restated for use with the calculator, plus many others. It is intended for users of all types of scientific calculators, from the simplest to the most advanced programmable types.

Since calculators vary considerably in their manner of operation, some using the algebraic and some the Reverse Polish Notation, with very considerable differences in the methods of keying in entries, we have confined ourselves for the most part to stating the formulae designed to solve the various problems and left the keying procedure to the readers, on the assumption that they are familiar with the operation of their own calculators. In some cases, however, it has appeared desirable to tabulate keying instructions, rather than formulae. All the formulae included may be solved by a calculator having trigonometric functions. Some solutions may be facilitated if the calculator is equipped to convert between polar and rectangular coordinates, while others may be speeded up if the calculator has a summation capability. Examples of the use of these features are included. We have made every effort to make these instructions, as well as the entire text, as understandable as possible to the mariner who has not majored in mathematics.

Among the new material in this text is a section including the basic formulae covering ship stability and trim, as well as new long-term almanacs which yield an improved degree of accuracy for the reduction of observations of the Sun and of the selected stars for the remainder of the twentieth century. A method of regaining longitude by lunar distance measurements with the sextant is included, that requires only a few minutes for "clearing," rather than the very time-consuming solution by use of log tables required in earlier times. Also presented is material that illustrates how modern methods and tools have simplified the practice of celestial navigation.

In the scientific calculator, the mariner has a new tool, capable of rendering a speedy solution of even highly complex problems, and with a degree of accuracy not attainable by the use of most tables. In celestial navigation, for example, the calculator permits the navigator to reduce a round of sights from a dead reckoning or estimated position, rather than having to employ a series of assumed positions, thus not only saving time in plotting, but also doing away with the errors arising from long intercepts sometimes caused by the use of assumed positions.

We trust this volume will help the mariner put his calculator to the best use; *however, we urge that he under no circumstances go to sea without almanac, reduction tables, and so on, and the knowledge of how to use them.*

In closing, we wish to express our thanks to Alan S. Bagley for the elegant and extremely short sight reduction algorithm, and to Frederick P. Blau for the use of the "best fit" method. Also we thank Mortimer Rogoff for pointing out the importance of a statistical approach in navigation, and Bruce C. Nehrling for contributing the section on ship stability. John S. Letcher, Jr. kindly permitted us to use his formulae for clearing the lunar distance, and Constance M. MacDonald assisted greatly in editing the text. Finally, Susan W. Wheatly not only did a superb job of typing, but was most helpful in arranging the material.

The Calculator Afloat

1

Review of Procedures

Introduction

What Is a Scientific Calculator?

Many navigators have used the slide rule to assist them in navigational calculations. They are familiar with its many different scales for doing various mathematical jobs: performing multiplication and division, providing trigonometric functions and their inverses, computing logarithms, and so on. Until the early 1970s, the only functions that could be handled by inexpensive electronic calculators were the four basic arithmetic operations +, −, ×, and ÷. With the advent of scientific calculators a whole new world of computing power was opened up. Virtually all of the slide rule's jobs could be done with the greatest of ease, in an instant, and with unprecedented accuracy.

Today, calculators having all the functions of a slide rule are available for only a few tens of dollars; these are the scientific calculators. Not only do they perform elementary arithmetic with nary an error, but also they compute trigonometric, logarithmic, and many other useful functions. Some are even able to remember a sequence of keystrokes, repeating it on command without a mistake. Having a programmable scientific calculator is like having a slide rule that moves its own cursor.

The scientific calculator not only has made possible a degree of accuracy not attainable with the conventional table of logarithms, but also has speeded problem solution. We are reminded of the words of

Edward Wright, in the second edition of his *Certaine Errors in Naviga-tion* (1610): ". . . in our time the whole Art of Navigation is growne to much greater perfection, then . . . ever it had in any former ages."

What Features Are Most Important?

One of the most important requirements of a scientific calculator purchased to perform navigational computations is the ability to handle trigonometric functions. Sine, cosine, tangent, and their inverses are essential to all but the simplest problems in navigation. Furthermore, the calculator intended for marine use should be able to evaluate trigonometric functions for all angles, not just those in the range of 0° to 90°. Preferably it should have the powerful feature of polar to rectangular coordinate conversion by which a sine and a cosine can be computed simultaneously or an arc tangent resolved into its proper quadrant without having to resort to applying a rule.

A second useful feature is memory, a place to save several intermediate results for later use, without having to reenter them.

Another desirable feature on a scientific calculator to be used for navigation is an ability to cope with elementary statistics: accumulating sums and computing mean and standard deviation. With such a feature it becomes easier to minimize errors in observational data.

A most desirable feature to seek in a scientific calculator is programmability: the ability to retain and reproduce a series of keystrokes to solve a particular type of problem. Although it is possible to carry out most, if not all, of the procedures in this book on virtually any scientific calculator, it is impractical to carry out some advanced procedures on any but a programmable calculator. The benefit of programmability can hardly be overemphasized. Having your keystrokes stored in a calculator's program memory means that they can be repeated the same way time after time.

Some calculators even have a "nonvolatile" memory which draws so little current that a program is retained even when the calculator is switched off.

Many programmable calculators have decision-making ability; for example, they can make a comparison between the contents of the x-register and that of the y-register. If x is greater than y, they follow a predetermined routine; alternatively, if y is the greater, they follow a different routine. Similarly, if the contents of the x-register has a positive value, they follow one routine to arrive at an answer; if x is negative, they follow a different routine.

The scientific calculator replaces tables of values. The programmable calculator looks up those values and then does meaningful calculations with them. Thus, the job of evaluating mathematical expressions is replaced with the more important one of evaluating the results of the calculations.

Keystroke Notation

Whereas scientific calculators are very similar in regard to the types of calculations they can perform, they often differ in the actual key-strokes used to effect those calculations. Throughout this book we shall deal with two idealized calculators, an algebraic model and the Reverse Polish Notation model. Keystrokes will be indicated by placing the name of the function in a box representing a key even though the actual keystrokes for that function on a given calculator may involve one or more other keys as well. For example, if we were to calculate the angle whose sine is 0.5, we would want to calculate $\sin^{-1}(0.5)$, which would be shown as

$$\text{Keystrokes}$$
$$0.5 \boxed{\text{SIN}^{-1}}$$

whereas on various calculators it could involve more than just one key:

$$0.5 \boxed{\text{h}} \boxed{\text{SIN}^{-1}} \qquad 0.5 \boxed{\text{SIN}^{-1}} \qquad 0.5 \boxed{\text{INV}} \boxed{\text{SIN}}$$

Numbers entered through the keyboard will be shown simply as numbers. It may be necessary to press $\boxed{\text{CHS}}$ or $\boxed{+/-}$ to change the sign of a number being entered. For example, the evaluation of the expression

$$y = \cos(-30°)$$

would be indicated as

$$-30° \boxed{\text{COS}}$$

even though the actual keystrokes might be

$$30 \boxed{\text{CHS}} \boxed{\text{f}} \boxed{\text{COS}} \qquad \text{or} \qquad 30 \boxed{+/-} \boxed{\text{COS}}$$

Relevant displays will be shown in a separate column:

Keystrokes	Display
$-30 \boxed{\text{SIN}}$	-0.5

Calculator Operation

Scientific calculators are available with two different methods of operation. On an algebraic calculator the expression

$$y = 2 + 3 - 4$$

is evaluated using these keystrokes:

Keystrokes   Display

2 $\boxed{+}$ 3 $\boxed{-}$ 4 $\boxed{=}$ 1

On an RPN calculator, the same expression is evaluated as follows:

Keystrokes   Display

2 $\boxed{\text{ENTER↑}}$ 3 $\boxed{+}$ 4 $\boxed{-}$ 1

the difference being that the algebraic calculator waits until the entire expression has been keyed in to evaluate it, whereas the RPN calculator evaluates small portions of the expression as each operation is performed. For more complicated expressions, the difference is more subtle. Suppose, for example, that we wished to evaluate the expression

$$x = 4 \sin 30° + 8 \tan 45°$$

We shall place the keystrokes side by side to show their surprising similarity:

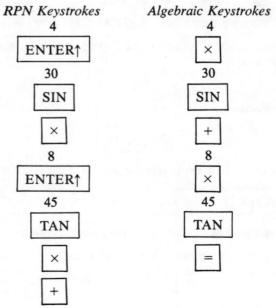

Notice that for any but the arithmetical operations, the keys are pressed in the same order in both calculation systems. In the RPN system, all operations are performed after the appropriate numbers have been keyed in. In the algebraic system, arithmetic operations are used between numerical inputs, and other operations are performed after the appropriate inputs.

In the example given above, the | ENTER↑ | function was used in the RPN keystrokes to tell the calculator that a first number was complete and that a second was to be keyed in. RPN calculators have a readily accessible *stack* or list of recently input values. This stack is manipulated by the | ENTER↑ |, | ROLL↑ |, | ROLL↓ |, and | x⇌y | keys. Algebraic calculators retain a stack of pending operations as well as a stack of values. However, this stack is not to be manipulated. (Note: For RPN calculators not having the "roll up" key, the same result may be achieved by substituting three strokes on the "roll down" key.)

Many of the examples in this book are sufficiently complicated that intermediate results have been shown in the equations. Usually these intermediate results are shown rounded to four places past the decimal point. The answers, however, are shown as they would be computed from carrying all intermediate results to their full precision.

Example: Evaluate the expression

$$X = \frac{a}{b} \times c$$

for $a = 2$, $b = 3$, and $c = 6$.

$$X = \frac{2}{3} \times 6$$

$$X = 0.6667 \times 6$$

$$X = 4.0000$$

The answer shown is 4.0000 even though starting with the intermediate expression would yield 4.0002.

Use of Scientific Functions

The functions on a scientific calculator can be somewhat intimidating at first. Perhaps an explanation of what the mnemonics mean will take away some of the mystery of the keyboard of the scientific calculator.

Mathematical Functions Found on Scientific Calculators

Symbol or mnemonic	Name (colloquial)	Meaning	Use for navigation
$\dfrac{1}{x}$	Multiplicative inverse (1 over x)	1 divided by x.	Used whenever you have computed the denominator first by mistake.
$10\uparrow x$ or 10^x	10 to the x	10 raised to the power x.	Used when computing anti-logarithms.
ABS or $|x|$	Absolute value	$|x| = \begin{cases} x; & \text{when } x \geq 0 \\ -x; & \text{when } x < 0 \end{cases}$	Used when the sign of a number would get in the way.
CHS or +/−	Change sign	Change the sign of x.	Used for negative number input or to correct a subtraction when the subtrahend was keyed in last.
D → R	Degrees to radians	Converts degrees to radians.	Sometimes used for spherical trigonometry.
R → D	Radians to degrees	Converts radians to degrees.	
$E\uparrow x$ or e^x	Exponential function (e to the x)	e raised to the power x.	
FACT or n!	Factorial	$n\,(n-1)(n-2)\cdots(1)$.	Determines odds in gambling games.
FRC or FP	Fractional part	The decimal-fraction portion of a number.	Useful for finding the proper quadrant for 28,799.24°.

HMS or H → HMS	Hours–minutes–seconds	Converts angles from sexagesimal representation to decimals.	Very useful for dealing with navigation's basic measurement: the angle.
HMS + HMS −	HMS addition HMS subtraction	Sexagesimal addition. Sexagesimal subtraction.	Useful for computing with times or angles. Super for interpolating in an almanac.
HR or HMS → H	Hours	Converts angles from sexagesimal representation to decimals.	Very useful for converting almanac values into calculator-compatible values.
INT	Integer part	The nonfraction portion of a number.	Useful for finding the number of cycles in 28,799.24°.
LST x or LAST x	Last x	Value of x before last operation (found on RPN calculators).	Convenient for undoing mistakes.
LN	Natural logarithm	Logarithm to the base e ($= 2.71828 \ldots$).	For rhumb-line calculations.
LOG	Common logarithm	Logarithm to the base 10.	
MEAN or $\bar{x}$	Mean of a set of values. x-bar	Statistical average.	Useful for improving accuracy of measurements by repetition.
MOD	Modulo	$a \bmod b = a - \left(\left[\dfrac{a}{b} \right] \times b \right)$ in which $\left[\dfrac{a}{b} \right]$ is the largest integer less than or equal to $\dfrac{a}{b}$	Useful for finding proper quadrant for 28,799.24°.

Symbol or mnemonic	Name (colloquial)	Meaning	Use for Navigation
OCT	Decimal to octal	Converts numbers in base 10 to base 8.	Not useful for navigation.
P → R	Polar to rectangular	Converts between two coordinate systems.	Extremely useful for vector problems and spherical trigonometry.
R → P	Rectangular to polar		
%	Percent	Computes percentage or percent of, depending on calculator.	Useless.
%CH	Percent change	Computes relative change.	Useful for interpolation.
SDEV or σ	Standard deviation	Square root of variance, a statistical parameter.	Useful for estimating improved accuracy of repeated measurements.
Σ+ Σ−	Summation plus and minus.	Accumulates data for statistical analysis.	Allows easy statistical analysis of data.
SQRT or $\sqrt{x}$	Square root of x.	Value of y satisfying $y^2 = x$.	Occurs often in vector problems.
x↑2 or x^2	Square of x.	x times x.	Occurs often in trigonometry.
y↑x or y^x	y to the x	y raised to the power of x.	Used in rhumb-line calculation.

ACOS or $\cos^{-1}$	arc cosine inverse cosine	The angle whose cosine is x.	
ASIN or $\sin^{-1}$	arc sine inverse sine	The angle whose sine is x.	
ATAN or $\tan^{-1}$	arc tangent inverse tangent	The angle whose tangent is x.	Don't buy a calculator without these functions.
COS	cosine	Ratio of adjacent side and hypotenuse of a right triangle.	
SIN	sine	Ratio of opposite side and hypotenuse of a right triangle.	
TAN	tangent	Ratio of opposite and adjacent sides of a right triangle.	

The keys are loosely grouped for reasons that seemed logical to the manufacturer. The numbers are located in the lower four- or five-row "numeric pad." The numeric pad also contains the decimal point key, a key for changing a number's algebraic sign, a key for entering powers of 10, the four arithmetic operators, and either an

| ENTER↑ | or an | = | key. The remainder of the keys are for

manipulation of numbers and for the other mathematical operations. Sometimes these functions are accessed by pressing a shift key and then another key. For the sake of this discussion, however, we shall mention the functions as if the calculator had a huge keyboard.

Elementary Statistics in Navigation

Navigators measure many things, often trying to attain great accuracy, but few employ measurement-improving statistical techniques. This neglect may be due, in part, to lack of knowledge of the benefits of these techniques, but probably it is due, mostly, to the apparent difficulty of the statistical formulae.

Statistical formulae should prove no barrier to the navigator armed with a little knowledge and a scientific calculator. Advanced scientific calculators have built-in statistical functions, and even the simplest calculators can be employed to reduce data by the methods discussed below.

All measurements are subject to error. Errors arise from many sources, but are primarily due to instrumentation accuracy, observer skill, and variations in the subject being measured. Various assumptions may be made regarding the distribution of errors, but it is sufficient for our purposes to assume that a given measurement will be the sum of some true value and a small random value that changes from measurement to measurement.

Suppose a horizontal sextant angle is to be measured between two stationary objects, say, a lighthouse and a prominent landmark. The true value of this angle might be 35°, but because it is difficult to superimpose the image of the lighthouse exactly on that of the landmark, various values, such as those tabulated below, might be obtained:

34°25'
35°18'
34°15'
34°42'
35°02'

In this example, some values measured are as close as 2' to the true value, and others are as much as 45' away. Our best guess, in this case, is the average of the five measurements, 34°44.4'. An average, or "mean" as it is sometimes called, is obtained by adding up the items and dividing the resulting sum by the number of items. Since it is impossible to know how many items there will be, we use this compact notation, involving the Greek Σ (sigma), equivalent to an English S for "sum":

$$\text{Mean} = \bar{x} = \frac{\sum_{i=1}^{n} x_i}{n}$$

The i is called an index; it is a counter enabling us to differentiate among the x's. The symbol for "mean," $\bar{x}$, is pronounced "x-bar." In the above example, $n = 5$, so we would write

$$\bar{x} = \frac{\sum_{i=1}^{5} x_i}{5} = \frac{x_1 + x_2 + x_3 + x_4 + x_5}{5}$$

A measure of how good our mean $\bar{x}$ is can be obtained by computing two statistical parameters: the *best estimate of the standard deviation,* usually denoted by s, and the *standard deviation of the mean,* usually denoted by σ_m. The value of s is given by the formula

$$s = \sqrt{\frac{\Sigma(x_i - \bar{x})^2}{n - 1}}$$

which can be rearranged to a form that is sometimes more convenient for calculation:

$$s = \sqrt{\frac{n}{n - 1} (\overline{x^2} - \bar{x}^2)}$$

and σ_m is given by the formula

$$\sigma_m = \frac{s}{\sqrt{n}}$$

in which

$$\overline{x^2} = \frac{\sum_{i=1}^{n} x_i^2}{n}$$

is the mean squared value or the average of the values squared, and

$$\bar{x} = \frac{\sum_{i=1}^{n} x_i}{n}$$

is the mean value, or the average of the values.

The statistical significance of $\bar{x}$ and σ_m is that any single measurement has a 68% chance of being within $\pm s$ of the true mean, and any mean of n measurements has a 68% chance of being within $\pm \sigma_m$ of the true mean. Thus, for our set of five measured angles, we can compute

$$\bar{x} = 34°44'24''$$

$$s \cong 26''$$

$$\sigma_m = 11''$$

We can say that although any one of our measurements is probably ($P = 68\%$) within $26''$ of the true mean value, the mean of the five measurements we took is probably ($P = 68\%$) no more than $11''$ away from the true mean. Incidentally, there is a 95% chance of being within $\pm 25''$ of the true mean.

Since, by taking only one measurement, we have no way of estimating the standard deviation, we can say very little about our measurement beyond reporting the single value. However, by taking as few as five measurements, not only do we have an idea of the size of the errors that may be perturbing our measurements, but also we obtain a reduction in the effect of those errors by a factor $\sqrt{5} \cong 2.2$. We can even determine how many more measurements must be made to reduce the error to some even smaller value, say, $\sigma_m = 5''$.

Since

$$\sigma_m = \frac{s}{\sqrt{n}} = \frac{26''}{\sqrt{n}}$$

we see that

$$n = \left(\frac{26''}{\sigma_m} \right)^2 = \left(\frac{26''}{5} \right)^2 = 27$$

Therefore, 27 readings are needed to reduce σ_m to $5''$.

Most scientific calculators have a statistical function called $\Sigma +$. This function accumulates the sums and the sums of the squares of values input in addition to maintaining a count of the inputs. That is, Σx, Σx^2, and n are saved in the calculator's memory. The mean is then obtained by pressing a key marked $\bar{x}$, mean, or m, and the standard deviation is obtained by pressing one marked s, σ, or DEV. Some calculators allow the input of two sets of values simultaneously. These calculators save not only Σx, Σx^2, and n, but also Σy, Σy^2 and a "cross-product" term Σxy. The utility of having these sums will be discussed later.

Should your calculator lack a $\Sigma +$ key, you need not despair. The following shows how countless means and standard deviations have been computed in other ways, the temporary answers being stored by that time-honored memory device, pencil and paper.

Example: You have measured the level of fuel in a tank using a dipstick. Because your vessel is moving, there is some variation in the level, and you would like to obtain an improvement in your measurement. The levels obtained were 13.5 in., 15 in., 14.25 in., and 14 in.

First, we compute the mean:

$$\bar{x} = \frac{\sum_{i=1}^{4} x_i}{4} = \frac{13.5 + 15 + 14.25 + 14}{4} = 14.1875 \cong 14.2$$

Then, we fill out this table column by column:

i	x_i	$x_i - \bar{x}$	$(x_i - \bar{x})^2$
1.	13.5	−0.7	0.49
2.	15	0.8	0.64
3.	14.25	0.05	0.0025
4.	14	0.2	0.04

and we can then compute s and σ_m:

$$s = \sqrt{\frac{\sum_{i=1}^{4} (x_i - \bar{x})^2}{4 - 1}}$$

$$= .6252$$

$$\sigma_m = \frac{s}{\sqrt{n}} = \frac{.6252}{\sqrt{4}} = .3126$$

So, you can be 68% sure that the level of fuel in your tank is between 13.9 in. and 14.5 in. You can be 95% sure that it is between 13.6 in. and 14.8 in.

Linear Regression

Introduction

Many measurements made by the navigator are of nonstationary objects; often these measurements are related to the time at which they are made. For example, the altitude of a celestial object is changing even as we measure it. Over the short period that we observe several altitudes, they will generally change in a linear fashion with respect to time. That is, when carefully plotted on graph paper, all the points should line up. That they never line up precisely is due to the multitude of perturbations mentioned in the section on averaging: instrument inaccuracy, operator skill, and such things as varying wave-height at the horizon, or rapidly changing atmospheric refraction. It would be nice to be able to reduce the combined effect of these errors by using averaging techniques. Let's give it a try.

Suppose we had observed the Sun and had obtained the following times and altitudes:

t	Ho
10 00 00	24°32′44″
10 01 00	24°47′59″
10 01 45	24°55′45″
10 02 30	25°04′42″
10 03 20	25°15′36″

We could simply average each of these sets of numbers to obtain $\bar{t} = 10{:}01{:}43$ and $\overline{Ho} = 24°52′44″$, and, indeed, such a technique will yield a more accurate sight than if we had taken only one measurement. However, we can't make a very good statistical statement about such an average, since the standard deviation we get is exceedingly large (21′) because Ho is increasing while we measure it. We should subtract out the effect of the known increase of altitude. The Sun is rising at a nearly constant rate over this short time; so what we actually need to determine is the amount by which each of our sights differs from those that lie on a straight line. The line to choose is usually taken to be the line that minimizes the sum of the squares of the deviations of the observations from the line. (See Figure 1-1.)

Mathematical Background

The job of determining the slope m and y-intercept b of a line from a set of points is called *linear regression*. Given a set of n points $\{(x_i, y_i),\ i = 1, 2, \ldots, n\}$, the constants m and b of the line $y = mx + b$ that fits the points best (in a least-squares sense) are given by

$$m = \frac{\Sigma x_i y_i - \dfrac{\Sigma x_i\, \Sigma y_i}{n}}{\Sigma x_i^2 - \dfrac{(\Sigma x_i)^2}{n}}$$

and

$$b = \bar{y} - m\bar{x}$$

Now with a scientific calculator having two-variable statistics, these two equations are easily evaluated; but, even so, you must consult your owner's manual to determine how to read values such as the sum of the products of x_i and y_i ($\Sigma x_i y_i$).

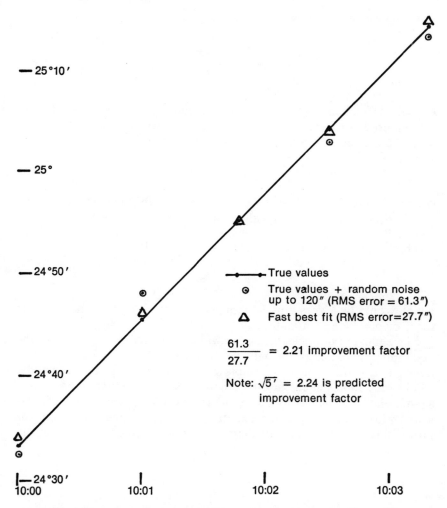

Figure 1-1. Plot of five Sun sights showing how an averaging technique can reduce error

Fast "Best Fit" Method

A look at yet another statistical parameter will resolve our difficulty. Having calculated the m and b that describe the best-fitting line to a set of points, many people like to compute a "goodness-of-fit" parameter, r^2 (r^2 is chosen because it is never negative as r might be). The value of r^2 is close to 1 if the line fits the points well.

This parameter is given by

$$r^2 = \frac{\left[\Sigma x_i y_i - \frac{1}{n}\Sigma x_i\,\Sigma y_i\right]^2}{\left[\Sigma x_i^2 - \frac{1}{n}(\Sigma x)^2\right]\left[\Sigma y_i^2 - \frac{1}{n}(\Sigma y)^2\right]}$$

which, although messy-looking, contains many pieces we have already encountered. In fact, except for a factor or two of $n/(n-1)$, which recede more and more as n increases, we can write

$$r^2 = \frac{m^2 s_x^2}{s_y^2}$$

where m is the slope of the best-fitting line, s_x is the best estimate of the standard deviation of the x values, and s_y is the best estimate of the standard deviation of the y values.

This equation can be rearranged to give

$$m^2 = \frac{r^2 s_y^2}{s_x^2}$$

which would be a very simple expression for m if only we had a value for r, or maybe an estimate, say, $r = 1$.

Since most of our celestial sights will be reasonably well aligned, the assumption $r = 1$ is not a bad one, and now the scientific calculator having one-variable or two-variable statistics can really come in handy.

The only things necessary to compute a nearly-least-squares fit for a set of points are the means and standard deviations of the two variables x and y (or t and Ho in the example above). We merely follow the protocol required by the calculator we are using to get those four values, and then we calculate m and b by

$$|m| = \frac{s_y}{s_x}$$

$$b = \bar{y} - m\bar{x}$$

assigning the correct sign to m, depending upon the usually readily observed slope of the line.

Using an RPN calculator having two-variable statistics, the FBF* (fast best fit) requires very few keystrokes:

---

* The FBF method was first brought to our attention by Frederick P. Blau of General Atomic Co., San Diego. He invented and used the FBF technique on his HP-45 while associated with the School of Engineering of the University of California at Los Angeles.

1(a). Input a y-value; press $\boxed{\text{ENTER}\uparrow}$.

(b). Input an x-value; press $\boxed{\Sigma+}$.

2.   Repeat step (1) until all points have been input.

3.   Then press $\boxed{\text{STD DEV}}$ (or $\boxed{\sigma}$ or whatever it is called),

and $\boxed{\div}$ to get the slope m ($\boxed{\text{CHS}}$ may be necessary).

4.   Next press $\boxed{\text{MEAN}}$ (or $\boxed{\bar{x}}$)

$\boxed{\text{LAST X}}$

$\boxed{\times}$

$\boxed{-}$ to get the y-intercept b.

To put the entire FBF into a neat shorthand notation:

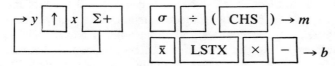

Using the FBF method to fit a line to the Sun altitude data presented earlier, we get

$$Ho = 12.6089\,t - 101.5271°$$

or

$$Ho = 12.61\,\frac{\text{degrees}}{\text{hour}}\,t - 101°31'38''$$

A full-blown least-squares fit gives

$$Ho = 12.5850\,t - 101.2879°$$

or

$$Ho = 12.60\,t - 101°17'16''$$

with a "goodness-of-fit" of

$$r^2 = 0.9962$$

See Figure 1-1.

Now that we have an equation for the line, what can we do with it? We can evaluate a probable value for an observed altitude at any time

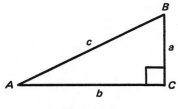

Figure 1-2.

during our period of observation instead of only at the average time. The FBF technique for line-fitting and error reduction will be very useful when we need improved accuracy as, for example, when trying to determine Greenwich Mean Time and longitude by the lunar distance method.

Plane Trigonometry

Trigonometry is the mathematics of angles. Certain properties of angles have been discovered to be very useful in all sorts of measurement situations. The basic figure used in trigonometry is the triangle—a plane figure having three sides and three angles. Nearly all measurement problems facing the navigator can be reduced, if necessary, to problems involving the plane right triangle, which contains a 90° angle. The sum of the three angles of any triangle is 180°; so the remaining two angles of a right triangle must add up to 90°. An especially interesting characteristic of right triangles is the relationship between the lengths of the sides and the length of the hypotenuse (the side opposite the right angle): $a^2 + b^2 = c^2$ where a and b are sides and c is the hypotenuse (Figure 1-2). The common drafting triangles are the 30°–60°–90° triangle and the 45° triangle. The hypotenuse of the 30°–60°–90° triangle is always twice the length of the side opposite the 30° angle (Figure 1-3). The two sides of the 45° triangle are equal. No matter how large or how small these triangles are drawn, these relationships between their sides remain the same.

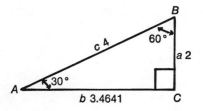 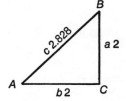

Figure 1-3.

Names have been given to the various possible ratios of pairs of sides of triangles. These are the *trigonometric functions:* sine, cosine, tangent, secant, cosecant, and cotangent. Each trigonometric function has a three-letter abbreviation to simplify its writing in mathematical expressions. The function definitions and their abbreviations follow.

Plane and Spherical Trigonometric Formulae

Functions of Right Plane Triangles (see Figure 1-2)

$$\text{Sine (sin)}A = \frac{\text{Side opposite}}{\text{Hypotenuse}} = \frac{a}{c} = \frac{1}{\csc A}$$

$$\text{Cosine (cos)}A = \frac{\text{Side adjacent}}{\text{Hypotenuse}} = \frac{b}{c} = \frac{1}{\sec A}$$

$$\text{Tangent (tan)}A = \frac{\text{Side opposite}}{\text{Side adjacent}} = \frac{a}{b} = \frac{1}{\cot A}$$

$$\text{Cotangent (cot)}A = \frac{\text{Side adjacent}}{\text{Side opposite}} = \frac{b}{a} = \frac{1}{\tan A}$$

$$\text{Secant (sec)}A = \frac{\text{Hypotenuse}}{\text{Side adjacent}} = \frac{c}{b} = \frac{1}{\cos A}$$

$$\text{Cosecant (csc)}A = \frac{\text{Hypotenuse}}{\text{Side opposite}} = \frac{c}{a} = \frac{1}{\sin A}$$

Solutions of Right Triangles

$$a = c \sin A = b \tan A$$

$$b = c \cos A = a \cot A$$

$$c = a \csc A = b \sec A = \frac{a}{\sin A} = \frac{b}{\cos A}$$

Inverse Trigonometric Functions

$$\sin^{-1}\frac{a}{c} = A$$

$$\cos^{-1}\frac{b}{c} = A$$

$$\tan^{-1}\frac{a}{b} = A$$

$$\cot^{-1}\frac{b}{a} = A$$

20

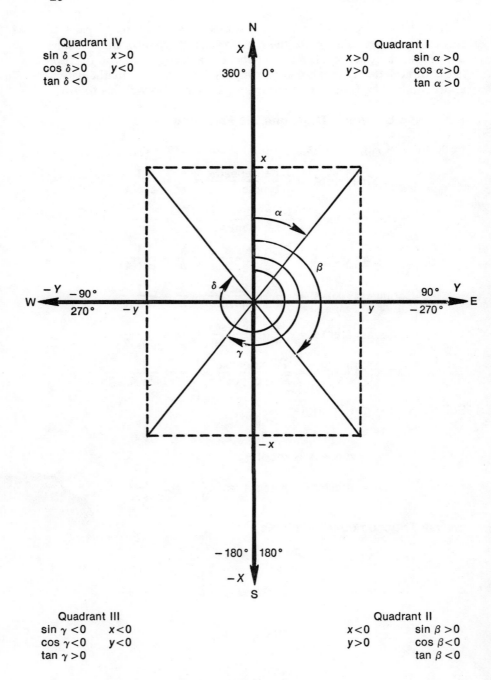

Figure 1-4. Trigonometric functions in all four quadrants

$$\sec^{-1}\frac{c}{b} = A$$

$$\csc^{-1}\frac{c}{a} = A$$

Before the use of calculators, people who wished to use trigonometric functions were obliged to seek the values from a table (or slide rule) and assign them the appropriate algebraic sign. Few navigators did this assignment, however, for most navigational formulae were written so that if all trigonometric functions were given positive values, the correct result could be obtained by applying one or more rules. With a scientific calculator in hand, there is no need to be burdened by a set of rules for various situations. Simply evaluate the expressions using the algebraic sign as given by the calculator, and no problems will arise.

There can be some problems with inverse trigonometric functions, however. Notice in Figure 1-4 that the sines of the angles α and β have a positive algebraic sign. If we were to take the inverse sine of that value, we would always get an angle in the first quadrant. Similarly, the inverse sine of a negative number will always be in the fourth quadrant, even though third-quadrant angles have negative sines, too. This effect is the result of the calculator's returning the "principal value" of an inverse trigonometric function. Since the calculator can't tell in which quadrant the original angle lay, it does the best it can by returning values between $-90°$ and $90°$ for $\sin^{-1}$ and $\tan^{-1}$ and between $0°$ and $180°$ for $\cos^{-1}$. In these cases, the calculator user must add $180°$ to the answer if he feels the answer is in the wrong quadrant.

Solutions of Oblique Plane Triangles (see Figure 1-5)

$$A = 180° - (B + C)$$

Law of sines
$$\frac{a}{\sin A} = \frac{b}{\sin B} = \frac{c}{\sin C}$$

Law of cosines
$$a^2 = b^2 + c^2 - 2bc\cos A$$

and
$$\cos A = \frac{b^2 + c^2 - a^2}{2bc}$$

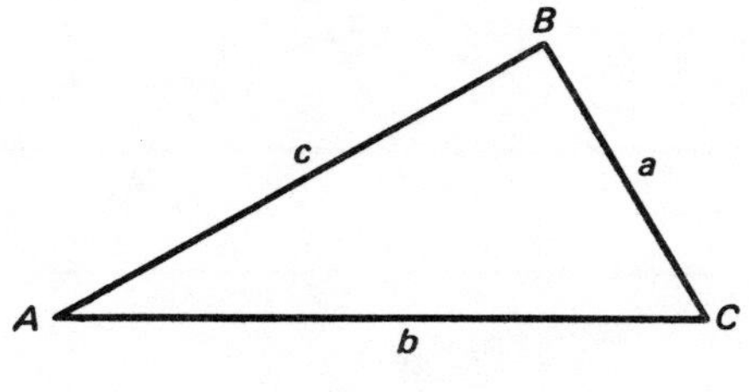

Figure 1-5.

1. Given two sides, b and c, and the included angle A,

$$a = \sqrt{b^2 + c^2 - 2bc \cos A}$$

and $$\sin B = \frac{b}{a} \sin A$$

Note: Since B and $180° - B$ have the same sine, the formula immediately above gives two possible solutions for the angle B, B_1 and B_2 (Figure 1-6). If the correct value of B is in doubt, it may be found by the law of cosines

$$\cos B = \frac{a^2 + c^2 - b^2}{2ac}$$

2. Given three sides, a, b, and c,

$$\cos A = \frac{b^2 + c^2 - a^2}{2bc}$$

and $$\sin C = \frac{c}{a} \sin A$$

Proceed as outlined in the note above.

3. Given two angles, A and B, and the side b,

$$C = 180° - (A + B)$$

$$a = \frac{b \sin A}{\sin B}$$

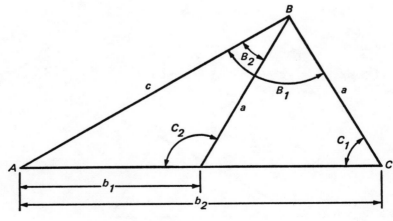

Figure 1-6.

and
$$c = \frac{b \sin C}{\sin B}$$

4. Given two sides, a and b, and an adjacent angle, A, it is assumed that A is less than 90°. If $c \sin A$ is less than a, and a is less than c, two solutions are possible:

$$\sin C_1 = \frac{c}{a} \sin A$$

$$B_1 = 180° - (A + C_1)$$

$$b_1 = \frac{a \sin B_1}{\sin A}$$

and

$$C_2 = 180° - C_1$$

$$B_2 = 180° - (A + C_2)$$

$$b_2 = \frac{a \sin B_2}{\sin A}$$

See Figure 1-6.

Some of the formulae for solving oblique plane triangles are given in Table 1-1. By reassigning letters to sides and angles, they can be used to solve for the unknown parts of such triangles.

Functions of Multiple Angles

$$\sin (A \pm B) = \sin A \cos B \pm \cos A \sin B$$

$$\cos (A \pm B) = \cos A \cos B \mp \sin A \sin B$$

$$\sin 2A = 2 \sin A \cos A$$

$$\cos 2A = \cos^2 A - \sin^2 A$$

$$= 1 - 2 \sin^2 A$$

$$= 2 \cos^2 A - 1$$

Area of Triangles

The area of a triangle equals one-half its base multiplied by its perpendicular height.

Right Spherical Triangles (see Figure 1-7)

According to "Napier's Rules," the sine of the middle part equals the product of the tangents of the adjacent parts, or the cosines of the

Table 1-1

Known	To find	Formula	Comments
a,b,c	A	$\cos A = \dfrac{c^2 + b^2 - a^2}{2bc}$	Cosine law
a,b,A	B	$\sin B = \dfrac{b \sin A}{a}$	Sine law. Two solutions if $b > a$
	C	$C = 180° - (A + B)$	$A + B + C = 180°$
	c	$c = \dfrac{a \sin C}{\sin A}$	Sine law
a,b,C	A	$\tan A = \dfrac{a \sin C}{b - a \cos C}$	
	B	$B = 180° - (A + C)$	$A + B + C = 180°$
	c	$c = \dfrac{a \sin C}{\sin A}$	Sine law
a,A,B	b	$b = \dfrac{a \sin B}{\sin A}$	Sine law
	C	$C = 180° - (A + B)$	$A + B + C = 180°$
	c	$c = \dfrac{a \sin C}{\sin A}$	Sine law

U. S. Naval Oceanographic Office, H.O. Pub. No. 9 (Bowditch).

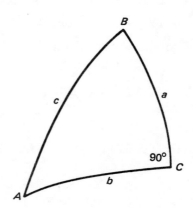

Figure 1-7.

opposite parts. Thus,

$$\sin a = \tan b \cot B = \sin c \sin A$$
$$\sin b = \tan a \cot A = \sin c \sin B$$
$$\cos c = \cot A \cot B = \cos a \cos b$$
$$\cos A = \tan b \cot c = \cos a \sin B$$
$$\cos B = \tan a \cot c = \cos b \sin A$$

In the above equations, the following rules apply:

1. An oblique angle and the side opposite are in the same quadrant.
2. The hypotenuse, c, is less than 90° when a and b are in the same quadrant, and greater than 90° when a and b are in different quadrants.

Oblique Spherical Triangles

An oblique spherical triangle can be solved by dropping a perpendicular from an apex to the opposite side, extending the latter, if necessary, to form two right spherical triangles. By reassigning letters as necessary, it can also be solved by the formulae given in Table 1-2.

The Navigational Triangle

The navigational triangle (Figure 1-8) is formed by arcs of great circles. The arc PZ is the arc of a meridian, passing through the elevated pole, P, and the observer's position at Z; its length equals the observer's colatitude, or 90° minus his latitude. The arc PM is the arc of

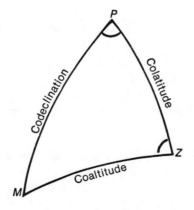

Figure 1-8. Navigational triangle

Table 1-2

Known	To find	Formula	Comments
a,b,c	A	$\cos A = \dfrac{\cos a - \cos b \cos c}{\sin b \sin c}$	
A,B,C	a	$\cos a = \dfrac{\cos A + \cos B \cos C}{\sin B \sin C}$	
a,b,C	c	$\cos c = \cos a \cos b + \sin a \sin b \cos C$	
	A	$\tan A = \dfrac{\sin D \tan C}{\sin(b - D)}$	$\tan D = \tan a \cos C$
	B	$\sin B = \dfrac{\sin C \sin b}{\sin c}$	
c,A,B	C	$\cos C = \sin A \sin B \cos c - \cos A \cos B$	
	a	$\tan a = \dfrac{\tan c \sin E}{\sin(B + E)}$	$\tan E = \tan A \cos c$
	b	$\tan b = \dfrac{\tan c \sin F}{\sin(A + F)}$	$\tan F = \tan B \cos c$
a,b,A	c	$\sin(c + G) = \dfrac{\cos a \sin G}{\cos b}$	$\cot G = \cos A \tan b$ Two solutions
	B	$\sin B = \dfrac{\sin A \sin b}{\sin a}$	Two solutions
	C	$\sin(C + H) = \sin H \tan b \cot a$	$\tan H = \tan A \cos b$ Two solutions
a,A,B	C	$\sin(C - K) = \dfrac{\cos A \sin K}{\cos B}$	$\cot K = \tan B \cos a$ Two solutions
	b	$\sin b = \dfrac{\sin a \sin B}{\sin A}$	Two solutions
	c	$\sin(c - M) = \cot A \tan B \sin M$	$\tan M = \cos B \tan a$ Two solutions

an hour circle, passing through the elevated pole and the geographic position of the body at M; its length equals the codeclination of the body. The arc MZ is the arc of a vertical circle, passing through the celestial body; its length represents the coaltitude of the body.

The angle at P is the body's local hour angle, figured from North toward the West from 0° to 360°; it may also be termed meridian angle, in which case it is figured to the East or West to 180°. The angle at Z represents the body's azimuth. It is measured from the elevated pole, East or West, to 180°; when measured from North clockwise to the body, to 360°, it is termed true azimuth, Zn. The angle at the geographic position of the body, M, is called the parallactic angle.

Any of the formulae given above for oblique spherical triangles may be used to solve the navigational triangle; however, it must be borne in mind that the three sides of this triangle represent the colatitude, the codeclination, and the coaltitude, respectively. However, the formulae used in the usual practice of celestial navigation and great-circle sailing will be found in the main body of the text.

Symbols Used in Navigation

Δ	Delta; difference; unit of change
λ	Lambda; longitude
θ	Theta; latitude
±	Plus or minus according to appropriate rule
~	Absolute difference, i.e., subtract smaller from larger
∴	Therefore
∵	Because
∞	Infinity
°	Degrees
′	Minutes of arc
″	Seconds of arc
∠	Angle
∟	Right angle
>	Greater than
<	Less than
☉	Sun
☉̄	Upper limb Sun
☉	Lower limb Sun
☽	Moon
☾̄	Upper limb Moon
☾	Lower limb Moon
♀	Venus
♂	Mars
♃	Jupiter
♄	Saturn
♈	Aries
✳	Star

Selected Abbreviations Used in Navigation

Note: In the following text, abbreviations are identified as they are used. The following are listed because of the frequency of their use or because of their confusing similarity.

a	Intercept
C	Centigrade, or Celsius, temperature; chronometer time; compass; correction; course; course angle
Cn	Course, referred to true North
D	Distance
d	Declination
DR	Dead reckoning; dead-reckoning position
EP	Estimated position
GHA	Greenwich hour angle
GP	Geographic position of celestial body
H	Altitude; horizon angle
HA	Hour angle
ha	Apparent altitude
Hc	Computed altitude
HE	Height of eye
Ho	Fully corrected observed altitude
hs	Sextant altitude
ht	Tabulated altitude
K	Knots; nautical miles per hour
LAN	Local apparent noon
LHA	Local hour angle
PZM	The navigational triangle
S	Speed, usually expressed in knots
t	Meridian angle
Z	Azimuth angle; zenith; time zone meridian
z	Zenith distance
ZD	Time zone description
Zn	True azimuth, reckoned clockwise from North to 360°

The Greek Alphabet

In navigational literature, Greek letters are often chosen to represent angular or other quantities, English letters having been used up for other values. Table 1-3 will help you to learn the Greek alphabet and its uses.

Table 1-3

Letter	Name	English equivalent	Typical use
α	alpha	a	Angle; designation of brightest star in a constellation.
β	beta	b	Angle; designation of second brightest star in a constellation.
γ	gamma	g	Angle.
Δ, δ	delta	d	Δ difference; Δ followed by a variable denotes "change in." δ represents angle; declination; small quantity.
ϵ	epsilon	ĕ	ϵ represents a very small quantity.
ζ	zeta	z	ζ represents zenith angle $(90° - H)$.
η	eta	e	
θ	theta	th	Angle; formerly used for latitude.
ι	iota	i	
κ	kappa	k	
λ	lambda	l	Angle; longitude.
μ	mu	m	μ (as a prefix) represents "micro" (1×10^{-6}).
ν	nu	n	(Q: "What's new?" A: "The 13th letter of the Greek alphabet.") ν is used for "true anomaly."
ξ	xi	x	
o	omicron	o	
Π, π	pi	p	$\pi = 3.14159 \ldots$; longitude of perihelion; Π denotes product.
ρ	rho	r	Ratio.
Σ, σ	sigma	s	Σ denotes "summation."
τ	tau	t	τ represents an astronomical epoch.
υ	upsilon	u	
ϕ	phi	ph	Angle.
χ	chi	ch	
ψ	psi	ps	Angle.
Ω, ω	omega	ō	Ω represents "ohms" (the unit of electrical resistance). ω represents angle; angular rate.

2
Inshore Navigation

Speed, Time, and Distance

Among the problems most frequently encountered at sea are those involving speed, time, and distance. After having traveled a certain distance in a certain time, what was the speed? Given a certain speed, how long will it take to travel a certain distance? After having spent a certain amount of time traveling at a given speed, what distance was covered? The answers to these questions can be supplied rapidly and accurately by use of the scientific calculator.

In formulae (1), (2), and (3) below, it is assumed that the time involved is short enough to be conveniently reckoned in minutes. When such is not the case, the factor "60" is dropped, and the time is obtained in hours and decimals of hours: to convert the decimals to minutes, multiply them by 60. When seconds are involved, they should be converted to decimals of a minute; that is to say, they should be divided by 60. In most instances, it is acceptable to work to the nearest tenth of a minute. Thus, 47 seconds, which is 0.783 minute, would ordinarily be written 0.8 minute.

Also, in formulae (1), (2), and (3), distance is stated in miles and decimals of miles.

To determine speed, when distance and time are known, the formula is:

$$\text{Speed} = \frac{\text{distance} \times 60}{\text{time, in minutes}} \qquad (1)$$

To determine time, when distance and speed are known, the formula is:

$$\text{Time, in minutes} = \frac{\text{distance} \times 60}{\text{speed}} \qquad (2)$$

To determine distance, when speed and time are known, the formula is:

$$\text{Distance} = \frac{\text{speed} \times \text{time, in minutes}}{60} \qquad (3)$$

From time to time, it is necessary to determine speed over the measured mile. In this instance, the time is taken in seconds, and the formula is:

$$\text{Speed} = \frac{3600}{\text{time, in seconds}} \qquad (4)$$

The following examples illustrate the use of these formulae.

Example 1: We have covered 9.6 miles in 32 minutes and 24 seconds, which equals 32.4 minutes, and want to determine our speed. Formula (1) becomes:

$$\text{Speed} = \frac{9.6 \text{ miles} \times 60}{32.4 \text{ minutes}} = 17.78$$

Our speed, therefore, is 17.78 knots.

Example 2: Our speed is 12.25 knots, and we want to know how many minutes and seconds will be required to travel 11.4 miles. Formula (2) becomes:

$$\text{Time} = \frac{11.4 \text{ miles} \times 60}{12.25 \text{ knots}} = 55.8367$$

The time required will, therefore, be 55.8367 minutes, or 55 minutes and 50 seconds.

Example 3: We are steaming at 12 knots, and wish to know how far we traveled in 43 minutes. Formula (3) becomes:

$$\text{Distance} = \frac{12 \text{ knots} \times 43 \text{ minutes}}{60} = 8.6$$

We have, therefore, steamed 8.6 nautical miles in 43 minutes.

Example 4: We steamed the measured mile in 4 minutes and 5 seconds, which equals 245 seconds, and wish to determine our speed in knots. Formula (4) becomes:

$$\text{Speed} = \frac{3600}{245 \text{ seconds}} = 14.7$$

Our speed, therefore, is 14.7 knots.

Example 5: The next leg of our voyage is 89.5 miles, we are steaming at 15.6 knots, and we wish to know how long it will take to traverse the next leg. Here we will use formula (2), omitting the factor 60, as the time obviously will run into hours:

$$\text{Time, in hours} = \frac{89.5}{15.6} = 5.7372$$

The time required, therefore, will be 5.7372 hours, which equals 5 hours, 44 minutes, and 14 seconds. Since time is ordinarily stated to the nearest minute, the answer would be written 5 hours and 44 minutes.

Distance to the Horizon

Because of the Earth's curvature, the distance to the sea horizon increases as the height of the observer's eye increases. Also, for any given height of eye, the distance increases because of terrestrial refraction, or the bending of the light rays caused by the atmosphere.

Knowing the distance to the horizon for your height of eye can be very helpful in estimating distances at sea. For example, when you sight an approaching steamer hull down, that knowledge allows you to determine the range with fair accuracy when her bow wave appears.

The formulae for determining the distance to the horizon for a given height of eye include a correction for terrestrial refraction calculated for normal atmospheric conditions.

For the distance in *nautical miles,* the formula is:

$$D_1 = 1.144 \sqrt{HE} \tag{1}$$

and for *statute miles* it is:

$$D_2 = 1.317 \sqrt{HE} \tag{2}$$

where D is the distance, and HE is the height, in feet, of the observer's eye above the surface.

When the height of eye is stated in meters, the distance to the horizon in nautical miles may be found by the formula

$$D_1 = 2.072 \sqrt{HE \text{ meters}} \tag{3}$$

Example 1: Your height of eye is 17 feet. What is the distance, in nautical miles, to the horizon?

$$D_1 = 1.144 \sqrt{17}, \text{ or } 4.72$$

The distance to the horizon is, therefore, 4.72 nautical miles.

Example 2: The height of eye is 15.25 meters; we require the distance to the horizon in nautical miles. Formula (3) becomes:

$$D_1 = 2.072 \sqrt{15.25 \text{ meters}}, \text{ or } 8.0914$$

We would, therefore, consider the distance to the horizon to be 8.1 nautical miles.

Distance by Sextant Angle

Distance by Horizon Angle

The distance to an object located between the horizon and the viewer may be determined by use of the angle subtended between the horizon and the object's waterline, as measured by sextant. To this angle, corrected for sextant index error, is applied the correction for the dip of the horizon for the observer's height of eye with the *sign reversed;* that is, the dip correction is added to the sextant angle. The sextant angle, thus corrected, is termed the horizon angle, *H*.

The distance, D, may now be found by the formula

$$D = \frac{HE}{\tan H} \tag{1}$$

where *HE* is the height of the observer's eye above water. Both *D* and *HE* are measured in feet.

If the distance is to be given in yards, the formula becomes

$$D, \text{ in yards} = \frac{1}{3}\frac{HE}{\tan H} \tag{2}$$

The greater the height of eye, the greater the accuracy obtained at shorter ranges, and the greater the ranges that can be obtained.

Example 1: The angle subtended between the horizon and the waterline of a buoy is 1°05.2′, the sextant's index error is −2.5′, and the observer's height of eye is 20 feet. What is the distance, in feet, between the buoy and the observer?

The first step is to determine the horizon angle, *H*, and the formula for doing so is:

Sextant angle		1°05.2′
Index correction	+2.5′	
Dip for 20 feet, sign reversed,	+4.3′	
	+6.8′	+ 6.8′
		H 1°12.0′

If a dip table is not available, the dip may be calculated by the formula for finding the dip of the horizon, given on page 95.

Formula (1) becomes:

$$D = \frac{20}{\tan 1°12.0'}$$
$$= 954.79$$

The distance to the buoy is, therefore, 955 feet.

Example 2: The height of eye is 95 feet, and the angle between the waterline of a boat and the horizon behind it, as measured by sextant, is 0°11.3'. The sextant is without index error. We need the range, in yards, to the boat.

We first determine *H*, as follows:

Sextant angle		0°11.3'
Index correction	0'	
Dip for 95 feet, sign reversed	+9.5'	
Net correction		+ 9.5'
		H 0°20.8'

Since the range is to be given in yards, we use formula (2), and it becomes:

$$D = \frac{95}{\tan 20.8'} \times \frac{1}{3}$$
$$= \frac{95}{.00605} \times \frac{1}{3} = 5,234$$

The range to the boat, therefore, is 5,234 yards.

Distance Short of Horizon

The sextant may be used as an accurate range finder when the height of an object is known, and when its base at the water, or waterline, does not lie beyond the observer's horizon. When the angle between top and base, measured by sextant, is less than about 10°, as it is in the majority of cases, we may assume for practical purposes that the distance to the top of the object and that to its waterline are the same. The index correction must, of course, always be applied to the sextant angle.

When the height of an object, such as the top of a lighthouse above the waterline, or the truck of a mast above the boot top or waterline, is known in feet, the distance, *D*, in feet, may be found by the formula

$$D, \text{ in feet} = \frac{A}{\sin H} \tag{1}$$

where *A* is the height of the object in feet, and *H* is the corrected sextant angle. In this formula, if the height of the object, *A*, is stated in meters, the distance, D, will be found in meters. If the distance is desired in yards, it is necessary only to divide the answer by three.

Example 1: The top of the light on a lighthouse is 224 feet above the water. The corrected angle between the water and the top of the light is found by sextant to be 29.5'. We require the distance, in yards, to the light.

Formula (1) becomes:

$$D = \frac{224 \text{ feet}}{\sin 29.5' \times 3} = \frac{224}{.00858 \times 3} = 8{,}701$$

The distance, therefore, is 8,701 yards.

The factor for converting feet to nautical miles is 0.0001646. Therefore, if the distance is to be determined in nautical miles, the formula becomes:

$$D, \text{ in nautical miles} = \frac{A, \text{ in feet} \times 0.0001646}{\sin H} \qquad (2)$$

Should the distance be required in statute miles, the factor would be 0.0001892.

Example 2: An object is known to be 183 feet above the water. The corrected sextant angle between its top and the waterline is 1°13.5'. What is the distance in nautical miles?

Formula (2) becomes:

$$D, \text{ nautical miles} = \frac{183 \text{ feet} \times 0.0001646}{\sin 1°13.5'} = 1.41$$

The distance, therefore, is 1.41 nautical miles.

Example 3: An object is known to be 247 feet high. The height, as measured by sextant, is 1°50.8'. What is the distance in statute miles?

Formula (2) becomes:

$$D, \text{ in statute miles} = \frac{247 \text{ feet} \times 0.0001892}{\sin 1°50.8'} = 1.45$$

The distance, therefore, is 1.45 statute miles.

Distance in nautical miles may also be determined by sextant angle if "the height in feet of the observed object is divided by the" sextant altitude, *in minutes,* and the result is multiplied by 0.566.

The formula, therefore, is:

$$D, \text{ in nautical miles} = \frac{\text{height of object, in feet} \times 0.566}{\text{sextant angle, in minutes}} \qquad (3)$$

Example 4: Using the same data as in Example 2, a height of 183 feet, and a corrected sextant angle of 1°13.5′, formula (3) becomes:

$$D, \text{ in nautical miles} = \frac{183 \text{ feet} \times 0.566}{73.5'} = 1.41$$

The distance, therefore, is 1.41 nautical miles.

Some years ago, a defender in the America's Cup races used this method to keep a regular check on the range between himself and his challenger, whose mast height he knew. He had, of course, to allow for the challenger's angle of heel, so that the actual height of the mast above the water could be used. Since his boat and the challenger were about equally stiff, he assumed that the challenger's angle of heel was the same as his own.

He then determined the current height of his challenger's mast truck above the water by multiplying vertical mast height by the cosine of the angle of the heel, and used this height, in conjunction with formula (1), above, to determine the range.

Distance Beyond the Horizon

In clear weather, a mountain top can often be seen when it is well beyond the horizon. If the mountain's altitude is known, its approximate distance can be determined by sextant angle. However, it must be borne in mind that a distance thus found is only an approximation, as it can be considerably affected by the vagaries of terrestrial refraction.

The formula for finding the distance is:

$$D = \sqrt{\left(\frac{\tan ha}{0.000246}\right)^2 + \frac{\text{Alt} - HE}{0.74736}} - \frac{\tan ha}{0.000246} \qquad (1)$$

where D is the distance to the object in nautical miles, Alt is the height of the distant object in feet, HE is the observer's height of eye in feet, and ha is the sextant altitude, corrected for instrumental error, index error, and dip.

Example: The sextant altitude of the highest point of a mountainous island, situated beyond the horizon, is 1°25.5′. The sextant is free of instrumental and index error; the height of eye is 45 feet. From the chart, we note that the mountain top has an altitude of 7,000 feet and that it is situated 22.7 miles inland from the seaward edge of a large offlying shoal. We require our approximate distance from the shoal.

We first correct the altitude, as read from the sextant:

hs	1°25.5′
IE	0
IC	0
Dip	−6.5
ha	1°19.0′

We can now write formula (1):

$$D = \sqrt{\left(\frac{\tan 1°19.0'}{0.000246}\right)^2 + \frac{7000 - 45}{0.74736}} - \frac{\tan 1°19.0'}{0.000246}$$

$$= \sqrt{\left(\frac{0.0230}{0.000246}\right)^2 + \frac{6955}{0.74736}} - \frac{0.0230}{0.000246}$$

$$= \sqrt{8729.5 + 9306.1} - 93.4$$

$$= 134.3 - 93.4 = 40.9$$

Our distance off the mountain peak is therefore about 40.9 miles, and as the reef lies 22.7 miles to seaward of the peak, our approximate distance from the reef is 18.2 miles.

Distance of Visibility of Objects

When the height of an object is known, it is simple to determine the distance at which, under normal atmospheric conditions, it should become visible for a given height of eye. All that is required is to solve the distance to the horizon for the observer's height of eye, and the distance to the horizon for the height of the object, and add the results.

The formulae used are those given for calculating distance to the horizon, where D represents distance and HE represents height of eye, in feet:

$$D_1, \text{ in nautical miles} = 1.144 \sqrt{HE} \tag{1}$$

$$D_2, \text{ in statute miles} = 1.317 \sqrt{HE} \tag{2}$$

Example 1: Your height of eye is 63 feet, and the height of a brilliant light is 178 feet. At what distance, in nautical miles, should the light become visible?

Formula (1) becomes:

$$D_1 = 1.144 \sqrt{63} = 9.08$$
$$+$$
$$D_1 = 1.144 \sqrt{178} = \underline{15.26}$$
$$24.34$$

Under normal atmospheric conditions, therefore, you would expect to pick up the light at a distance of 24.3 nautical miles.

Example 2: Your height of eye is 6 feet, and the height of the brilliant light is 97 feet. At what distance, in statute miles, should the light become visible?

Formula (2) becomes:

$$D_2 = 1.317 \sqrt{6} = 3.23$$
$$+$$
$$D_2 = 1.317 \sqrt{97} = \underline{12.97}$$
$$16.20$$

Under normal atmospheric conditions, therefore, you would expect to see the light at a distance of 16.2 statute miles.

When the height of eye is stated in meters, the distance to the horizon, in nautical miles, may be found by the formula

$$D_1 = 2.072 \sqrt{HE}, \text{ meters} \tag{3}$$

With the height of eye stated in meters and the distance to the horizon desired in kilometers, the formula is:

$$D_3 = 3.8373 \sqrt{HE}, \text{ meters} \tag{4}$$

Distance by Bearings

Distance Off Abeam by One Bearing and Run to Beam

The distance off when abeam of a fixed object can be determined by taking a bearing on the bow, and noting the distance run from the time of that bearing to the time the object is abeam. Solution is by the law of sines:

$$D = \frac{R \times \sin A}{\cos A}$$

where D is the distance off when abeam, R is the run, and A is the angle on the bow.

Example: We pick up a light bearing 319° relative, and after we have run 6.0 miles, it is abeam. We wish to know the distance off when the light was abeam.

Since 319° relative is 41° on the bow, the formula becomes:

$$D = \frac{6.0 \times \sin 41°}{\cos 41°} = 5.22$$

We were, therefore, 5.2 miles off the light when it was abeam.

Distance Off at Second Bearing by Two Bearings on Bow and Run Between

The distance from a fixed object can readily be determined by two bearings on the bow, if the ship's run between the bearings is known. Best results are obtained when the change in bearing is considerable.

Solution is by the law of sines:

$$D = \frac{R \times \sin A}{\sin (A \sim B)}$$

where D is the distance off at the time of the second bearing, A is the first bearing on the bow, B is the second bearing on the bow, and R is the run between bearings.

Example 1: A landmark bears 20° on the bow. After we steam 5.0 miles, the mark bears 70° on the bow. We require the distance off at the time of the second bearing.

The formula becomes:

$$D = \frac{5.0 \times \sin 20°}{\sin (20° \sim 70°)} = \frac{5.0 \times \sin 20°}{\sin 50°} = 2.23$$

At the time of the second bearing, therefore, our distance from the mark was 2.23 miles.

Example 2: We are on course 323° True, and obtain a bearing of 347° True on a light. After we steam 8.0 miles, the light bears 016° True. We require the distance off the light at the time of the second bearing.

The first bearing is 24° (347° − 323°) on the bow, and the second is 53° (376° − 323°). The formula becomes:

$$D = \frac{8.0 \times \sin 24°}{\sin 29°} = 6.7$$

The light was, therefore, 6.7 miles distant at the time of the second bearing.

Distance Off When Abeam by Two Bearings on the Bow and Run Between

The distance off a fixed object when abeam can be determined from two bearings on the bow, and the run between them. Here, again, solution is by the law of sines.

In this case, the first step is to determine the distance between the ship and the object, at the time of the first bearing. This can be done when the second bearing is obtained by determining the angle at the object formed by the two bearing lines, and considering this angle to be the apex of a triangle. For example, if the first bearing were 30° on the bow, and the second were 50°, the angle at the object would be 20° [180° − (130° + 30°)]. This distance off the object at the time of the first bearing is then found by the formula

$$D_1 = \frac{R \times \sin B_2}{\sin C} \qquad (1)$$

where D_1 is the distance off at the first bearing, R is the run between the first and second bearing, B_2 is the second bearing on the bow, and C is the angle between the two bearing lines at the object.

Having solved that equation, we find the distance off the object when it is abeam by the formula

$$D_2 = \frac{D_1 \times \sin A}{\sin 90°} \qquad (2)$$

or

$$D_2 = D_1 \times \sin A, \ \sin 90° \text{ being equal to } 1$$

where A is the first angle on the bow, D_1 is the distance off the object at the time of the first bearing, and D_2 is the distance off when the object is abeam.

Example: We sight a light bearing 28° on the bow. After we steam 6.5 miles, it bears 52° on the bow. We wish to know the distance off the light when it is abeam.

First, we determine the angle at the light, C in formula (1) above, and to do so, we subtract the first bearing, 28°, from the second, 52°; and we get 24°. Formula (1) becomes:

$$D_1 = \frac{6.5 \times \sin 52°}{\sin 24°} = 12.6$$

Formula (2) then becomes:

$$D_2 = 12.6 \times \sin 28° = 5.92$$

The light will, therefore, be distant 5.9 miles when it is abeam.

Run to a Given Bearing and Distance Off When on That Bearing

It is at times necessary to determine the distance to steam to bring a fixed object to a given bearing, and the distance off the object when it is on that bearing. The problem is illustrated in Figure 2-1.

Two bearings on the bow are obtained, and the run between them is noted. The distance off at the time the first bearing was obtained can then be determined by the formula

$$D_1 = \frac{R_1 \times \sin B}{\sin C} \tag{1}$$

D_1 being the distance off at the first bearing, R_1 the run between the first and second bearing, B the second bearing on the bow, and C the angle between the two bearing lines at the object.

After we have found the distance off the object at the time of the first bearing, the distance to steam to bring the object to the given or second bearing is calculated by the formula

$$R_2 = \frac{D_1 \times \sin E}{\sin F} \tag{2}$$

R_2 being the run from the first bearing to the given bearing, D_1 the distance off the object at the first bearing, E the angle at the object formed by the first bearing line and the bearing of the object when on

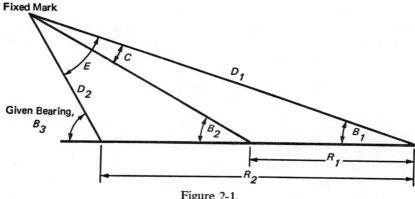

Figure 2-1.

the given bearing, and F the bearing on the bow of the object when on the given bearing.

The distance off the object at the time of the given bearing, D_2, is found by the formula

$$D_2 = \frac{D_1 \times \sin A}{\sin F} \tag{3}$$

A being the first bearing on the bow.

Example: We are steaming on course 273°, speed 12.0 knots, when a navigational light on shore comes into sight. Course is to be altered to 305° when the light bears 333° per gyro compass. At 2207 the light bears 293° per gyro; at 2257 it bears 308°. At what time will the course be changed, and how far will we be off the light at that time?

As we are on course 273°, the first bearing is 20° on the bow, and the second is 35°; at 12.0 knots we have steamed exactly 10 miles in 50 minutes. The angle at the light formed by our two bearing lines is 15°. Formula (1) becomes:

$$D_1 = \frac{10.0 \times \sin 35°}{\sin 15°} = 22.16$$

At the time of the first bearing, 2207, we were, therefore, 22.16 miles from the light.

The course change is to take effect when the light bears 333° per gyro. The bearing on the bow will then be 60°; the angle at the light between this bearing line and the first bearing line is therefore 40° (60° − 20°). Formula (2) becomes:

$$R_2 = \frac{22.16 \times \sin 40°}{\sin 60°} = 16.448$$

So the run from the first bearing to the turning bearing is 16.4 miles. The time of the first bearing was 2207; at 12.0 knots it will take us 82 minutes to steam 16.4 miles. We can, therefore, expect to change course at 2329. Formula (3) becomes:

$$D_2 = \frac{22.16 \times \sin 20°}{\sin 60°} = 8.75$$

We will, therefore, be 8.7 miles off the light when course is changed.

Distance Off Two Landmarks or Seamarks

When the distance between two fixed marks and the bearing of one from the other are known, a vessel's distance from each mark can be determined, without plotting, by true bearings taken on each mark. The problem is illustrated in Figure 2-2.

Solution is by the law of sines:

$$\frac{s}{\sin \angle S} : \frac{a}{\sin \angle A} : \frac{b}{\sin \angle B}$$

In this ratio, $\angle A$ represents the angular difference between the true bearing of A from the ship and the bearing of B from A; $\angle B$ represents the angular difference between its bearing from A and its true bearing from the ship. The ship is located at S. $\angle S$ represents the angular difference between the true bearings of A and B. The known distance from A to B is represented by s. The distance of the ship from A is represented by b, while the distance of the ship from B is represented by a.

Example: Cuttyhunk Light bears 074° True from Buzzards Light, and is distant 3.96 miles. We obtain a bearing of 015° True on Buzzards, which we will call A, and of 050° on Cuttyhunk, which we will call B. We wish to determine our distance from both lights.

In this case, the angle S is 35° (050° − 015°), while the side s is 3.96 miles. For the angle A, we will use 59° (074° − 015°), and for the angle B 24° (074° − 050°). Our distance off Buzzards Light is represented by b, and our distance off Cuttyhunk Light by a. The ratio becomes:

$$\frac{3.96}{\sin 35°} = \frac{a}{\sin 59°} = \frac{b}{\sin 24°}$$

or

$$\frac{3.96}{\sin 35°} = \frac{5.92}{\sin 59°} = \frac{2.81}{\sin 24°}$$

The distance off Buzzards Light, therefore, is 2.81 miles, and off Cuttyhunk Light it is 5.92 miles.

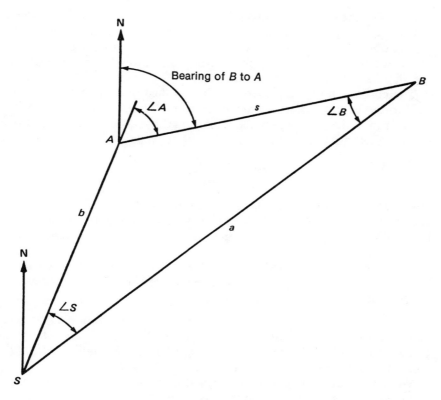

Figure 2-2.

Heading to Bring a Light to a Specified Bearing and Distance, and the Run Thereto

At night, under conditions of good visibility and normal refraction, it is possible to approximate quite closely the course correction required to bring a light to a specified bearing and distance, and to estimate the time at which the ship will arrive at that point. Alternatively, a similar situation may arise when radar is used to obtain range and bearing.

Once the light is sighted, the first step is to determine any correction to the ship's present heading that may be required to bring her to the specified distance off the light when on the specified bearing. This correction may be found by the formula

$$\tan A = \frac{a \times \sin C}{b - (a \times \cos C)} \qquad (1)$$

where A is the bearing on the bow *relative to the present heading* to which the light must be brought so that it will be at the specified distance, *a* is the specified distance, *b* is the range of visibility of the light for the observer's height of eye, and *C* is the angle at the light formed by the difference between the initial true bearing and the bearing when the ship has reached the specified point.

The correction to the present heading is then made by bringing the light to the bearing found by means of formula (1).

The run to the point where the light is on the required bearing and at the specified distance is computed by the formula

$$D = \frac{a \times \sin C}{\sin A} \tag{2}$$

where *D* is the run, *A* is the angle found by formula (1), *a* is the specified distance off the light, and *C* is the angle at the light formed by the initial bearing and the bearing when the ship has reached the specified point.

To determine the time of arrival at the specified point, the distance, *D*, is divided by the ship's speed to give the time in hours and decimals required to reach the turning point.

Example: We are on course 140°, speed 13.0 knots. Our course is to be changed when Light *X* bears 205° True, distant 9.0 miles. For our height of eye, Light *X* will become visible at a range of 18.6 miles. At 2217 Light *X* is sighted bearing 160° T, or 20° on the bow.

We wish to determine any change that must be made to our present heading to bring us to the required distance off the light when it bears 205° and to find the time at which we shall arrive at that point.

Our first step is to find what the relative bearing of the light should be when the ship is headed for the specified point; this we determine by formula (1), in which the angle *C* is 45° (160° ~ 205°).

$$\tan A = \frac{9 \times \sin 45°}{18.6 - (9 \times \cos 45°)} = \frac{6.3640}{12.2360} = 0.5201$$

$$A = 27.4789°$$

The relative bearing of the light should therefore be 027.5°; we accordingly come left 7.5°, to a heading of 132.5°.

We can now find the distance of the run to the turning point, using formula (2) which becomes:

$$D = \frac{9 \times \sin 45°}{\sin 27.5°} = 13.7823$$

The distance from where the light first came into view to the point where the course is to be changed is therefore 13.8 miles. At 13.0 knots it will take us 63.6 minutes to get there, so we can expect to come to the new course at 2321.

An alternate solution to this type of problem is available for use with calculators having the polar to rectangular conversion feature. The keying procedures for both the algebraic and RPN-type calculators are given below. The symbols shown are typical of those used on most calculators: ↑ means "enter," →R means "convert to rectangular coordinates," →P means "convert to polar coordinates," R↑ means "roll up," and R↓ means "roll down."

To solve the example given above by this method, the keystrokes for a RPN calculator are:

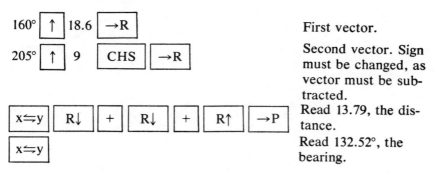

160° ↑ 18.6 →R   First vector.

205° ↑ 9 CHS →R   Second vector. Sign must be changed, as vector must be subtracted.

x⇌y R↓ + R↓ + R↑ →P   Read 13.79, the distance.

x⇌y   Read 132.52°, the bearing.

For calculators using the algebraic notation, the keystrokes, typically, would be:

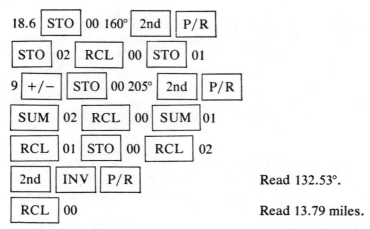

18.6 STO 00 160° 2nd P/R

STO 02 RCL 00 STO 01

9 +/− STO 00 205° 2nd P/R

SUM 02 RCL 00 SUM 01

RCL 01 STO 00 RCL 02

2nd INV P/R   Read 132.53°.

RCL 00   Read 13.79 miles.

The problem in this example is represented graphically in Figure 2-3. *AB* represents the course to which the ship must come to reach point *B*,

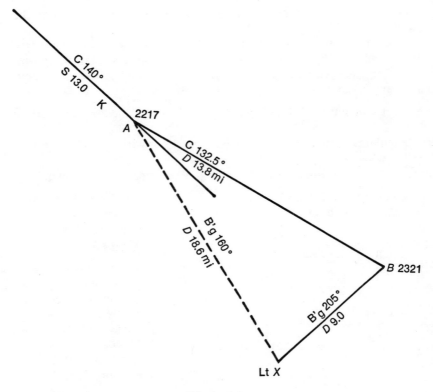

Figure 2-3.

A is the ship's position when Light *X* is sighted, *AX* is the initial bearing and range of Light *X*, *B* is the specified turning point, and *AC* represents ship's heading when the light is sighted. Angle *A* is the angle on the bow, relative to the original heading, to which the light must be brought, and angle *C* is the angle at the light between the original true bearing and the bearing of point *B* from the light. *D* represents the distance to steam from the point where the light was sighted to point *B*.

Tides

The Moon's gravitational pull is the primary cause of tides; while the Sun also affects the tides, its gravitational pull is materially less than that of the Moon, owing to the much greater distance separating the Sun from the Earth.

These gravitational attractions set up oscillations in the oceans, the periods of these oscillations depending upon the dimensions of the body of water. No ocean appears to be a single oscillating body; rather, each one is made up of a number of oscillating basins. As such basins are acted upon by the tide-producing forces, some respond more readily to diurnal or daily forces, others to semi-diurnal forces, and still others respond about equally to both. Hence, tides at a given place are classified as diurnal, semi-dirunal, or mixed, according to the characteristics of the tidal pattern occurring at that place.

With diurnal tides, only a single high and a single low water occur each tidal day; such tides are encountered along the northern shores of the Gulf of Mexico.

Semi-diurnal tides produce two high and two low waters during each tidal day, with relatively small inequality in the high and low water heights. Tides along the Atlantic coast of the United States are representative of the semi-diurnal type.

In mixed tides, both the diurnal and semi-diurnal oscillations are important factors, and the tide is characterized by a large inequality in the high water heights, the low water heights, or both. Usually there are two high and two low waters each tidal day, but occasionally the tide may become diurnal. Such tides are found along the Pacific coast of the United States.

In some localities the normal height of the tide can be greatly affected by strong winds blowing for a considerable period of time. Barometric pressure also affects the height of tide; a difference of one inch of barometric pressure causes a difference of about one foot in the water level.

A cautionary note should be introduced at this point—the expression "height of tide" must not be confused with "depth of water." The former refers to the vertical distance from the water surface to an arbitrarily chosen "reference plane" or "datum plane," such planes being based on a selected low water average, whereas the latter refers to a vertical distance from the surface of the water to the bottom. "Charted depth" is the vertical distance from the reference plane to the ocean bottom.

Early Tidal Predictions

The tides and currents about Britain and the western coast of Europe have presented a serious problem to mariners since time immemorial. Many ports dry out completely at low water, and the currents run strong in the English Channel.

Apparently, the relationship between the Moon and the tides was realized by the ancients. Voyaging in the first part of this millenium was generally quite restricted; the wine carrier usually sailed from his home port in Britain to either one or two ports in France. He therefore did not require tidal information of a general nature.

As commerce increased, so did the requirement for more general information. The methods used in the sixteenth and seventeenth centuries to cope with this problem, outlined below, may be of interest before we go on to discuss modern solutions for these problems.

The *Tide Tables,* as we know them, are a fairly modern invention. Tidal predictions were originally based on the time of the full Moon, called "Full," or of the new Moon, usually called "Change."

The earliest known tidal predictions covering ports over a fairly large area appeared on a chart prepared by Thomas Hood, an Englishman, in 1596, covering the southern portion of Ireland, southern England, the English Channel, and the Bay of Biscay. Against the various ports, a capital letter appeared.

The eastern half of a compass rose also appeared on the chart; against every point—11.25°—on the rose appeared a capital letter, *A* through *R, J* being omitted. *A* was located at North, representing midnight, and *R* at South, representing noon. Each letter therefore represented 45 minutes of time; thus, the letter *E,* appearing at NE, or at 45°, represented 3 A.M. and 3 P.M. This lettering system of giving tidal information had originally been suggested by William Bourne, in his *Regiment of the Sea,* published in 1574.

The letter *E,* appearing against the name of a port on the chart, therefore indicates that on the days of Full or Change high water occurred at that port at 3 A.M. and 3 P.M. To find the time of high water on other days, the Moon's age was taken into account, the time of high water being moved back 45 minutes of time for each day. Thus, for a port labeled *E* (3 hours) when the Moon is 4 days old, high water would occur at noon and midnight (3 hours − 4 × 45 minutes).

This lettering system was subsequently replaced by roman numerals, to which quarter hours in arabic numerals were sometimes appended, to give greater precision. This system yielded acceptably accurate results, and in many areas its use continued well into the present century. The information thus presented was variously called "The Vulgar (Common) Establishment," "The Establishment of the Port," "High Water, Full and Change," and "Mean Highwater Unitidal Interval."

This system of using roman numerals to indicate the time of high water was subsequently expanded to give tidal current information in the English Channel. About 1702 Edmond Halley, a noted English scientist, and subsequently Astronomer Royal, completed a study of tidal currents and magnetic variation in the channel; the results were presented on a chart.

Halley's roman numerals, with arabic quarters appended where necessary, appeared in many areas of the chart. They indicated the hours of high water on the days of new and full Moon, these hours coinciding with the end of the easterly set. Arrows indicating the direction of the easterly set were also shown. The flow of the current at intermediate days and times could then be determined in a manner similar to that for finding the time of high water.

Finding the Height of the Tide at a Specified Time

The *Tide Tables* tabulate the local standard times of high and low water; the navigator must frequently calculate the height of water at a specified time, or determine the time at which the water will be at a desired height.

If the vessel's clocks are set to daylight saving time, allowance must be made for the difference between ship's time and standard time.

The formula for finding the height of tide, H, at a specified time is:

$$H = \frac{Hh + Hl}{2} - \left[\frac{R}{2} \times \cos \left(\frac{Td \sim Tl}{Th \sim Tl} \times 180° \right) \right] \qquad (1)$$

in which Hh is the height of high water, Hl is the height of low water, R is the range of the tide (the difference in feet between high water and low water), Td is the specified time, Tl is the time of low water, and Th is the time of high water.

In regard to the range of the tide, if Hh is 7.0 feet, and Hl is −3.0 feet, R = 10 feet.

Example 1: On 3 June, at Humboldt Bay, California, low water comes at 0713, PST, the height being −2.0 feet, and high water is at 1353, height 5.4 feet. Our clocks are set to Pacific daylight saving time; we require the height of tide at 1200 ship's time.

1200 PDT equals 1100 PST, for which time we will find the height of tide, using formula (1), which we write:

$$H = \frac{5.4 + (-2.0)}{2} - \left[\frac{7.4}{2} \times \cos \left(\frac{11:00 \sim 7:13}{13:53 \sim 7:13} \times 180° \right) \right]$$

$$= \frac{3.4}{2} - \left[3.7 \times \cos \left(\frac{3.7833}{6.6667} \times 180° \right) \right]$$

$$= 1.7 - [3.7 \times \cos 102.15°]$$

$$= 1.7 - [-0.7787] = 2.4787 \text{ feet}$$

We would, therefore, expect the height of the tide to be about 2.5 feet at 1200 ship's time.

Example 2: We require the height of the tide in meters at Port Orford, Oregon, at 2200 PST on 17 June. We find that Port Orford's tides are based on those of Humboldt Bay, California, and that high water comes 24 minutes earlier and low water 21 minutes earlier than at Humboldt Bay; high water is 0.9 foot higher at Port Orford, and low water is 0.1 foot higher. We shall first find the height of tide in feet at the required time and then convert it to meters, using the conversion factor 0.30480.

Humboldt Bay, 17 June	Low water	18:18	2.8 feet
Differences		− :21	+ 0.1 foot
Port Orford	Low water	17:57	2.9 feet
Humboldt Bay, 17 June	High water	23:59	6.3 feet
Differences		− :24	+ 0.9 foot
Port Orford	High water	23:35	7.2 feet

Formula (1) is now written:

$$H = \frac{7.2 + 2.9}{2} - \left[\frac{4.3}{2} \times \cos\left(\frac{4.0500}{5.6333} \times 180°\right)\right]$$
$$= 5.050 - [2.150 \times \cos 129.4083°] = 5.050 - [-1.3649]$$

equals 6.4149, the height of tide in feet at 2200 PST; multiplying this figure by 0.3048, we get 1.9553 meters. We would therefore expect the height of tide to be 1.96 meters at 2200 PST.

It is, at times, necessary to determine the time at which the tide will reach a certain height. This problem may be solved by means of the following formula, in which T represents the desired time:

$$T = Tl + (Th - Tl)\left[\frac{\cos^{-1}\left\{1 - 2\left(\frac{Hd - Hl}{Hh - Hl}\right)\right\}}{180°}\right] \quad (2)$$

in which Tl is the time of low water, Th is the time of high water, Hd is the desired height of tide, Hl is the height of water at low tide, and Hh is the height of high tide.

Example 3: On the morning of 16 June, we require the time when the rising tide will reach a height of 3.5 feet at Humboldt Bay, California. From the *Tide Table* for Humboldt Bay, we extract data as follows:

16 June	At 0607	Height is −0.8 foot
	At 1254	Height is 4.6 feet

We can now write formula (2):

$$T = 6.1167 + (12.90 - 6.1167) \left[\frac{\cos^{-1}\left\{1 - 2\left(\frac{3.5 - (-0.8)}{4.6 - (-0.8)}\right)\right\}}{180°} \right]$$

$$= 6.1167 + 6.7833 \left[\frac{\cos^{-1}\left\{1 - 2\left(\frac{4.3}{5.4}\right)\right\}}{180°} \right]$$

$$= 6.1167 + 6.7833 \left[\frac{\cos^{-1}\{1 - 1.5926\}}{180°} \right]$$

$$= 6.1167 + 6.7833 \left[\frac{126.3412°}{180°} \right]$$

$$= 6.1167 + 6.7833[0.7019] = 10.8779 = 10h\ 52m\ 40s$$

We would, therefore, say the tide would reach a height of 3.5 feet at 1053.

Example 4: We are anchored in the harbor at Cape May, New Jersey, on the evening of 11 July and intend to leave the following morning to proceed North in Delaware Bay, departing via the Cape May Canal. We note that a fixed highway bridge, with a clearance of 55 feet above mean high water, crosses the canal. Our mast head stands 57.1 feet above the waterline.

From the *Tide Tables* we note that low tide will occur at Cape May Harbor on the morning of 12 July at 0320, the height being −1.0 foot; high water will occur at 0937, with a height of 5.0 feet. We are in need of a good night's sleep, and therefore wish to determine the last possible time on the following morning when we can pass under the highway bridge.

The first step is to determine the height of tide at which the clearance under the bridge will be 57.1 feet. To find this tidal height, we use the formula

$$\text{Tidal height} = MTL + \frac{MR}{2} + C - H$$

where MTL is the mean tide level, MR is the mean range of tide, C is the clearance above mean high water, and H is the height of the mast head above the water.

Only when chart datum is mean low water may this formula be abbreviated to

$$\text{Tidal height} = MR + C - H$$

From the *Tide Tables* we note that the mean tide level at Cape May Harbor is 2.2 feet and that the mean range is 4.4 feet; we know the bridge clearance is 55 feet and that we require a minimum clearance of

57.1 feet. To find the maximum tidal height on the morning of 12 July that will give a clearance of 57+ feet, the full formula becomes:

$$\text{Tidal height} = 2.2 \text{ feet} + \frac{4.4 \text{ feet}}{2} + 55 \text{ feet} - 57.1 \text{ feet}$$
$$= 59.4 \text{ feet} - 57.1 \text{ feet} = 2.3 \text{ feet}$$

To permit us to pass under the bridge, the tidal height therefore must not exceed 2.3 feet.

The next step is to determine the time on the morning of 12 July when the rising tide will reach a level of 2.3 feet:

$$\text{Time} = 0320 + (0937 - 0320) \times \left[\frac{\cos^{-1}\left\{ 1 - 2\left(\frac{2.3 - (-1.0)}{5.0 - (-1.0)} \right) \right\}}{180°} \right]$$
$$= 3.\overline{3} + 6.2833 \times \left[\frac{\cos^{-1}\left\{ 1 - 2\left(\frac{3.3}{6.0} \right) \right\}}{180°} \right]$$
$$= 3.\overline{3} + 6.2833 \times 0.5319 = 6.6754 = 06h \ 40m \ 31s$$

We, therefore, know that we will have to be at the bridge well before 0640 in order to pass underneath it safely.

Tidal Currents

Offshore, tidal currents are generally rotary in nature; during a complete tidal cycle, the set moves through 360°, although not in equal hourly increments. The drift, also, tends to vary considerably from hour to hour.

In harbor entrances, straits, narrows, and so on, the drift can be predicted for normal weather conditions with great accuracy; it can, however, be considerably affected by strong winds, and to a lesser degree by large changes in barometric pressure. However, the calculator can be used to advantage in conjunction with the *Current Tables* in determining (1) the drift under normal conditions at the majority of locations for any date and time, and for finding (2) the time when the drift will be of a specified strength. A third formula permits the calculation of the duration of the period of comparatively slack water.

These three formulae are for use with all reference and substations tabulated in the U. S. *Tidal Current Tables,* with the exception of the following:

Cape Cod Canal, Massachusetts
Hell Gate, New York
Chesapeake and Delaware Canal, Delaware and Maryland
Deception Pass, Washington

Seymour Narrows, British Columbia
Sergius Narrows, Alaska
Isanotski Strait, Alaska

and all stations referred to them. For these stations, the actual drift may exceed the drift as calculated by as much as 20%.

The same caveat applies to the formula for calculating the period of comparatively slack water.

It must be borne in mind that all times given in both the *Current Tables* and *Tide Tables* are standard times. If daylight time is in use on board ship, allowance must be made for the difference.

Predicting Current Drift at a Specified Time

To find the drift at a given time, the formula is:

$$D = Dm\left[\cos\left\{90° - \left(\frac{Td \sim Ts}{Tm \sim Ts} \times 90°\right)\right\}\right] \qquad (1)$$

where D is the drift at the specified time, Dm is the maximum tabulated drift, Td is the specified time, Ts is the time of slack water, and Tm is the time of maximum drift. In using this and formula (2), minutes are stated as decimals of an hour.

Example: Our ETA off Naruto, Japan, is 1440 local time on 16 May. We wish to determine the set and drift for that time and date.

From the *Current Tables* for 16 May, we note:

Slack water time	Maximum current time	Velocity
1559	1258	5.2 K, Flood
		Set northward

To determine the drift of the flood current at 1440, we write formula (1):

$$\text{Drift} = 5.2\left[\cos\left\{90° - \left(\frac{15.9833 - 14.6667}{15.9833 - 12.9667} \times 90°\right)\right\}\right]$$
$$= 5.2\left[\cos\left\{90° - \left(\frac{1.3166}{3.0166} \times 90°\right)\right\}\right]$$
$$= 5.2[\cos\{90° - 39.2806°\}]$$
$$= 5.2[\cos 50.7194°] = 3.2922$$

The current at 1440 will, therefore, be flooding at about 3.3 knots.

Predicting the Time When the Drift Will Be of a Specified Speed

The second formula is for use in determining the time at which the drift will be at a specified velocity.

$$\text{Time} = Ts \pm \left[\left(\frac{90° - \cos^{-1} \dfrac{Dd}{Dm}}{90°} \right) \times (Tm - Ts) \right] \qquad (2)$$

in which Ts is the time of slack water, Dd is the velocity of the desired drift, Dm is the velocity of the maximum drift, Tm is the time of maximum drift, and Ts is the time of slack water.

The sign following Ts is + when the required time will be after the time of slack water, and − when it will occur before the time of slack water.

Example 2: Having, in Example 1, established the set and drift of the current for the time of our ETA, 1440 on 16 May, off Naruto, using formula (1), we decide that the drift is too strong for safe maneuvering, and decide to wait until the drift of the flood current is 2.0 knots. Using the same current data as given in Example 1, at what time can we expect the drift to be 2.0 knots?

We write formula (2) as follows, using a − sign because, in this instance, the required time will occur before the time of slack water.

$$\text{Time} = 15.9833 - \left[\left(\frac{90° - \cos^{-1} \dfrac{2.0}{5.2}}{90°} \right) \times (15.9833 - 12.9667) \right]$$

$$= 15.9833 - [(0.2513) \times (3.0166)]$$

$$= 15.9833 - 0.7582 = 15.2251 \text{ hours}$$

We would, therefore, expect that the drift would be 2.0 knots at about 1514.

Duration of Slack Water

The predicted time of slack water, tabulated in the *Current Tables,* is only momentary. There is, however, a period on each side of the time of slack water when the drift is weak.

The formula given below permits the calculation of the total period, in minutes, during which weak currents, with a drift not exceeding 0.5 knot, may be expected. This formula applies to all stations listed in the *Current Tables,* with the exception of those listed at the beginning of the section on tidal currents. For these latter stations, the times calculated by the formula may be shorter by 25 to 45%.

$$T = \frac{115}{Dm} \times 2 \times Ds \qquad (1)$$

in which T is the total duration in minutes during which the drift should not exceed the specified velocity, Dm is the maximum drift, and Ds is the specified drift.

Example: We wish to determine the total period during which the drift will not exceed 0.25 knot, when the maximum drift is 5.5 knots.

Formula (1) becomes:

$$T = \frac{115}{5.5} \times 2 \times 0.25 = 10.45$$

We would assume, therefore, that there would be a period of at least 10 minutes during which the set would not exceed 0.25 knot.

Wind Currents at Sea

Surface currents are generated at sea by wind. As a general rule, it is held that a wind must blow for a minimum of 12 hours before generating appreciable surface motion. Well offshore a steady wind will cause a surface drift of up to 2% of the wind speed.

The set of a wind current will be deflected to the right in the Northern Hemisphere by the Coriolis force, and to the left in the Southern Hemisphere; the Coriolis force increases with latitude. In general, the difference between the wind direction and the wind-current direction varies from about 15% in shallow coastal areas to a maximum of 45% in the deep oceans.

Prolonged strong winds can materially affect the surface set and drift of the great ocean currents, such as the Gulf Stream. A prolonged nor'east gale off the Florida coast will materially slow the Gulf Stream, and cause extremely steep, breaking seas.

Current Sailing

Finding Correction Angle and Speed of Advance

When a current of known set and drift is flowing, the course a ship must steer in order to offset it, as well as the speed of advance (i.e., the speed made good over the bottom) may be readily calculated. Using the law of sines, both the correction angle (i.e., the angle between the desired track and the heading to be used to make good that track) and the speed of advance may be readily determined.

Figure 2-4a represents a situation in which the current is fair, while Figure 2-4b represents a foul current situation. In both parts of the figure, the direction of the vector c represents the desired track; its length represents the speed of advance. The vector b represents the set and drift of the current, while a represents the ship's heading and speed through the water. Angle B is the correction angle.

The first step is to determine the value of the correction angle, B, using formula (1):

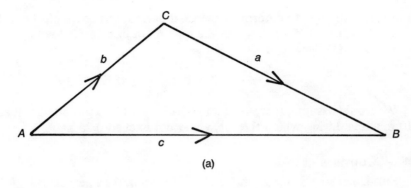

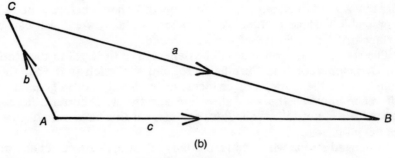

Figure 2-4.

$$\sin B = \frac{b \times \sin A}{a} \tag{1}$$

The next step is to calculate the speed of advance, c, for which we use the formula

$$c = \frac{a \times \sin [180° - (A + B)]}{\sin A} \tag{2}$$

Example 1: The current is setting 248°, and the drift is 1.5 knots. We wish to make good a track of 289°, and are sailing at 11.0 knots. What should be our heading, and what will be our speed of advance?

Formula (1) is written:

$$\sin B = \frac{1.5 \times \sin (289° - 248°)}{11.0} = 0.0895$$

$$B = 5.1327°$$

The correction angle is, therefore, 5.1327°; for practical purposes, we shall call it 5°. The current being on our starboard quarter, we shall steer 5° to the right of the desired track, or 294°.

The next step is to determine the speed of advance, c, using formula

(2), which becomes:

$$c = \frac{11.0 \times \sin [180° - (41° + 5°)]}{\sin 41°} = 12.0610$$

Our speed of advance, therefore, will be 12.0 knots.

Example 2: We wish to make good a track of 160°, and are steaming at 12.0 knots. The current is setting 015°, with a drift of 2.0 knots. What course should we steer, and what will be our speed of advance?

We write formula (1):

$$\sin B = \frac{2.0 \times \sin (160° - 15°)}{12.0} = 0.0956$$
$$B = 5.4856°$$

The current being on the starboard bow, we would, therefore, steer 165.5°.

To find the speed of advance, formula (2) is written:

$$c = \frac{12.0 \times \sin [180° - (145° + 5.5°)]}{\sin 145°} = 10.3022$$

Our speed of advance, therefore, will be 10.3 knots.

Current Sailing When Track and Speed of Advance Are Specified

A somewhat different problem arises when both the track and speed of advance are specified. In such a case, returning to Figure 2-4a,b, we know the angle A, which represents the difference between the track and the current's set, we know the length of the vector b, the drift of the current, and we know the vector c, the specified speed of advance.

As previously, we must compute the correction angle, B, but in this instance we must also compute the length of the vector a, which represents the speed at which we must steam.

The value of the correction angle, B, is found by means of the formula

$$\tan B = \frac{b \times \sin A}{c - b \times \cos A} \qquad (3)$$

Having computed the value of the angle B, we apply it to the direction of the track, in order to obtain the course to be steered.

The next step is to calculate the speed at which we must steam, represented by the length of the vector a, in order to maintain the specified speed of advance. This we find by means of the formula

$$a = \frac{b \times \sin A}{\sin B} \qquad (4)$$

Example 3: We are to make good a track of 230°, at a speed of advance of 15.0 knots. The current is setting in the direction 350°, and the drift is 2.0 knots. We require the heading and the steaming speed to comply with orders.

Formula (3) becomes:

$$\tan B = \frac{2.0 \times \sin 120°}{15.0 - 2.0 \times \cos 120°} = \frac{1.7321}{16.0} = 0.1083$$

B, therefore, is 6.1784°.

Because the current is on our port bow, we would, therefore, come 6° to the left of the track and steer 224°.

The next step is to determine the speed to steam. We write formula (4):

$$\text{Steaming speed} = \frac{2.0 \times \sin 120°}{\sin 6.1784°} = \frac{1.7321}{0.1076} = 16.0935$$

We should, therefore, make turns for 16.1 knots to maintain a speed of advance of 15.0 knots.

Note that in solving the first formula, we could have stored the dividend, 1.7321, and subsequently would have recalled it as for use as the dividend in the second formula.

Set and Drift from Track Between Fixes

Sometimes a vessel unexpectedly passes into an area where the current drift is strong, and finds that she is being badly set. The problem here is to determine the set and drift of the current, in order that corrective action may be taken.

In determining the set and drift, departure must be taken from a fixed or known position, and a second fix must be obtained. When the second fix is plotted on a chart, the current vector is represented by a line drawn from the DR position for the time of the second fix, to that fix. Alternatively, unless the distance traveled between fixes is great, it may be found by a plane sailing solution, using the calculator. If the distance is great, the current vector should be found by mid-latitude sailing. It must be borne in mind that when a considerable amount of time has elapsed between obtaining fixes, the current may not have been flowing during the whole period. In this case, the current is stronger than is indicated in the solution.

Example: We are on course 340°, speed 10.6 knots, headed for the sea buoy at the entrance to the main ship channel at Key West. At 2200, we get a good radar fix which puts us in L 24°13.1′ N, λ 81°42.2′ W. At 2300 we obtain another radar fix which puts us in L 24°24.1′ N, λ 81°43.0′ W.

We wish to determine the set and drift of the current.

We first determine what our 2300 position would have been, if no current had existed. Using 20° for course (360° − 340°), by plane sailing formula the difference of latitude is 9.96 miles North, which we call 10.0 miles, and the departure is 3.625 miles West, which converts to 3.98' of longitude and which we call 4.0'. At 2300, therefore, our DR latitude is 24°23.1' N (24°13.1' + 10.0') and our DR longitude is 81°46.2' W (81°42.2' + 4.0').

We now compare our 2300 fix with our 2300 DR:

Fix	L 24°24.1' N	81°43.0' W
DR	L 24°23.1' N	81°46.2' W
Difference	1.0' N	3.2' E

To convert 3.2' of longitude in L 24°24' N to departure, p, we use the formula

$$p = DLo \text{ in minutes} \times \cos L$$

which makes p 2.9142, which we shall call 2.91 miles. Consequently, in one hour, the current has set us 1.0 mile to the North and 2.91 miles to the East of our DR position; the set is, therefore, North and East.

To determine the direction of the set, we use the formula:

$$\cot \text{ direction, N \& E} = \frac{l}{p}$$

The cotangent of the direction is therefore 2.9142, which makes the set N 71.0605° E, or, for our purposes, 071°.

To find the drift, as the period between fixes was exactly 1 hour, we can use the formula

$$\text{Drift} = \frac{l}{\cos \text{ set}}$$

which makes the drift 3.077; we shall call it 3.1 knots.

Current Sailing Problems with Calculators Having Polar–Rectangular Conversion Capability

The use of the polar–rectangular interconversion feature can also be very helpful in the solution of current sailing problems. Without this feature, an inverse tangent of some ratio, say y/x, is required. With the rectangular to polar conversion capacity, instead of our performing the division, and having to accept a principal value, the R → P function can be executed, and the angle in its correct quadrant is obtained.

Example: We are on course 180° at 10 knots. The current is setting 270°, with a drift of 3 knots. We wish to determine our course over the bottom, using the rectangular to polar conversion feature.

As our course is southerly, and the set of the current is westerly, both the drift and ship's speed will be entered as minus quantities. In essence, what we are doing is finding the angle whose tangent is $-3/-10$.

For calculators using the Reverse Polish Notation, the keying sequence is:

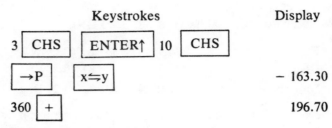

Keystrokes	Display
3 CHS ENTER↑ 10 CHS	
→P x⇆y	− 163.30
360 +	196.70

which is our course made good, or track.

With calculators using the algebraic notation, the keying sequence is:

Keystrokes	Display
10 +/− STO 00	
3 +/− →P	− 163.30
+ 360 =	196.70

which is our track.

Current Sailing Using Vector Addition

The vector addition capability, combined with the capability to interconvert polar and rectangular coordinates, available on many scientific calculators, is illustrated by the following current sailing problem.

We are to make good a track of 230°, with a speed of advance of 15 knots. The current is setting 350°, with a drift of 2.0 knots. We require course to steer, and the speed at which to steam.

To obtain the steaming speed and the course, using both the vector addition and coordinate conversion capabilities of our calculator, we proceed as follows:

Remarks

Clear all registers.

Key in track, 230°, ENTER↑

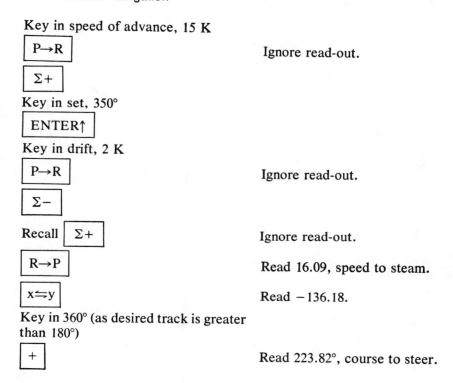

Key in speed of advance, 15 K

P→R   Ignore read-out.

Σ+

Key in set, 350°

ENTER↑

Key in drift, 2 K

P→R   Ignore read-out.

Σ−

Recall Σ+   Ignore read-out.

R→P   Read 16.09, speed to steam.

x⇆y   Read −136.18.

Key in 360° (as desired track is greater
than 180°)

+   Read 223.82°, course to steer.

Direction and Speed of True Wind

Given the course and speed of the ship, and the direction and speed of the apparent wind, the direction and speed of the true wind may be found by solving a vector triangle. The form this triangle takes depends upon whether the apparent wind is from forward of the beam (see Figure 2-5) or from abaft the beam (see Figure 2-6).

In both these triangles, side a represents the speed of the true wind and its direction relative to the ship's heading; side b represents the speed of the apparent wind and the direction in which it is moving relative to the ship; side c represents the speed and course of the ship. In Figure 2-5, the ship's travel vector is in the direction AB, and in Figure 2-6 it is in the direction BA.

The direction of the true wind is found by means of the formula

$$\tan B = \frac{b \times \sin A}{c - b \times \cos A} \tag{1}$$

in which A is the angle of the apparent wind relative to the ship's heading, and B is the angle to be applied to the ship's heading to obtain

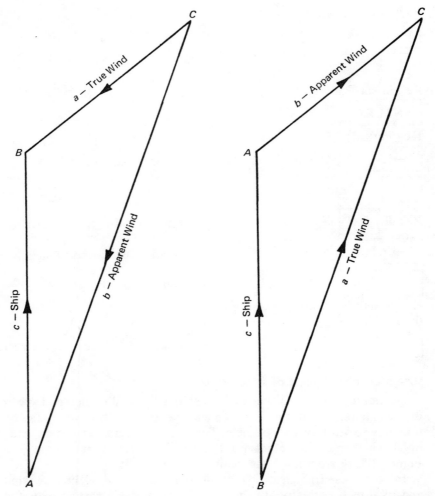

Figure 2-5. Apparent wind forward of beam

Figure 2-6. Apparent wind abaft beam

the direction of the true wind. The ship's vector is c, the apparent wind vector is b, and the true wind is a.

The speed of the true wind is found by means of the formula

$$a = \frac{b \times \sin A}{\sin B} \qquad (2)$$

Example 1: We are on course 090°, speed 12 knots, and the apparent wind is blowing from 120° True, speed 25.0 knots. For our heading, 120°

True is 030° relative. We require the direction and speed of the true wind.

We write formula (1):

$$\tan B = \frac{25 \times \sin 30°}{12 - 25 \times \cos 30°} = -1.2953$$

This converts to −52.3300°, so the angle B in the vector triangle is 127.6700°, and the true wind direction is from 052.3300° relative, or 142.3300° True. We would therefore write the wind as being from 142°, or as SE.

To find its speed, we write formula (2):

$$a = \frac{25 \times \sin 30°}{\sin 52.33°}$$

The true wind speed is, therefore, 15.7919 knots, which we would note as 16 knots.

Example 2: Our course is 305°, speed 15.0 knots, and the apparent wind is from 230° relative, or 175° True at 8 knots. What is the direction and speed of the true wind?

In this case, the angle A equals 130° as the wind's relative vector, it lies in the direction 230° − 050°, it intersects the ship's vector at 50° + 130°, and the latter is the angle required in the vector triangle.

We now write formula (1):

$$\tan B = \frac{8 \times \sin 130°}{15 - 8 \times \cos 130°} = 0.3043$$

B, therefore, equals 16.9225°, or 17°, and the true wind is from 197° (180° + 17°) relative to our ship's heading. This makes it from 142° True (305° + 197° − 360°).

To find the true wind speed, we write formula (2):

$$a = \frac{8 \times \sin 130°}{\sin 16.9225°} = 21.0540$$

The true wind is, therefore, blowing from 142° True at 21 knots.

Wind Triangle Solution by Calculators Having the Polar–Rectangular Conversion Capability

The wind triangle may be solved rapidly with calculators having the polar–rectangular conversion feature. The keying sequences for both RPN and algebraic calculators are tabulated below. The first step is to determine the direction *toward* which the apparent wind is blowing. Thus, if the apparent wind is from 110° True, it is blowing toward 290°; this vector we will call *TWT*.

RPN Keystrokes   Comments

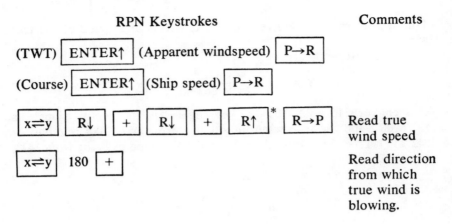

Read true
wind speed

Read direction
from which
true wind is
blowing.

Algebraic Keystrokes

The order of entry for these calculators is slightly different from the above. *TWT* is here used as with the RPN calculators.

Algebraic Keystrokes   Comments

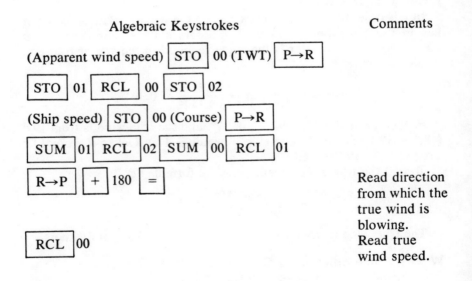

Read direction
from which the
true wind is
blowing.
Read true
wind speed.

To illustrate, we shall use the data given in Example 1 above.

* For calculators not equipped with a "Roll Up" key, substitute three "Roll Down" entries (R↓ R↓ R↓).

Our course is 090°, speed 12 knots, and the apparent wind is blowing from 120°, speed 25 knots. We require the direction and speed of the true wind.

For the RPN calculation, the steps are as follows:

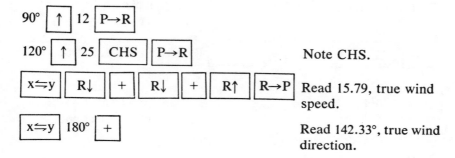

Note CHS.

Read 15.79, true wind speed.

Read 142.33°, true wind direction.

For the algebraic notation calculators, the keystrokes, typically, would be as follows:

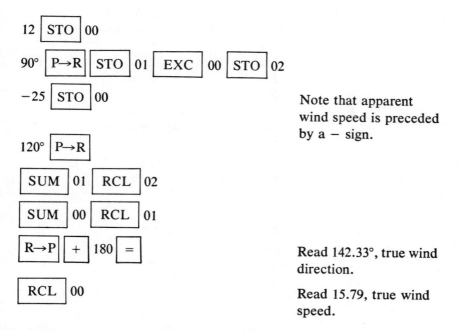

Note that apparent wind speed is preceded by a − sign.

Read 142.33°, true wind direction.

Read 15.79, true wind speed.

In Example 2 above, we are on course 305°, speed 15 knots; the apparent wind is from 230° relative, at 8.0 knots. We require the direction and speed of the true wind.

In this case, the RPN keystrokes are as follows:

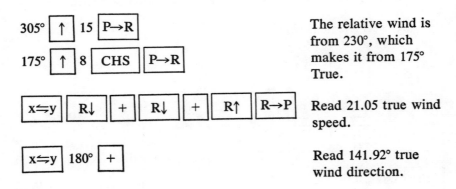

305° ↑ 15 P→R   The relative wind is
                        from 230°, which
175° ↑ 8 CHS P→R   makes it from 175°
                        True.

x⇌y R↓ + R↓ + R↑ R→P   Read 21.05 true wind
                        speed.

x⇌y 180° +   Read 141.92° true
                        wind direction.

Beaufort Wind Scale

Beaufort number	Knots	World meteorological organization
0	Under 1	Calm
1	1–3	Light air
2	4–6	Light breeze
3	7–10	Gentle breeze
4	11–16	Moderate breeze
5	17–21	Fresh breeze
6	22–27	Strong breeze
7	28–33	Near gale
8	34–40	Gale
9	41–47	Strong gale
10	48–55	Storm
11	56–63	Violent storm
12	64–72	Hurricane
13	72–81	Hurricane
14	81–89	Hurricane
15	90–99	Hurricane
16	100–108	Hurricane
17	109–118	Hurricane

For algebraic calculators, the keystrokes are as follows:

15 | STO | 00 305° | P→R | STO | 01

EXC | 00 | STO | 02 −8 | STO | 00

175° | P→R | SUM | 01 | RCL | 02 | SUM | 00

RCL | 01 | R→P | + | 180° | =   Read true wind
                                   direction 141.92°.

EXC | 00   Read 21.05 true
              wind speed.

Great-Circle Direction Converted to Mercator Direction, and Vice Versa

On board ship, it is frequently necessary to convert a great-circle bearing, or direction, to a rhumb line, which is its equivalent Mercator value, so that it can be plotted on a Mercator chart. This problem most frequently involves radio-direction-finder bearings, which, of course, are great-circle bearings, and it can be solved by determining the conversion angle. Conversely, given a Mercator bearing, the conversion angle permits determination of the equivalent great-circle bearing.

Where the difference of longitude between the two points involved, DLo, is less than 5°, the conversion angle may be found by means of the formula

$$\tan \text{ conversion angle} = \sin Lm \times \tan \frac{DLo}{2}$$

in which Lm is the mid-latitude.

In determining the sign of the conversion angle, it must be remembered that the great circle lies toward the elevated pole from the rhumb line. Alternatively, the sign may be taken from Table 2-1.

Where the difference of longitude exceeds 5°, one of the formulae given in the section on great-circle sailing should be used to determine the great-circle direction.

Example 1: Our DR position is L 35°51.0′ N, λ 84°25.0′ W when we receive a radio bearing of 128.0° from a beacon located at L 32°47.0′ N, λ 79°55.0′ W. In order to plot a line of position on a Mercator chart, we need the conversion angle and its sign.

We tabulate the data:

Table 2-1

	Radio bearings			Great-circle sailing	
Latitude of receiver	Radio beacon lies to	Correction sign	Latitude of departure	Destination lies to	Correction sign
N	Eastward	+	N	Eastward	−
N	Westward	−	N	Westward	+
S	Eastward	−	S	Eastward	+
S	Westward	+	S	Westward	−

	L	λ	
Ship	35°51.0′ N	84°25.0′ W	
Beacon	32°47.0′ N	79°55.0′ W	
Difference	3°04.0′	4°30.0′	Half difference = 2°15.0′
Lm	34°19.0′ N		

With the above data, the formula above becomes:

tan conversion angle = sin 34°19.0′ × tan 2°15.0′ = 0.0222

The conversion angle, therefore, is 1°16.0′, or 1.3°, and the sign is
+. Thus, the Mercator bearing is 129.3° (128.0° + 1.3°).

Example 2: We are in L 47°19.0′ N, λ 49°23.6′ W, and wish to
determine the great-circle bearing of Point A, located in L 51°47.5′ N,
λ 53°31.7′ W. From a Mercator chart, Point A bears 329.0°.
We tabulate the data, as in Example 1:

	L	λ	
Ship	47°19.0′ N	49°23.6′ W	
Point A	51°47.5′ N	53°31.7′ W	
Difference	4°28.5′	4°08.1′	Half difference = 2°04.0′
Lm	49°33.3′ N		

and write the formula

tan conversion angle = sin 49°33.3′ × tan 2°04.0′ = 0.0275

The conversion angle, therefore, equals 1°34.5', or, for our purpose, 1.6°. In this case we are converting a rhumb-line bearing to a great-circle bearing, we are in North latitude, and Point A lies to the west-ward. Therefore, the sign of the conversion angle is +, and the great-circle bearing is 330.6° (329.0° + 1.6°).

3
Offshore Navigation

The Sailings

A sailing, as traditionally defined, is a method of solving the various problems involving course, distance, difference of latitude, difference of longitude, and departure. Departure, in turn, is defined as the distance between any two meridians at any given parallel of latitude, expressed in linear units, such as nautical miles.

Plane Sailing. For centuries, the only sailing employed by the mariner was plane sailing, which is based on the assumption that the Earth is a flat surface. Plane sailing still yields satisfactory results over comparatively small areas when plotted on a Mercator chart.

Traverse Sailing. Traverse sailing derives its name from the travas, a circular board with lines radiating in 32 directions, one for each point of the compass. Holes were drilled at equal distances along each line; a peg could be inserted in one of these holes to denote the length of time as determined by an hour or half-hour sand glass; sometimes a peg was used to denote the estimated distance sailed on a given course. This device enabled the mate of the watch to keep track of the ship's courses for a considerable period of time, even when forced to tack frequently, without the almost impossible alternative of resorting to pen and ink, the prerogative of the master.

However, the unenviable task of reducing a number of traverses mathematically to an updated position remained. This need led to the invention of the traverse table, such as Table 3 of *Bowditch*. The first such table apparently was prepared by Andrea Biancho in 1436.

Parallel Sailing. Because of the early navigator's inability to determine longitude, parallel sailing came into use. Knowing the latitude of his destination, as he neared land he came to this latitude, and then ran either due East or West.

Middle-Latitude Sailing. The inaccuracies inherent in plane sailing over considerable distances led to the development of middle-latitude sailing (usually abbreviated mid-latitude sailing), supposedly by Ralph Handsen, about 1640. This sailing is based on the assumption that the use of a parallel midway between those of the point of departure and of the destination will eliminate the errors in plane sailing caused by the convergence of the meridians. This assumption is reasonably accurate, and yields acceptable results for distances up to about 1,200 miles. However, when accuracy is a prime consideration, Mercator or rhumb-line sailing should be used.

Mercator Sailing. In 1569 Gerardus Mercator, a Flemish cartographer, published a chart of the world, constructed on a system that since then has borne his name. However, he failed to publish any data on the mathematics he had employed. In 1599, an Englishman, Edward Wright, explained the Mercator projection, and published a table of meridional parts. This table not only made possible the construction of other charts on the Mercator projection, but also led to the development of Mercator sailing, which provides a mathematical solution of the plot, as made on a Mercator chart, by using meridional difference and difference of longitude.

Rhumb-line Sailing. Rhumb-line sailing considers the Earth to be a perfect sphere, rather than a spheroid or a plane surface; it can, however, be modified to allow for the asphericity of the Earth. A rhumb line, or loxodrome, is a line on the surface of the Earth making the same oblique angle with all meridians. This sailing is a comparatively recent concept.

Great-Circle Sailing. That a great circle is the shortest distance between two points on a sphere has long been known. In 1498, Sebastian Cabot argued in favor of the concept, and in 1524, the Italian Giovanni da Verrazano attempted to sail a great-circle track to North America. The first printed description of great-circle sailing appeared in Pedro Nunes's *Tratado de Sphera,* published in 1537.

It was, however, difficult for square-rigged sailing vessels to take much advantage of this sailing, except on some routes in the Pacific; with the advent of steam, on the other hand, great-circle sailing came into general use on long passages.

In great-circle sailing, the Earth is considered to be a perfect sphere;

the problems involved in this sailing are solved by spherical trigonometry.

Composite Sailing. Composite sailing is a modified form of great-circle sailing; it is used when it is desired to limit the highest latitude to be reached on a passage.

In connection with great-circle sailing, it may not be amiss to mention the Lambert projection charts, published by the National Ocean Survey primarily for air use. These charts can be extremely useful in planning long ocean voyages, in that a straight line on such a chart very closely approximates a great-circle track, so that distances can readily be measured with only small error. In addition, whereas land masses represented on great-circle charts prepared on the gnomonic projection tend to appear distorted in shape, on Lambert projection charts they appear very much as we are used to seeing them on Mercator charts.

The coordinates of points at which a great-circle track is to be broken into rhumb lines can readily be taken off a Lambert projection chart.

The first four of the above sailings all offer one great advantage, in that they permit the calculation of a single course, which may be followed from the point of departure to the destination. Great-circle sailing, on the other hand, permits the calculation of the shortest track. However, to follow such a track, the course would have to be changed constantly. Thus, when great-circle sailing is employed, it is customary to break the track into a series of rhumb lines of convenient lengths.

Plane Sailing

In plane sailing the figure formed by the meridian passing through the point of departure, the parallel of latitude passing through the destination, and the course line, is considered to be a plane right-angled triangle (see Figure 3-1). As in any right triangle, if a second angle and the length of any side are known, the remaining angle and the length of either other side can readily be found by means of the formulae given below.

In Figure 3-1, P_1 represents the point of departure and P_2 the destination. Side p of the triangle, called the "departure," is the distance, in nautical miles, East or West, made good in proceeding to the destination. Side l is the portion of a meridian drawn from the point of departure to the parallel of latitude of the destination; it represents the difference of latitude and is measured in nautical miles, which are equal to minutes of arc along a meridian. Side D represents the distance sailed in nautical miles, and angle C represents the course angle.

Note: In plane sailing, the course is reckoned as course angle from North or South to 90° East or West. Thus, *Cn* 162° would be written as S 18° E, and *Cn* 341° as N 19°W.

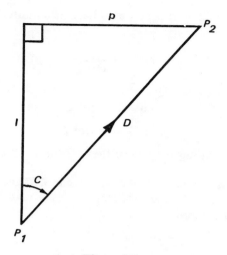

Figure 3-1.

Plane sailing formulae are:

Given C and D, to find l:

$$l = \cos C \times D \qquad (1)$$

Given C and D, to find p:

$$p = \sin C \times D \qquad (2)$$

Given l and p, to find C:

$$\tan C = \frac{p}{l} \qquad (3)$$

In connection with formula (3), it must be remembered that if l is greater than p, C will be less than 45°; if it is less, C will be greater than 45°.

Given C and l, to find D:

$$D = \frac{l}{\cos C} \qquad (4)$$

Given C and p, to find D:

$$D = \frac{p}{\sin C} \qquad (5)$$

Knowing p, it is often necessary to convert it to difference of longitude, DLo. Strictly speaking, this problem does not belong under the heading of plane sailing; it is included here as a matter of convenience. The formula is:

$$DLo = \frac{p}{\cos L} \qquad (6)$$

where L represents latitude.

Alternatively, if DLo is known, p may be found:

$$p = DLo \times \cos L \qquad (7)$$

Examples illustrating the use of these formulae are given below.

Example 1: We have steamed 90 miles on Cn 320° and need to find the difference of latitude, l. The first step is to convert 320° to N 40° W. Formula (1) then becomes:

$$l = \cos 40° \times 90 = 68.94$$

The difference of latitude, therefore, is 68.9' or 1°08.9' North.

Example 2: Given the same data as in Example 1, find p. Formula (2) becomes:

$$p = \sin 40° \times 90 = 57.85$$

The departure, therefore, is 57.9 miles West.

Example 3a: Given an l of 69.0' South and a p of 57.9 miles West, we wish to find C. Formula (3) becomes:

$$\tan C = \frac{57.9}{69} = 0.839$$

The course angle, therefore, is S 40° W, or Cn 220°.

Example 3b: Given an l of 57.9' North and a p of 69 miles East, find C. Formula (3) becomes:

$$\tan C = \frac{69}{57.9} = 1.19$$

The course angle is, therefore, N 50° E, or Cn 050°.

Example 4: Given Cn 273.5°, or N 86.5° W and an l of 5 miles, find D. Formula (4) becomes:

$$D = \frac{5}{\cos 86.5°} = 81.9$$

The distance, therefore, is 81.9 miles.

Example 5: Given *Cn* 030°, or N 30° E, and *p* 41.5 miles, find *D*. Formula (5) becomes:

$$D = \frac{41.5}{\sin 30°} = 83.0$$

The distance, therefore, is 83.0 miles.

Example 6: Given L 46° N and *p* 57.9 miles West, find the *DLo*. Formula (6) becomes:

$$DLo = \frac{57.9}{\cos 46°} = 83.4$$

The difference of longitude, therefore, is 83.4' West.

Example 7: Given L 43° N and *DLo* 41.0' W, find *p*. Formula (7) becomes:

$$p = \cos 43° \times 41 = 30.0$$

The departure, therefore, is 30.0 miles West.

Mid-latitude Sailing

Mid-latitude sailing is based on approximations that simplify solutions and yield results sufficiently accurate for ordinary navigation over medium distances, say, to 1,200 miles. When the distance is greater, or in high latitudes, or when a rigorous solution is required, Mercator or great-circle sailing should be used.

When course and distance steamed are given, mid-latitude sailing permits determination of the difference of latitude, *l*, and the departure, *p*, expressed as a difference of longitude, *DLo*, in minutes of arc. Alternatively, when the coordinates of two points are given, it permits determination of the rhumb-line course and the distance between the points, *D*.

In mid-latitude sailing, departure and difference of longitude may be interconverted, using the mean, or mid-, latitude, *Lm*. The formulae are:

$$p = DLo, \text{ in minutes} \times \cos Lm \qquad (1)$$

$$DLo, \text{ in minutes} = \frac{p}{\cos Lm} \qquad (2)$$

$$\tan C = \frac{p}{l} \qquad (3)$$

where *l* is in minutes of arc and *C* is the course angle, expressed from North or South toward East or West to 90°.

$$D = \frac{l}{\cos C} \qquad (4)$$

Example 1: By mid-latitude sailing, what is the course and what is the distance from Brenton Reef Light (off Newport, Rhode Island), L 41°26′ N, λ 71°23′ W, to St. David's Light, Bermuda, L 32°22′ N, λ 64°39′ W?

We set up the problem:

L_1	41°26′ N		λ_1	71°23′ W
L_2	32°22′ N		λ_2	64°39′ W
l	9°04′ S = 544′ S		*DLo*	6°44′ E = 404′ E
½l	4°32′ S			
L_1	41°26′ N			
Lm	36°54′ N			

Having obtained *Lm,* we proceed to find p, using formula (1):

$$p = 404 \times \cos 36.9° = 323.1 \text{ miles}$$

Having found p, 323.1, we find the course, using formula (3):

$$\tan C = \frac{323.1}{544} = 0.594 = \text{S } 30.7° \text{ E}$$

The true course, therefore, will be 149.3° (180° − 30.7°).

The final step is to determine the distance, using formula (4):

$$D = \frac{544}{\cos 30.7°} = 632.7 \text{ miles}$$

Thus, the course to reach St. David's Light is 149.3°, and the distance is 632.7 miles. This calculation compares quite well with a rigorous great-circle solution, which makes the distance 632.2 miles and the initial heading 147.79°.

Example 2: We steam 960 miles on course 230° from L 33°16′ N, λ 29°43′ W, and need to find the latitude and longitude of our position. By transposing formula (4), we can find l:

$$l = 960 \times \cos 230° = -617.0761′$$

Knowing that l equals 617.1′ S, or 10°17.1′ S, and consequently that L_2 is 22°58.9′ N (L 33°16′ N − 10°17.1′ S), we can find p, by transposing formula (3):

$$p = \tan 230° \times 617.1′ = 1.1918 \times 617.1 = 735.4 \text{ miles}$$

To find the *DLo,* we must first determine *Lm*:

$$l = 10°17' \text{ S and } \tfrac{1}{2}l = 5°08.5' \text{ S}$$

$$\begin{array}{lr} L_1 & 33°16.0' \text{ N} \\ & - \\ \tfrac{1}{2}l & 5°08.5' \text{ S} \\ Lm & 28°07.5' \text{ N} \end{array}$$

Then formula (2) becomes:

$$DLo = \frac{735.4}{\cos 28.1250°} = 833.8613'$$

Converting 833.8613' to degrees and minutes, we get 13°53.9' W.

Finally, we can obtain the latitude and longitude of our destination as follows:

$$\begin{array}{lrlr} L_1 & 33°16.0' \text{ N} & \lambda_1 & 29°43.0' \text{ W} \\ \sim & & + & \\ & 10°17.1' \text{ S} & DLo & 13°53.9' \text{ W} \\ L_2 & 22°58.9' \text{ N} & \lambda_2 & 43°36.9' \text{ W} \end{array}$$

Solution of Plane-Sailing Problems with Calculators Having the Polar–Rectangular Interconversion Feature, and of Vector Addition Problems

Under the heading "Current Sailing," we saw how useful the rectangular to polar conversion feature could be. The polar to rectangular conversion can be equally useful in solving plane-sailing problems. Given course and speed, it can convert them into North–South and East–West components; equally, it can convert course and distance into change of latitude and departure, and can compute the sine and cosine of an angle simultaneously.

Example 1: We have sailed 53 miles on course 137°, and wish to determine our change in latitude, l, and departure, p.

For calculators using the Reverse Polish Notation, the keystrokes are:

137 | ENTER↑ | 53 | P→R   Display −38.76, which indicates that l is South (minus) 38.76'.

x⇆y   Display 36.15, which is p 36.15 miles, named East as it is positive.

Example 2: At 0634 our position is L 33°23.2' N, λ 74°40.6' W. We estimate that we made good a course of 043° T until 1150, and covered 36.9 miles. At 1150, we tacked, came to course 316° T, and sailed 41.3 miles. At 1729, we tacked again, coming to C 040°, and by 1932 we had logged 12.7 miles on this leg.

During the entire day, we estimate that the current was setting 020° T, with a drift of 1.2 knots.

We derive our 1932 position, using the polar to rectangular conversion capability of our calculator.

We tabulate the data for each leg as shown on the left below, course and distance constituting polar coordinates. These data, converted to rectangular coordinates, are tabulated on the right for each leg, l being minutes of latitude, and p minutes of departure.

1 C 043° T,	36.9 miles	*l* 26.99' N,	*p* 25.17' E	
2 316°	41.3 miles	29.71' N	−28.69'W	
3 040°	12.7 miles	9.73' N	8.16' E	
Total for boat	__	*l* 66.43' N	*p* 4.64' E	

Current:
Set 020°; drift 1.2 knots for
12h 58m = 15.56 miles l 14.62' N p 5.32' E

l 81.05' N p 9.96' E

Our change in latitude for the entire run, and allowing for the current, is 1°21.0' N. We are 9.96 miles farther east than we were in the morning.

We convert this departure, p, of 9.96 miles E to a difference of longitude, by dividing it by the cosine of the mid-latitude of the run, which we shall call 34.0°:

$$\frac{9.96 \text{ miles}}{\cos 34°} = DLo \; 12.01' \text{ E}$$

Our 1932 position was therefore L 34°44.2' N (33°23.2' + 1°21.0') and λ 74°28.6' W (74°40.6' − 12.0').

Mercator Sailing

Materials here, of every kind
May soon be found, were Youth inclin'd,
To practice the Ingenious Art
Of sailing by Mercanter's Chart.

Ebenezer Cooke, circa 1778
Maryland Patriot and poet (?)

At the equator, a degree of longitude is approximately equal in length to a degree of latitude. As distance from the equator increases, the degrees of latitude remain about the same length (varying slightly because of the Earth's oblateness); at the same time, degrees of longitude become progressively shorter. Since, on a Mercator chart, the degrees of longitude appear everywhere to be of the same length, it is necessary to increase the length of the degrees of latitude in order that the expansion remain the same in all directions.

The length of a degree of latitude, as thus increased between the equator and any specified parallel, expressed in minutes of arc as measured at the equator, constitutes the number of meridional parts, M, corresponding to that latitude.

Meridional parts not only make possible the construction of Mercator projection charts, but also the solution of problems in Mercator sailing. This sailing yields a constant course to be steered from the point of departure to the destination; in addition, the distance as obtained by Mercator sailing will be more accurate than that obtained by a mid-latitude sailing solution.

To compute the course C, in Mercator sailing, the formula is:

$$\tan C = \frac{DLo'}{m} \qquad (1)$$

in which DLo' is the difference in longitude between the point of departure and the destination, expressed in minutes of arc, and m is the difference in meridional parts between M_1, the value of the meridional parts for the latitude of the point of departure, and M_2, that for the latitude of the destination. When L_1 and L_2 are of contrary name, the sum of M_1 and M_2 is used for m.

Distance, D, is computed by the formula

$$D = \frac{l}{\cos C} \qquad (2)$$

where l is the difference in latitude between the point of departure and that of the destination, expressed in minutes of arc.

A third formula is used to determine the difference of latitude, l, when a ship has sailed a known distance on one course:

$$l = D \times \cos C \qquad (3)$$

Other formulae used in Mercator sailing are:

$$DLo = m \times \tan C \qquad (4)$$

and

$$p = \frac{l \times DLo}{m} \qquad (5)$$

in which p is the departure, expressed in nautical miles.

In using Mercator sailing, the course should be calculated to four decimal places, since, if it lies near 090° or 270°, a large error may otherwise be introduced in calculating the distance.

The value of the meridional parts, M, for any given latitude may be calculated by the formula

$$M = 7915.7045 \times \log \tan \left(45° + \frac{L}{2} \right) - 23.2689 \sin L \qquad (6)$$

M should be calculated to the nearest decimal place, which is sufficient for all ordinary navigation.

Example 1: Our position is L 32°14.7' N, λ 66°28.9' W, and we wish to determine the course and distance to a point near Chesapeake Light, in L 36°58.7' N, λ 75°42.2' W, by Mercator sailing.

We first determine the difference between L_1 and L_2 in minutes of arc, and note it:

$$
\begin{array}{ll}
L_1 & 32°14.7'\ N \\
L_2 & \underline{36°58.7'\ N} \\
l & 284.0'\ N
\end{array}
$$

The next step is to calculate the value of the meridional parts, M_1 and M_2, for each latitude, using formula 6, and then go on to find the difference, m, between the values of M_1 and M_2.

To find the value of M for our present latitude, we write formula (6):

$$M_1 = 7915.7045 \times \log \tan \left(45° + \frac{32.2450}{2} \right) - 23.2689 \times \sin 32.2450°$$
$$= 2045.7409 - 12.4149 = 2033.3$$

We next compute M_2 for L_2, 36°58.7' N, which we find to be 2377.0. We now have:

$$
\begin{array}{llll}
L_1 & 32°14.7'\ N & M_1 & 2033.3 \\
\ \sim & & \ \sim & \\
L_2 & \underline{36°58.7'\ N} & M_2 & \underline{2377.0} \\
l & 284.0'\ N & m & 343.7
\end{array}
$$

The next step is to find the difference in longitude, expressed in minutes of arc:

$$
\begin{array}{ll}
\lambda_1 & 66°28.9'\ W \\
\ \sim & \\
\lambda_2 & \underline{75°42.2'\ W} \\
DLo & 553.3'\ W
\end{array}
$$

We can now write formula (1):

$$\tan C = \frac{553.3'}{343.7} = 1.6098$$

The course is therefore N 58.1522° W; the course to steer will be Cn 301.8°.

To find the distance D, we write formula (2):

$$D = \frac{284.0'}{\cos 58.1522°} = 538.2206$$

The distance is, therefore, 538.2 miles.

Example 2: We are situated in Baffin Bay, in L 75°31.7′ N, λ 79°08.7′ W. If we steam 263.5 miles on Cn 155.0°, what will be the coordinates of the point of arrival?

We first determine the change of latitude by restating formula (2):

$$l = 263.5 \times \cos 155.0° = -238.8'$$

The change of latitude is therefore S 238.8′, or S 3°58.8′, making the latitude of the point of arrival 71°32.9′ N (75°31.7′ − 3°58.8′).

Using formula (6), we compute the values of M_1 and M_2, and then proceed to determine the value of m:

L_1	75°31.7′ N	M_1	7072.4
L_2	71°32.9′ N	M_2	6226.1
		m	846.3

To find the longitude of the point of arrival, we write formula (4):

$$DLo = 846.3 \times \tan 155.0° = -394.6362'$$

which equals −6°34.6′. Subtracting this from the longitude of the point of our departure, 79°08.7′ W, we find the present longitude to be 72°34.1′ W.

Our new position therefore will be L 71°32.9′ N, λ 72°34.1′ W.

Rhumb-line Sailing

In the introduction to the sailings, we stated that the basic rhumb-line sailing formulae are designed for a perfectly spherical Earth, but that they could be modified for use with a spheroid. While Mercator sailing, as we know it in the United States, is designed for use with Clarke's spheroid of 1866, the basic rhumb-line formulae may be adapted for use with any spheroid, such as Clarke's spheroid of 1880, the International spheroid, or Bessel's spheroid, among others.

We shall first consider the two basic formulae used in rhumb-line sailing. The formula for finding the course, C, is:

$$\tan C = \frac{\pi(\lambda_1 \sim \lambda_2)}{180°[\ln \tan (45° + \tfrac{1}{2}L_2) \sim \ln \tan (45° + \tfrac{1}{2}L_1)]} \qquad (1)$$

Note that this formula employs natural logs (base e) rather than common logs (base 10); for these natural logs, we shall use the abbreviation ln.

The distance, D, is computed by formula (2), except when the course is 090° or 270°:

$$D = 60 \frac{L_2 - L_1}{\cos C} \qquad (2)$$

When the course is 090° or 270°, the distance is found by the formula

$$D = 60 (\lambda_2 \sim \lambda_1) \times \cos L \qquad (3)$$

Example 1: We wish to determine the course and distance from Brenton Reef Light, Rhode Island, L 41°26′ N, λ 71°23′ W, to St. David's Light, Bermuda, L 32°22′ N, λ 64°39′ W, using rhumb-line sailing formulae. (This example uses the same data as used in Example 1 of mid-latitude sailing.)

To calculate the course, C, we write formula (1):

$$
\begin{aligned}
\tan C &= \frac{\pi \times 6.7333°}{180[\ln \tan 61.1833° - \ln \tan 65.7167°]} \\
&= \frac{21.1534}{180[\ln 1.8177 - \ln 2.2165]} \\
&= \frac{21.1534}{180[0.5976 - 0.7959]} = \frac{21.1534}{-35.6987} \\
&= -0.5926
\end{aligned}
$$

The course, therefore, is S 30.6490° E, or *Cn* 149.4°.

To find the distance, formula (2) is written:

$$D = 60 \frac{32.3667° \sim 41.4333°}{\cos 30.6490°} = 60 \frac{9.0667}{0.8603}$$

The distance, therefore, is 60 × 10.5389°, or 632.3 miles.

Example 2: We are in L 10°17.5′ N, λ 120°33.6′ W, and wish to determine the course and distance to L 12°43.0′ S, λ 137°23.8′ W by rhumb-line sailing. We write formula (1):

$$\tan C = \frac{\pi(120.5600° - 137.3967°)}{180°\left[\ln \tan\left(45° - \frac{12.7167}{2}\right) - \ln \tan\left(45° + \frac{10.2917}{2}\right)\right]}$$

$$= \frac{\pi(-16.8369)}{180°[-0.2238 - 0.1806]}$$

$$= \frac{-52.8939}{-72.7902} = 0.7267$$

$$C = 36.0045°$$

The course, therefore, is S 36.0045° W, or *Cn* 216.0045°.
To find the distance, we write formula (2):

$$D = 60\,\frac{(-12.7167° - 10.2917°)}{\cos 216.0045°} = 60\,\frac{-23.0083°}{-0.8090}$$

$$= 60 \times 28.4414 = 1706.4868 \text{ miles}$$

The course, therefore, would be *Cn* 216.0° and the distance 1706.5 miles. It may be of interest to note that, in this particular example, where we cross the equator from one low latitude to a second low latitude, the rhumb-line sailing yields almost exactly the same solution as great-circle sailing, which makes the course 216.4° and the distance 1706.5 miles.

When we wish to modify rhumb-line sailing to allow for the eccentricity of the Earth, the formula to compute the course is:

$$\tan C = \frac{\pi(\lambda_1 - \lambda_2)}{180\left[\ln\left(\frac{\tan\left(45 + \frac{L_2}{2}\right)}{\left(\frac{1 + e\sin L_2}{1 - e\sin L_2}\right)^{e/2}}\right) - \ln\left(\frac{\tan\left(45 + \frac{L_1}{2}\right)}{\left(\frac{1 + e\sin L_1}{1 - e\sin L_1}\right)^{e/2}}\right)\right]} \quad (4)$$

where e is the value of the eccentricity factor of the ellipsoid to be used. The values of e found for various modifications include:

Clarke of 1866	$e = 0.082\ 271\ 854\ 22$
Clarke 1880	$e = 0.082\ 483\ 399\ 04$
International	$e = 0.081\ 991\ 889\ 97$
Caltech Seismological Lab.	$e = 0.081\ 839\ 952\ 6$
Airy	$e = 0.081\ 673\ 374$
Australian National–South American of 1969	$e = 0.081\ 820\ 2$
Bessel	$e = 0.081\ 696\ 83$
Everest	$e = 0.081\ 472\ 98$
Fischer—1960 (Mercury)	$e = 0.081\ 813\ 334$
Fischer—South Asia	$e = 0.081\ 813\ 334$

Fischer of 1968 $e = 0.081\ 813\ 33$
Hough $e = 0.081\ 991\ 89$
International Astronomical $e = 0.081\ 820\ 2$
Krassovsky $e = 0.081\ 813\ 33$
World Geodetic System $e = 0.081\ 818\ 8$

The formula for distance remains unchanged:

$$D = 60 \frac{L_2 \sim L_1}{\cos C}$$

Example: We wish to determine the course and distance from L36°57.7' N, λ 75°42.2' W, to L 45°39.1' N, λ 1°29.8' W, using the value for *e* given for Clarke's ellipsoid of 1866, $e = 0.082\ 271\ 854\ 22$. Substituting into formula (4), we obtain the following:

$$\tan C = \frac{233.1271189}{180\left[\ln\left(\dfrac{2.453586896}{1.004857646}\right) - \ln\left(\dfrac{2.004010604}{1.004081494}\right)\right]}$$

$$\tan C = \frac{233.1271189}{180(0.201627819)}$$

$$\tan C = 6.433472022$$

$$C = 81.15127722°$$

Thus the course is N 81.151 277 22°.
To find the distance, we write formula (2):

$$D = 60 \frac{8.690°}{\cos 81.15127722°} = 3389.540868$$

Our course, therefore, is 081.2°, and the distance is 3389.5 miles.

Great-Circle Sailing

The shortest distance between any two points on the Earth lies along the great circle that passes through them. Great-circle sailing is used when the distance between the points of departure and arrival, measured along a great circle, is materially shorter than along the rhumb line drawn between them. It is impossible for a ship to steam along a great circle on the same course, unless she is moving due North, due South, or along the equator. It is customary, therefore, to select a number of points along the great-circle track, usually 5° of longitude apart, and steam rhumb-line courses between them; the distance thus steamed closely approximates that of the great-circle track.
Alternatively, the great-circle track may be broken up into equal

segments of arc, each of which in the following example is 6°, or 360 nautical miles, in length.

A great-circle voyage should not, of course, be undertaken if the great circle crosses land or dangerous waters, or if such a voyage would take the ship into too high a latitude. Another factor that must be taken into account is the location of the vertex, or point of greatest latitude, through which the circle passes. The vertex might lie beyond the destination, behind the point of departure, or between the two.

The calculator permits easy solution of great-circle problems by means of various spherical trigonometric formulae. The Lambert projection charts, intended primarily for aviators, which show land masses in very much the same shape we are used to seeing them on Mercator projection charts, are often very helpful, as a straight line very closely approximates a great-circle track, and distances may be measured easily, with very considerable accuracy.

In order to obtain a complete solution of a great-circle problem, it is necessary first to establish the distance along the great-circle track to the destination, and the initial heading; usually the latitude and longitude of the vertex are also required. Even when the vertex lies beyond the destination, or behind the point of departure, its position may be calculated. If it is located between the point of departure and the destination, its position is useful in determining whether the track will take the vessel into an undesirably high latitude, and if the track is to be broken down into segments of equal length in distance, its position is required in order to obtain the coordinates of the intermediate points at which rhumb-line course changes are to be made.

In working the following great-circle formulae with a calculator, South latitude and East longitude should be entered as negative values.

Distance and Initial Heading

The formula for finding the distance, D, is:

$$\cos D = \sin L_1 \times \sin L_2 + \cos L_1 \times \cos L_2 \times \cos DLo \qquad (1)$$

where L_1 is the latitude of the point of departure, L_2 is the latitude of the destination, and DLo is the difference of longitude between the two places.

To find the initial heading C, two formulae are available:

$$\cos C = \frac{\sin L_2 - \cos D \times \sin L_1}{\sin D \times \cos L_1} \qquad (2)$$

and

$$\tan C = \frac{\sin DLo}{\cos L_1 \times \tan L_2 - \sin L_1 \times \cos DLo} \qquad (3)$$

In both formulae, L_1 is the latitude of the point of departure, and L_2 the latitude of the destination. D is the distance expressed in arc, and DLo is the difference in longitude between the point of departure and the destination. If the latitude is South, it should be prefixed with a − sign when entered into the calculator. When the cosine C formula (formula 2) is used, the initial heading will always be computed from North, toward either the East or the West, according to the change in longitude. Formula (3) computes C from the elevated pole, toward either the East or the West.

Computing the Coordinates of the Vertex

The nearer vertex of the great circle may lie between the point of departure and the destination, behind the point of departure, or beyond the destination. Its latitude may be found by the formula

$$\cos L_v = \cos L_1 \times \sin C \tag{4}$$

The longitude of the vertex may be obtained by calculating the difference of longitude between the point of departure and the vertex, using the formula

$$\sin DLo_v = \frac{\cos C}{\sin L_v} \tag{5}$$

The angular distance between the point of departure and the vertex D_v may now be calculated by means of the formula

$$\sin D_v = \cos L_1 \times \sin DLo_v \tag{6}$$

Alternatively, the longitude of the vertex may be calculated directly, using the formula

$$\tan \lambda_v = \frac{\tan L_2 \times \cos \lambda_1 - \tan L_1 \times \cos \lambda_2}{\tan L_1 \times \sin \lambda_2 - \tan L_2 \times \sin \lambda_1} \tag{7}$$

Computing Coordinates of Intermediate Points Along the Great-Circle Track

The great-circle track may be broken up into segments of equal angular length, mid-latitude, Mercator, or rhumb-line sailing then being used to determine the course for each leg. When the great-circle track is so segmented, the next step is to determine the latitude, L_x, of each point (X_1, X_2, etc.) along the great-circle track where the course is to be changed. The formula for this purpose is:

$$\sin L_x = \sin L_v \times \cos D_{v-x} \tag{8}$$

D_{v-x} being the angular distance to the vertex, less the angular distance along the great circle at which the course is to be changed.

Finally, the longitude of each of these change points is obtained by the formula

$$\sin DLo_{v-x} = \frac{\sin D_{v-x}}{\cos L_x} \tag{9}$$

DLo_{v-x} being the difference between the meridian of DLo_v found in formula (5) and that between each course change point, X_1, X_2, etc.

The DLo_v and D_v of the nearer vertex are never greater than 90°, and the nearer vertex is usually employed in making the above calculations. However, when the latitude of the point of departure and that of the destination are of contrary name, it may be more convenient to use the far vertex, if it is nearer to the midpoint of the track.

Example: We are bound from San Francisco, L 37°47.5′ N, λ 122°27.8′ W, to Sydney, Australia, L 33°51.7′ S, λ 151°12.7′ E, and wish to obtain the distance along the great circle, the initial heading, the latitude and longitude of the vertex, and the latitude and longitude of the first point where we shall make a course change; the course change points are to be 6° or 360 miles apart along the great circle.

Our first step is to obtain the *DLo;* it is 86°19.5′ [360° − (λ$_1$ W + λ$_2$ E)]. We can now write formula (1):

$$\cos D = \sin(37°47.5′) \times \sin(-33°51.7′) + \cos(37°47.5′)$$
$$\times \cos(-33°51.7′) \times \cos(86°19.5′)$$

This gives us

$$\cos D = -0.34144 + 0.04206 = -0.2994$$

The distance therefore is 107.4204°, which, multiplied by 60, is 6445.2243 miles.

We next compute the initial great-circle heading C. Formula (2) becomes:

$$\cos C = \frac{\sin(-33.8617°) - \cos(107.4204°) \times \sin(37.7917°)}{\sin(107.4204°) \times \cos(37.7917°)}$$
$$= \frac{-0.5572 - (-0.1835)}{0.7540} = \frac{-0.3737}{0.7540} = -0.4957$$

The initial heading therefore is N 119.7137° W (*Cn* 240.2863°).

We can now calculate the latitude of the vertex, using formula (4), which we write:

$$\cos L_v = \cos(37.7917°) \times \sin(119.7137°) = 0.6863$$

The latitude of the vertex is therefore 46.6591° (46°39.5′); we shall be able to name it N or S after we calculate its longitude.

To obtain the longitude of the vertex, we first determine the difference of longitude between San Francisco and the vertex, DLo_v, and then convert this difference to the actual longitude of the vertex. Formula (5) becomes:

$$\sin DLo_v = \frac{\cos(119.7137°)}{\sin(46.6591°)} = -0.6815$$

The DLo_v is therefore $-42.9634°$, or $-42°57.8'$, which, when applied to the longitude of our point of departure, $122°27.8'$ W, makes the longitude of the vertex $79°30.0'$ W. The longitude of the southern vertex would therefore be $100°30.0'$ E; since this vertex is farther away from the midpoint of the great-circle track, we shall use the northern vertex in computing the coordinates of the intermediate positions.

The next step is to compute the distance from the vertex to the point of departure, D_v, using formula (6), which becomes:

$$\sin D_v = \cos(37.7917°) \times \sin(42.9634°) = 0.5386$$

which makes the distance $32.5867°$ (1955.2049 miles).

We next need the latitude of the first point, X_1, where we shall change course; this we obtain by formula (8), which becomes:

$$\sin L_{x_1} = \sin(46.6591°) \times \cos(38.5867°) = 0.5685$$

L_{x_1} therefore is $34.6451°$ N, or $34°38.7'$ N. We go on to find the longitude of the point X_1 by means of formula (9):

$$\sin DLo_{v-x_1} = \frac{\sin D_{v-x_1}}{\cos L_{x_1}} = \frac{\sin 38.5867°}{\cos 34.6451°} = 0.7581$$

which makes DLo_{v-x_1} $49.2989°$. This, when added to the longitude of the vertex, $79.50°$, found above, gives us the longitude of our first turning point, $128.7989°$ or $128°47.9'$ W.

We would then proceed to calculate the coordinates of the other turning points (X_2, X_3, etc.) in a similar manner, those for X_2, for example, being L_{x_2} $31.1957°$ (L $31°11.7'$ N), and λ_{x_2} $134.6501°$ (λ $134°39.0'$ W).

All that remains is to determine the rhumb-line course and distance from San Francisco to Point X_1; as the great-circle distance is only 360 miles, solution by mid-latitude sailing should be entirely satisfactory. By this sailing, Cn is $238.4°$, and the distance is 360.1 miles.

To Find the Latitude at Which a Great-Circle Track Crosses A Selected Meridian

The navigator may at times wish to determine the latitude in which a great circle crosses a selected meridian. Some navigators use this method of breaking up a great-circle track into a series of segments, or legs. Under such circumstances, a latitude, L_d, may be found by means of the formula

$$\tan L_d = \frac{\tan L_2 \times \sin(\lambda_d - \lambda_1) - \tan L_1 \times \sin(\lambda_d - \lambda_2)}{\sin(\lambda_2 - \lambda_1)} \quad (10)$$

in which L_1 is the latitude of the point of departure, L_2 that of the destination, λ_d the selected longitude, λ_1 longitude of the point of departure, and λ_2 longitude of the destination.

It should be noted that in this formula absolute differences are not used; rather, negative values are employed. Thus, in this formula, should we encounter $40° - 60°$, we use $-20°$.

Example: We desire to determine the latitude in which a great-circle track between L 40° N, λ 80° W and L 50° N, λ 10° W passes through λ 31°04.3' W; we write formula (10):

$$\tan L_d = \frac{\tan L_2 \sin(\lambda_d - \lambda_1) - \tan L_1 \sin(\lambda_d - \lambda_2)}{\sin(\lambda_2 - \lambda_1)}$$

$$\tan L_d = \frac{\tan 50° \sin(31.0717° - 80°) - \tan 40° \sin(31.0717° - 10°)}{\sin(10° - 80°)}$$

$$\tan L_d = \frac{1.1918 \sin(-48.9283°) - 0.8391 \sin 21.0717°}{\sin(-70°)}$$

$$\tan L_d = \frac{-0.8984 - 0.3017}{-0.9397} = \frac{-1.2001}{-0.9397} = 1.2772$$

$$L_d = 51.9394°$$

The required latitude is therefore 51.9394° N, or 51°56.4' N.

Composite Sailing

When a great-circle track would carry a vessel to an undesirably high latitude, a modification of great-circle sailing, called composite sailing, may be used to advantage; it can be used only when the vertex lies between the point of departure and the destination. The composite track consists of a great circle from the point of departure and tangent to the limiting parallel, a course line along the parallel, and a great circle tangent to the limiting parallel and through the destination.

The formula for finding the difference of longitude, DLo, between that of the point of departure and that of the point where the limiting latitude is reached, is:

$$\cos DLo = \tan L_1 \times \cot L_v \quad (1)$$

where L_1 is the latitude of the point of departure, and L_v is the limiting latitude.

After finding the longitude at which the limiting latitude is reached by applying the difference of longitude to the longitude of the point of departure, the next step is to find the longitude at which to depart the limiting latitude for the destination. To compute this longitude, the same formula is used, but L_2, the latitude of the destination, is substituted for L_1.

Example: A ship bound from Baltimore for Bordeaux takes her departure from L 36°57.7' N, λ 75°42.2' W, near the Chesapeake Light, for L 45°39.1' N, λ 1°29.8' W, near the entrance to the Grande Passe de l'Ouest. The limiting latitude is to be 47° N. We write formula (1):

$$\cos DLo = \tan(36°57.7') \times \cot(47°) = 0.7525 \times 0.9325 = 0.7017$$

$$DLo = 45.4346°$$

The difference of longitude between the point of departure, and the point where L 47° N is to be reached is therefore 45°26.1'; so the ship will reach L 47° N in λ 30°16.1' W (75°42.2' W − 45°26.1').

To find the longitude in which the ship will depart the 47th parallel, formula (1) is written:

$$\cos DLo = \tan(45°39.1') \times \cot(47°) = 1.0230 \times 0.9325 = 0.9540$$

$$DLo = 17.4513°$$

The ship will therefore leave the 47th parallel in λ 18°56.9' W (*DLo* 17°27.1' + $λ_2$ 1°29.8').

To find the distance the ship will steam along the 47th parallel, we first find the difference in longitude between that where she arrives at the 47th parallel, λ 30°16.1' W, and the one where she leaves, at λ 18°56.9' W. This difference is 11°19.2' or 679.2'; multiplying this difference in longitude by the cosine of latitude 47°, we get the distance steamed along the 47th parallel, 463.2133 miles.

Time Conversion

Time to Arc

Time may readily be converted into arc by a series of steps on the calculator. The conversion may be facilitated if the following values are kept in mind:

1 hour = 15°	4 minutes = 1° or 60'	4 seconds = 1'
	1 minute = 0.25° or 15'	1 second = 0.25'

1. Multiply the number of hours by 15, and note the resulting number as degrees.

2. Divide by 4 the number of minutes, and note the resulting whole number as degrees.
3. Multiply by 15 the number of minutes remaining, and note the resulting number as minutes of arc.
4. Multiply by 0.25 the number of seconds, and note the resulting number as minutes of arc.
5. Add together the number of degrees and minutes of arc obtained in the above four steps.

Example: We wish to convert 13 hours, 46 minutes, 58 seconds, to arc.

		D	*M*
1. 13 hours × 15	= 195		
2. $\frac{46}{4}$ minutes = 11, with 2 left over	= 11		
3. 2 minutes × 15	=		30
4. 58 seconds × 0.25	=		14.5
5.	= 206		44.5

13 hours 46 minutes 58 seconds converted to arc is, therefore, 206°44.5′.

Arc to Time

Arc may readily be converted into time by a series of steps on the calculator. The conversion may be facilitated if the following values are kept in mind:

15° = 1 hour	15′ = 1 minute	1′ = 4 seconds
1° or 60′ = 4 minutes		0.25′ = 1 second

1. Divide the number of degrees by 15, and note the resulting whole number as hours.
2. Multiply by 4 the remaining number of degrees, and note the result as minutes.
3. If the number of minutes of arc is greater than 15, divide it by 15, and note the whole number in the dividend as minutes of time. If it is less than 15, treat as in Step 4.
4. Multiply by 4 the remaining number of minutes of arc and the decimal of a minute, and note the answer to the nearest second.
5. Add together the number of hours, minutes, and seconds found in the above four steps.

Example: We wish to convert 329°59.6′ to time.

$$\begin{array}{llr}
 & & H \quad M \quad S \\
1. \ \dfrac{329°}{15} = 21 \text{ hours} + 14° & = 21 & \\
2. \ 14° \times 4 & = & 56 \\
3. \ \dfrac{59.6'}{15} = 3 \text{ minutes} + 14.6' & = & 3 \\
4. \ 14.6' \times 4 = 58.4 \text{ seconds} & = & \underline{\qquad 58} \\
5. & = 21 & 59 \quad 58
\end{array}$$

329°59.6′ converted to time is, therefore, 21 hours 59 minutes 58 seconds.

Local Mean Time to Zone Time

The times of some celestial phenomena are first determined as local mean time, LMT; that is, time based on the mean or average sun, and applying to one particular meridian. However, our clocks on board ship are almost never set to LMT; they are usually set to zone time, ZT. Zone time is the local mean time of a zone or reference meridian, and is kept throughout a designated zone. Our clocks, therefore, read LMT only when we are exactly on the reference meridian of our zone. If the LMT of sunrise, for example, is to be useful, it must be converted to the time kept by our clocks.

In zone time, the nearest meridian exactly divisible by 15° is usually used as the time zone meridian. Thus, within a time zone extending 7.5° on each side of the zone meridian, the clock time is the same, and the time in adjacent zones will differ from ours by exactly one hour. Our ZT, therefore, can differ from our LMT by as much as one-half hour.

To convert LMT to ZT, we must find the difference in longitude between our own meridian, and our time zone meridian. This difference is then converted into time, one degree being equal to 4 minutes of time, and one minute of arc being equal to 4 seconds of time. Thus 3°43′ of longitude would equal 14 minutes 52 seconds ($4 \times 3 = 12$ minutes + 43×4 seconds).

If our ship's longitude is West of our zone meridian, our LMT will be earlier than ZT, and to convert the LMT to ZT, the difference in longitude between our meridian and the zone meridian, converted to time, must be added to our LMT. Conversely, if we are East of our zone meridian, our LMT will be later than our ZT, and the difference in longitude, stated as time, must be subtracted from our LMT.

Example 1: We are in λ 69°42.3′ W, and our clocks are set to zone + 5 time (zone meridian 75° W). The LMT is 17 53 42. We require zone time.

			H	M	S	
Our longitude	69°42.3′ W					
Zone meridian	75°00.0′ W					
Difference in longitude	5°17.7′ E					
5°	=			20		
17.7′	=			1	11	
Difference of longitude in time	= −			21	11	E
LMT	=		17	53	42	
Zone time	=		17	32	31	

The sign is negative because we are East of our zone meridian.

Example 2: We are in λ 117°22.6′ E, and our clocks are set to zone − 8 time (zone meridian 120° E). The LMT is 05 12 32. We require the zone time.

			H	M	S	
Our longitude	117°22.6′ E					
Zone meridian	120°00.0′ E					
Difference in longitude	2°37.4′ W					
2°	=			8		
37.4′	=			2	30	
Difference of longitude in time	= +			10	30	W
LMT	=		05	12	32	
Zone time	=		05	23	02	

The sign is positive because we are West of our zone meridian.

Interconversion of Minutes and Seconds of Arc or Time and Decimals of Degrees or Hours

Position at sea and in the heavens is usually stated in degrees, minutes, and seconds (or minutes and tenths) of arc; similarly, time is usually stated in hours, minutes, and seconds. The calculator, however, is geared to work only with decimals; it is, therefore, often necessary to convert input data to decimals in order to enter them into the calculator, and usually it is desirable to reconvert the decimal portion of the answer, as read from the calculator, to minutes and seconds, or minutes and tenths.

Many models of scientific calculators can make these conversions at the touch of one or two keys. For the others, the conversion must be made arithmetically, as discussed below.

When arc is stated in minutes and tenths, we divide the minutes and tenths by 60 to convert to decimals. Thus, if we wish to convert 29°37.6' to decimals, we divide 37.6' by 60 and obtain 0.6267; thus 29°37.6' becomes 29.6267°.

When arc or time is stated in minutes and seconds, we first divide the minutes by 60 and then divide the seconds by 3600; the sum of the two dividends gives us the answer in decimals. For example, suppose we wish to convert 53m 37s to decimals of an hour:

$$53m/60 \ = 0.883 \ 33$$

$$37s/3600 = 0.010 \ 28$$

The answer, therefore, is 0.893 61 hour.

When arc is stated in minutes and seconds, and precision is not of primary importance, we can round off the seconds to the nearest one-tenth of a minute, and proceed as above. If, however, precision is required, we divide the seconds by 3600, and then divide the minutes by 60; the sum of the dividends gives us the conversion. Thus, to convert 57'49", we divide 49" by 3600 and get 0.01361; we next divide 57' by 60 and get 0.9500. Adding the two dividends, we obtain the sum, 0.96361°.

The conversion from decimals of degrees to minutes and seconds is equally simple: the first two digits in the decimal are multiplied by 60 to obtain minutes and decimals of a minute. The number of whole minutes is noted, and the decimals of a minute are multiplied by 60 to convert them to seconds. The remaining digits in the decimal are then multiplied by 3600 to convert them to seconds, and then added to the number of seconds found in the first step.

Example: We wish to convert 0.81971° to minutes and seconds:

$$0.81° \times 60 = 48.6' = \quad 48'36''$$
$$+$$
$$0.00971° \times 3600 = \quad \underline{34.96''}$$
$$49'10.96''$$

Ordinarily, when dealing with arc, we work to the nearest one-tenth of a minute; we would, therefore, call this value 49.2'. When working with time, we ordinarily work to the nearest second, and this quantity would then be written 49m 11s.

4

Celestial Observations

Sextant Altitude Correction

Dip of the Horizon

The dip of the horizon, caused by the fact that the Earth is a sphere, is the angle by which the visible horizon differs from the true horizontal at the observer's eye. Its value increases as the height of the observer's eye increases; it is also affected by terrestrial refraction, the bending of the light rays as we look at the horizon, which increases the distance to the horizon. Furthermore, it can be very considerably affected by anomalous atmospheric conditions, such as a difference between the temperature of the water surface and that of the air above it.

The following formula for determining dip allows for terrestrial refraction in "normal" atmospheric conditions:

$$D = 0.97 \sqrt{h}$$

D being the dip in minutes of arc, and h being the observer's height of eye above sea level, in feet.

The value of the dip is subtracted from the sextant altitude for all celestial observations.

Example: Your height of eye is 63 feet. What is the correction for dip? The above formula becomes:

$$D = 0.97 \sqrt{63} = 7.7$$

The correction for dip, therefore, is $-7.7'$.

95

Dip Short of the Horizon

A celestial observation may be necessary when land or some other obstruction located directly below the body makes the sea horizon invisible. In such a case, provided the distance to the obstruction is known, the waterline of the obstruction may be used as the horizontal reference.

Under such conditions, the dip short of the horizon may be closely approximated by use of the formula

$$D_s = 0.416d + 0.566\,\frac{h}{d}$$

where D_s is the dip short of the sea horizon, in minutes of arc; d is the distance to the waterline of the obstruction, expressed in nautical miles; and h is the observer's height of eye above sea level, in feet.

This formula is a simplified version of the one given in *Bowditch;* in the great majority of cases it gives the value of the dip correct to the nearest tenth of a minute. Only when the height of eye is great, and the range to the obstruction is very short does some error arise; for example, if the height of eye were 100 feet, and the range 0.1 mile, the above formula would give a dip of 566.0′, whereas the correct dip would be 565.8′.

The value of the dip is subtracted from the sextant altitude for all celestial observations.

Example: The height of eye is 24 feet, and the distance to the obstruction is 0.75 nautical mile. We require the value of the dip short of the horizon. The formula becomes:

$$D_s = (0.416 \times 0.75) + 0.566\,\frac{24}{0.75} = 0.312 + (0.566 \times 32)$$
$$= 0.312 + 18.112 = 18.424$$

The correction for dip, as here calculated, is, therefore, $-18.4′$, which is correct to the nearest tenth of a minute.

Mean Refraction

Mean refraction is based on a temperature of 50°F (+10°C) and a barometric pressure of 29.83 inches (1010 millibars), conditions that are considered standard. Corrections for "nonstandard" temperature and for "nonstandard" barometric pressure are given in the following sections. It is particularly important to correct the mean refraction when observations are made at low altitudes, and it should always be done when the utmost accuracy is desired.

The index and instrumental errors, as well as the correction for dip, should always be applied to the altitude as read from the sextant before the refraction is determined; the sextant altitude, so corrected, is termed the apparent altitude, *ha*.

The mean refraction, *Rm*, stated in minutes of arc, may be determined with sufficient accuracy for all ordinary navigation by means of the following formula:

$$Rm = 0.97' \: [\tan\{ha - \tan^{-1} 12(ha + 3°)\}] \qquad (1)$$

in which *ha* is the apparent altitude, expressed in degrees and decimals.

Example 1: We observed Aldebaran to have an *ha* of 17°13.6' and wish to determine the mean refraction correction.
    We write formula (1):

$$
\begin{aligned}
Rm &= 0.97' \: [\tan \{17.2267° - \tan^{-1} 12(17.2267° + 3°)\}] \\
&= 0.97' \: [\tan \{17.2267° - \tan^{-1} 242.7204°\}] \\
&= 0.97' \: [\tan \{17.2267° - 89.7639°\}] \\
&= 0.97' \: [\tan \{-72.5372°\}] \\
&= 0.97' \times -3.1788' = -3.0834'
\end{aligned}
$$

Rm, therefore, is −3.1' for practical purposes.
    The mean refraction may be corrected for nonstandard atmospheric temperature and pressure, as discussed below.

Mean Refraction Correction for a Nonstandard Temperature

The value of the correction for mean refraction, *Rm*, is based on a standard temperature of 50°F. The correction to be applied to *Rm* for a nonstandard temperature may be found by the following formula, taken from *Bowditch*.

$$\text{Correction} = Rm \left(1 - \frac{510}{460 + T}\right) \qquad (2)$$

Temperatures above 0°F are added to 460 in the divisor; those below 0°F are subtracted. *Rm* is entered in the formula without a negative sign. The correction for temperature as found will be applied to *Rm* according to its sign; the corrected refraction thus found will then have the minus sign restored.

Example 2: We observed the Sun to have an *ha* of 5° when the temperature was 10°F. The computed *Rm* proved to be −9.8985'; we wish to correct it for the temperature.
    Formula (2) is written:

$$
\begin{aligned}
\text{Correction} &= 9.8985' \left(1 - \frac{510}{460 + 10}\right) \\
&= 9.8985' \times -0.0851 \\
&= -0.8424'
\end{aligned}
$$

The correction to Rm $-9.9'$ is, therefore, $-0.8'$, making the corrected refraction correction $-10.7'$.

Mean Refraction Correction for Nonstandard Barometric Pressure

The value of the mean refraction, Rm, is based on a standard atmospheric pressure of 29.83 inches, or 1010 millibars. When the existing pressure varies considerably from the standard, it may be desirable to correct for it, particularly if the body was observed at a low altitude.

The correction to be applied to Rm for nonstandard barometric pressure may be found by the following formula, taken from *Bowditch:*

$$\text{Correction} = Rm \left(1 - \frac{P}{29.83''}\right) \text{ or } Rm = \left(1 - \frac{P}{1010 \text{ mbs}}\right) \quad (3)$$

in which Rm is entered without sign, and P is the existing pressure in inches of mercury, or millibars, as appropriate.

Example 3: We observed the Sun to have an *ha* of 5° when the barometric pressure was 31.2 inches. The computed Rm proved to be $-9.8985'$. We wish to correct the Rm for the existing pressure.

We write formula (3):

$$\text{Correction} = 9.8985' \left(1 - \frac{31.2''}{29.83''}\right) = -0.4546'$$

The correction for barometric pressure is, therefore, $-0.5'$, making the net correction for refraction $-10.4'$.

Combining Corrections to *Rm* for Nonstandard Temperature and Pressure

When Rm is to be corrected for nonstandard conditions of both temperature and pressure, the two corrections are added algebraically, and then applied to Rm to obtain the net correction for refraction to be applied to *ha* in order to obtain *Ho*.

Thus, if Rm is $-7.4'$, and the correction for temperature is $-0.6'$, while the correction for pressure is $+0.2'$, the net correction for refraction is $-7.8'$.

A Single Formula for Finding the Refraction Correction under Nonstandard Conditions of Temperature and Pressure

The *Almanac for Computers* gives a single formula that permits calculating the net correction for refraction under any condition of temperature and pressure, to be applied to altitudes observed on board ship. It is quite lengthy and therefore lends itself best for use with programmable calculators.

$$R = \frac{P}{273 + T} [3.430\ 289\ \{z - \sin^{-1}(0.998\ 604\ 7 \times \sin[0.996\ 761\ 4z])\}$$
$$- 0.011\ 159\ 29z]$$

in which R is the refraction corrected for temperature and pressure, and expressed in minutes of arc, P is the atmospheric pressure in millibars, T is the temperature in degrees Celsius, and z is the zenith distance, 90° − ha.

Sea–Air Temperature Difference

The preceding formula for calculating the dip of the horizon is based, as are the values for dip given in the *Nautical Almanac,* on the fact that as altitude increases, standard or "normal" temperature and pressure in the atmosphere decrease. When there is a difference between the temperature of the seawater and the temperature of the air in contact with it, the normal decrease in air temperature is upset, and the normal value of the dip is affected.

Considerable study, with varying results, has been devoted to determining the exact effect of such a temperature difference on the value of the dip, with varying results. However, it has been determined that where the water is warmer than the air, the horizon is depressed, resulting in sextant altitudes that are too great; the converse is true if the water is the cooler substance.

The Japanese Hydrographic Office, after much empirical testing, found that the value of the dip would be affected by 0.11 minute of arc for each degree Fahrenheit of difference between sea and air temperatures.

As a formula this is stated:

Sea–air temperature correction = 0.11′ × difference in temperature in degrees Fahrenheit between sea and air

The correction is subtractive if the air is colder than the water, and additive if it is warmer.

In practice, the dry-bulb temperature is taken in the shade at the observer's height of eye, and the water temperature is taken either from a sample obtained in a dip bucket, or from the intake water temperature obtained from the engine room.

If temperatures are stated in degrees Celsius, the formula becomes:

S–A correction = 0.198′ × difference in temperature in degrees Celsius between sea and air

As before, the correction is stated in minutes of arc.

Example: The air temperature is 32°F, and the water temperature is 48°F. We require the sea–air temperature correction.

We write the formula:

$$S\text{–}A \text{ correction} = 0.11' \times 16 = 1.76'$$

The correction to the sextant altitude for the sea–air temperature difference is, therefore, −1.8′, the correction being subtractive because the water is warmer than the air.

Coriolis Effect

Observations of celestial bodies made with sextants fitted with artificial horizons, such as the bubble, and so on, are affected by the Earth's rotation, which tends to move objects to the right in the Northern Hemisphere, and to the left in the Southern. This Coriolis effect or acceleration varies with the observer's speed, his latitude, and his track angle, and manifests itself as a deflection of the apparent vertical. The amount of this deflection, *Def,* in minutes of arc, may be found by means of the following formula:

$$Def = 2.62\,V \times \sin L + 0.146\,V^2 \times \sin T \times \tan L - 5.25\,V \times T' \quad (1)$$

where *V* is the speed over the ground in hundreds of knots, *L* is the latitude, *T* is the true track, and *T'* is the rate of change of track angle in degrees per minute of time.

Under ordinary conditions, sufficient accuracy may be obtained by abbreviating the formula to

$$Def = 2.62\,V \times \sin L \quad\quad\quad (1A)$$

The deflection of the apparent vertical having been determined by means of formula (1) or (1A), the correction for Coriolis effect to be applied to the body's altitude, as read from an artificial horizon sextant, may be computed by use of the formula

$$\Delta h = Def \times \sin(Zn - T) \quad\quad\quad (2)$$

in which Δh is the altitude correction in minutes of arc, *Def* is the deflection of the vertical found by formula (1) or (1A), *Zn* is the body's true azimuth, and *T* is the track angle.

In the Northern Hemisphere, the altitude correction, Δh, is additive for bodies observed to the right of the vehicle, and subtractive for those observed to the left. In the Southern Hemisphere, the correction is subtractive for bodies observed to the right, and additive for those observed to the left.

Review of Corrections to be Applied to Celestial Observations

Sun, Stars, and Planets

1. To all sights, apply:

   a. The instrument correction, if any, obtained from the sextant certificate, which may be + or −.
   b. The index correction, obtained by observation, which may be + or −.
   c. The correction for height of eye, or dip, which is always −.
   d. The correction for the difference between sea temperature and air temperature, which may be + or −.

The above corrections, applied to the sextant altitude, give the apparent altitude, *ha.*

2. To the apparent altitude of all bodies, apply:

   a. The correction for mean refraction, which is always −.
   b. If required, the correction for nonstandard air temperature, which may be + or −.
   c. The correction for nonstandard barometric pressure, which may be + or −.

That completes the corrections for observations of the stars and planets.

For observations of the Sun, in addition to the above, apply:

   a. The correction for semidiameter for the date, found in the *Long-Term Sun Almanac.* This is + for the lower limb sights, and − for upper limb sights.
   b. The correction for parallax, +0.1′, for observations at all altitudes below 65°.

For observations of the Moon, in addition to the above, apply the corrections as found on the inside back cover of the *Nautical Almanac.*

Sight Reduction

Brief History

   Sight reduction is defined as the process of deriving from a sight the information needed for establishing a line of position. This entails computing the body's altitude or azimuth, using either the estimated or an assumed position.

   As we know it, sight reduction is a comparatively recent development, whether the computations are made by log tables or sight reduction tables; the concept of the position line dates back only about 140 years.

For centuries, the only sights the navigator could use were those of bodies transiting his meridian; from these he could obtain his latitude. Otherwise, with the exception of Polaris, which served to indicate latitude and direction in the Northern Hemisphere, without an accurate time source, the celestial bodies were of little use except as steering references.

The need for developing a method of determining longitude became ever more urgent as longer voyages of commerce and exploration were undertaken. During the fifteenth through the eighteenth centuries, the best mathematical and scientific minds in Europe worked on this problem. It was known that the apparent motion of the heavenly bodies was extremely regular, and that the Moon changed its position relative to the Sun and the stars at a constant rate.

It was apparent, therefore, that there were two possible solutions: either the Moon must be made to furnish time, and therefore longitude, or an accurate time piece must be designed and built. The latter choice was long unattainable; the great majority, therefore, turned their attention to the Moon.

The Moon's rate of motion, as it crosses the sky, differs by roughly 30′ per hour, about the Moon's diameter—or 12° per day—from the motions of the Sun and stars. If the exact angular difference between the center of the Moon and the center of some other celestial body could be measured, the time of the observation, and therefore the longitude, could be determined.

The first determination of longitude by lunar distance is variously attributed to Regiomontanus in 1472, Amerigo Vespucci in 1497, and John Werner in 1514; however, for centuries it was very little used, because of lack of accurate ephemeral data on the Moon, poor instruments, and the complexity of the necessary computations.

In 1675 the Royal Observatory was established at Greenwich, England, and accurate ephemeral data on the Moon were slowly accumulated there, as well as at various observatories on the Continent. In 1767 the English *Nautical Almanac* appeared, combining much astronomical data in a single source. Incidentally, this publication eventually led to the universal adoption of the meridian of Greenwich as the prime meridian for establishing longitude.

The advent of the *Nautical Almanac* facilitated the working of lunar distance observations, and the invention of the sextant in 1730 made it possible to obtain such observations with considerable accuracy. On his first voyage to the Pacific, 1768–1771, Captain James Cook did not carry a chronometer, and determined his longitude by lunar distances. In 1769–1770 he charted New Zealand with remarkable accuracy. Observations were all made afloat by Cook, himself, and Charles Green, an astronomer, using Hadley sextants.

By our standards, these instruments were quite primitive; however, the latitudes obtained were all very accurate. The longitudes were somewhat more uncertain. The South Island he placed about 25', or 18 miles, too far to the East; one of the greatest errors was 40'.

However, the lengthy mathematical calculations involved deterred many navigators from making use of lunar distance observations, and the habit of coming to the latitude of the vessel's destination, and then sailing down the easting or westing to the port, remained in wide use. The simplification of the lunar method by Nathaniel Bowditch in 1802 considerably widened the use of the lunar distance observation.

Even with a chronometer on board, lunar distance observations continued to be used in isolated areas as a check on chronometers until the invention of radio. The lengthy tables of "Maritime Positions," listed in *Bowditch* through the 1962 edition, were included primarily to permit checking the accuracy of the chronometer by means of celestial observations.

John Harrison developed a prototype chronometer in 1720, and submitted a perfected instrument to the Royal Navy for sea trials in 1735. Improved models were produced by him over the next 40 years; they ran well, but were extremely expensive, and their use was long highly restricted. Only in this century did the chronometer come into wide use, greatly facilitating the determination of longitude. The invention of radio permitted a regular and easy check on its accuracy.

With the invention of the chronometer, when the latitude was known, it became possible to compute the longitude, using the time sight method; this method of navigation remained popular into this century, as a position could be determined without plotting. The discovery of the line of position by Captain Thomas H. Sumner in 1837 heralded a new era in navigation. The Sumner line of position was originally obtained by reducing the same sight twice; the estimated latitude was used for the first reduction. A slightly different latitude, say, 10' or 20' from the first, was then selected to reduce the sight a second time; a line of position was then drawn through the two positions on the chart. With the invention of azimuth tables in the latter part of the nineteenth century, it became possible to work only one time sight, and then draw a line through the resulting position, perpendicular to the body's azimuth.

The era of the "new navigation" came with the introduction of the altitude-difference method of determining a line of position by Commander Adolphe-Laurent-Anatole Marcq de Blonde de Saint-Hilaire, of the French Navy, in 1875. This method remains the basis of almost all celestial navigation used at sea today.

The Marcq Saint-Hilaire method, as it is generally called, remained in common use on board U. S. naval ships through the first decades of this century. Computed altitude and azimuth angle were calculated by means of the log sine, cosine, and haversine, and natural haversine tables included in *Bowditch*.

Subsequently sight reduction was greatly simplified by the coming of the various so-called short-method tables—such as the Weems *Line of Position Book,* Dreisonstok's *H.O. 208,* and Ageton's *H.O. 211.* Even greater simplification was achieved when the inspection tables, H.O. 214, H.O. 249, and H.O. 229, were published.

The final step is use of the electronic calculator. However, the wise navigator will always have familiar back-up methods to rely upon if necessary; he may even need to find his longitude by a lunar distance observation on occasion.

Computing Altitude

To plot the line of position, LOP, resulting from the observation of a celestial body, two computations are required: both the body's altitude, *Hc,* and its azimuth angle, *Z,* must be calculated. Alternatively, the body's true azimuth, *Zn,* or azimuth reckoned clockwise from true North through 360°, may be determined by a somewhat longer formula.

In all the formulae for computing altitude and azimuth, *L* represents the latitude, *d* the declination, and *LHA* the local hour angle, reckoned from the observer's meridian westward through 360°. It is sometimes convenient to measure the arc in either an easterly or a westerly direction from the local meridian, through 180°, when it is called meridian angle (*t*) and labeled E or W to indicate the direction of measurement. *Hc* is the body's computed altitude, and *Ho* is the fully corrected sextant altitude. Where *H* is used, it implies that either *Ho* or *Hc* may be employed.

Having obtained *Hc,* we compare it with *Ho* to obtain the intercept, *a.* The LOP may then be plotted, toward the body, in the direction *Zn* by the length of the intercept if *Ho* is greater than *Hc,* and away in the direction *Zn* − 180° if *Hc* is greater.

While some formulae for computing altitude require that *Z* must first be determined, they are but rarely used, and it seems desirable to start with the determination of altitude.

In *Slide Rule for the Mariner,* three formulae for obtaining *Hc* were included—the classic sine formula,

$$\sin Hc = \sin L \sin d \pm \cos L \cos d \cos t \qquad (1)$$

the cosine *Hc* formula,

$$\cos Hc = \frac{\cos L \sin d \pm \sin L \cos d \cos t}{\cos Z} \tag{2}$$

and the tangent *Hc* formula,

$$\tan Hc = \frac{\dfrac{\sin M}{\tan t} \pm \sin d \cos M}{\cos d} \tag{3}$$

in which *M* is the parallactic angle at the geographic position of the body in the navigation triangle *PZM*. To find the value of *M*, it was first necessary to compute the value of *Z*. The value of *M* was then computed by the formula

$$\tan M = \frac{\sin Z}{\cos H \tan L \pm \sin H \cos Z} \tag{4}$$

In each of these formulae, *t* is the meridian angle stated to 180° East or West, from the observer's meridian, *L* is the ship's estimated or DR latitude, and *H* is the observed body's altitude.

Formulae (2) and (3) were included because of the compression of the sine scale on the slide rule, as the angle increased. With a 10-inch rule, accuracy within about 2' of arc may be obtained to about 30°. With a 20-inch rule, the same accuracy can be obtained to about 50°.

The calculator is plagued by no such limitation. The slide rule does not lend itself well to handling negative values, as with South latitude or declination, or when angles are greater than 90°. Consequently, rules were required as to when the sign was to be positive and when negative; these rules are not required with the calculator.

For use with the calculator, formula (1) is slightly changed:

$$\sin Hc = \sin L \times \sin d + \cos L \times \cos d \times \cos LHA \tag{5}$$

Here, the sign is always positive, and local hour angle, *LHA*, measured to the West to 360° from the observer's meridian, is substituted for meridian angle, *t*. Latitude and declination, if named South, are prefixed with a minus sign in entering them into the calculator. This permits us always to add the two terms in the equation and does away with the rules previously required.

In the reduction of celestial observations, the sine *Hc* formula, when used with the calculator, offers a considerable advantage over the various sight reduction tables, in that a round of sights can be plotted from the same DR or estimated position, thus doing away with the long intercept frequently encountered when plotting from an assumed position.

Example 1: Our DR latitude was 37°16.3′ N when we observed the Sun to have a corrected altitude of 58°26.3′; its declination was N 20°42.3′ and its *GHA* such that when we applied our longitude, the *LHA* was 329°02.7′. We require the *Hc*.

Formula (5) becomes:

$$\sin Hc = \sin 37.2717° \times \sin 20.7050° + \cos 37.2717°$$
$$\times \cos 20.7050° \times \cos 329.0450°$$
$$= 0.2141 + 0.6384 = 0.8525$$

so that:

Hc		58°28.9′
Ho		58°26.3′
a	A	2.6′

Hc being greater than *Ho*, the intercept, *a*, is away 2.6 miles.

Example 2: Our estimated latitude was 31°17.8′ S when we observed the planet Mars to have an *Ho* of 34°49.7′. At the time of the observation the planet's declination was N 15°06.4′, and its *LHA* was 31°20.6′. We require *Hc* and *a*.

In this instance, formula (1) becomes:

$$\sin Hc = -0.1354 + 0.7046 = 0.5692$$

so that:

Hc	34°41.6′	
Ho	34°49.7′	
a	8.1′ Toward	

Cosine–Haversine Formula

Another sight reduction formula, which was widely used in the first part of this century, before the advent of the "short-method" tables, such as those prepared by Ogura, Weems, Ageton, and so on, and then the inspection tables, H.O. 214, 218, 229, and 249, was the cosine–haversine formula:

$$\text{hav } z = \text{hav } (L \sim d) + \cos L \cos d \text{ hav } t$$

in which z is zenith distance, L either an assumed or the DR latitude, d the declination, and t the meridian angle. The haversine of an angle, incidentally, is half the versine of an angle, or $(1 - \cos ine)/2$.

This formula simplified matters somewhat for the navigator, as the sign is always positive—there are no cases, as in the sine–cosine formula, in which meridian angle rather than local hour angle is used;

haversines are always positive, and increase in value continuously from 0° to 180°.

In using this formula, the natural haversine of $(L \sim d)$ was first found; then the log cosine of L and d and the log haversine of t were added, and this sum was converted to a natural haversine (log + natural values of haversines were listed side by side). The two natural haversines were then added to obtain z, which was subtracted from 90° to obtain Hc.

Azimuth angle was found by means of the formula $\sin Z = \cos d \times \sin t \times \sec H$. Here, again, logs were used to substitute addition for multiplication.

Computing Azimuth Angle and Azimuth

In sight reduction we must determine azimuth as well as altitude in order to plot a line of position. Azimuth angle, Z, may be computed from either North or South, toward either the East or the West. Some formulae compute it only to 90°; others compute it to 180°. However, to plot a line of position, we must convert azimuth angle to azimuth, Zn, figured from true North, clockwise to 360°. Various formulae for determining either azimuth or azimuth angle with the calculator are available; the latter tend to be somewhat longer than the former.

The following formulae may be helpful in converting azimuth angle to true azimuth:

Z North X degrees East	$Z = Zn$
Z South X degrees East	$180° - Z = Zn$
Z North X degrees West	$360° - Z = Zn$
Z South X degrees West	$180° + Z = Zn$

Computing Azimuth Angle

The simplest formula for computing azimuth angle is

$$\sin Z = \frac{\cos d \sin LHA}{\cos H}$$

This formula yields a rapid solution for Z; however, it gives no indication as to the quadrant in which the body lies. It is essential, therefore, when this formula is used, that the quadrant (NE, SW, etc.) be noted, in order that proper conversion may be made. When LHA is greater than 180°, Z will be preceded by a $-$, indicating that it is toward the East.

At times, the body may be located near the prime vertical (PV), the azimuth being close to 090° or 270°, leaving doubt as to whether Z is stated from the North or South. In such a case the doubt may be resolved by determining whether the body has crossed the PV. This may easily be determined; the altitude on the PV is found by the formula

$$\sin H = \frac{\sin d}{\sin L}$$

If the observed altitude is greater than that on the PV, the body lies away from the elevated pole; that is, in North latitude the body lies to the South of the PV, and Z will bear the prefix "S."

Example: In latitude 40°00.0' N, we observed the Sun to have an altitude of 28°21.4' at a time when its declination was North 21°00.0', and its *LHA* was 290°. We wish to compute Z using the $\sin Z$ formula, and to convert Z to Zn.

Formula (1) becomes:

$$\sin Z = \frac{0.9336 \times -0.9397}{0.8800} = \frac{-0.8773}{0.8800}$$

Z, therefore, is −85.4862°, that is, to the East.

We are not sure whether the Sun was located in the NE or SE quadrant at the time of the observation. To resolve this question, we find its altitude on the PV using the $\sin H = \sin d / \sin L$ formula. The altitude on the PV thus proves to be 33°53.1', which is greater than the observed altitude. The Sun's Z at the time of the observation for plotting purposes was N 85.5E°, making Zn 085.5°.

Cosine Z Formula

The second formula for computing Z is the cosine azimuth formula:

$$\cos Z = \frac{\sin d - \sin L \times \sin H}{\cos L \times \cos H} \tag{2}$$

This formula has the advantage of always computing Z from true North, provided that South latitude is entered as a minus quantity; declination, when South, should, of course, also be entered as a minus quantity.

Unlike the $\sin Z$ formula, this formula does not indicate whether the body lies toward the East or the West; the value of the *LHA* is used to make this determination.

The rules for obtaining Zn from Z when using the cosine Z formula are:

1. In both North and South latitudes, when *LHA* is less than 180°, $Zn = 360° - Z$.
2. In both North and South latitudes, when *LHA* is greater than 180°, $Zn = Z$.

Example 1: Our latitude was 30°00.0' N when we observed the Sun to have an *Ho* of 32°42.9'; its *d* was N 20°, and the *LHA* was 297°. We wish to find *Zn* using the cosine Z formula.

We write formula (2):

$$\cos Z = \frac{0.3420 - 0.50 \times 0.5405}{0.8660 \times 0.8414}$$

$$= \frac{0.0718}{0.7286} = 0.0985$$

$$Z = 84.3458°$$

Z, therefore, is 84.3°, and the *LHA* being greater than 180°, *Zn* is 084.3°.

Example 2: We were in L 45° N, when we observed Jupiter to have a corrected altitude 19°25.1'. Its *d* at the time was S 15° and the *LHA* was 41°. We require *Zn*, using the cosine Z formula. Formula (2) becomes:

$$\cos Z = \frac{-0.2588 - 0.2351}{0.6669} = \frac{-0.4939}{0.6669} = -0.7406$$

$$Z = 137.8°$$

Z is, therefore, 137.8°, and as the *LHA* is less than 180°, we subtract *Z* from 360° to obtain *Zn*, 222.2°.

Example 3: In latitude 37° S we observed the Sun to have an *Ho* of 33°11.9'; its declination at the time was N 10°00.0', and the *LHA* was 34°. We require *Z* and *Zn*.

Formula (2) becomes:

$$\cos Z = \frac{0.5032}{0.6683} = 0.7529$$

$$Z = 41.2°$$

LHA in this case being less than 180°, we subtract *Z* from 360° to obtain *Zn* 318.8°.

Computing Altitude and True Azimuth in Single Operation

Most formulae for computing azimuth produce a quantity termed azimuth angle, *Z*, the smallest angle measured from the nearest pole, or, in the case of the cosine *Z* formula, azimuth angle to 180°, figured East or West from true North. In either case, the azimuth angle must then be converted to true azimuth, *Zn*. Below, we discuss algorithms that will supply both *Zn* and computed altitude in a single operation.

Normally when we wish to compute azimuth, we know the local

hour angle, *LHA*, latitude, *L,* and declination, *d*. By preserving the algebraic signs of these values (negative for southerly latitudes and declinations), we can use the Dozier formula on our handheld scientific calculator to obtain true azimuth without the necessity of having to figure out which quadrant contains the angle.

The Dozier formula is normally seen as

$$\tan Zn = \frac{\sin LHA}{\cos LHA \sin L - \cos L \tan d}$$

However, it is not really enough to evaluate the right-hand side of the equation and then simply push [TAN^{-1}]. Instead, because valuable information is retained by the algebraic signs of the numerator and denominator of the expression, it is best to use the rectangular-to-polar function to return *Zn* directly. It turns out that the result is always 180° off, so the formula is better written

$$\tan (Zn - 180) = \frac{\sin LHA}{\cos LHA \sin L - \cos L \tan d}$$

which, using an invented notation, can be rewritten as

$$Zn = 180 + R \rightarrow P (\sin LHA \cos d, \cos LHA \cos d \sin L - \cos L \sin d)$$

This formula for *Zn* can be evaluated in the usual way, paying attention to the quadrant in which *Zn* lies by computing numerator and denominator. Since there is an expression for *Hc* that contains similar-looking terms, one is generally wise to compute both *Zn* and *Hc* together by a method such as one of the following:

for RPN calculator (HP-67, -97, -41C)			*for AOS calculator* (SR-52, TI-58, -59)		
input	*function*		*input*	*function*	
LHA	ENTER↑		LHA	STO 01	
L	"		L	STO 02	
d	"		d	STO 03	
1	P>R	①	1	STO 00	
	R∧			RCL 03	
	X⇌Y			P>R	①
	P>R	②		EXC 01	
	R∧			P>R	②
	STO I			EXC 02	
	X⇌Y			STO 03	
	P>R	③		P>R	③
	X<>I			EXC 01	
	R∧			EXC 02	
	P>R	④		EXC 03	④

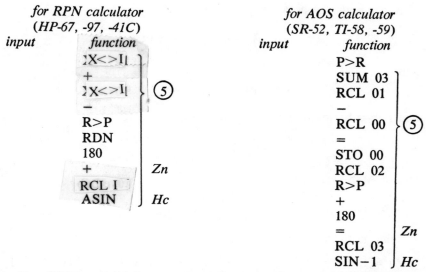

for RPN calculator
(HP-67, -97, -41C)

input	function
ΣX<>I₁	
	+
ΣX<>I₁	⑤
	−
	R>P
	RDN
	180
	+	*Zn*
RCL I	
ASIN	*Hc*

for AOS calculator
(SR-52, TI-58, -59)

input	function
	P>R
	SUM 03
	RCL 01
	−
	RCL 00	⑤
	=
	STO 00
	RCL 02
	R>P
	+
	180
	=	*Zn*
	RCL 03
	SIN−1	*Hc*

For RPN calculators not having the roll up (R↑) and register exchange features, such as the HP 25, 19-C, 33, and 65, the routine is:

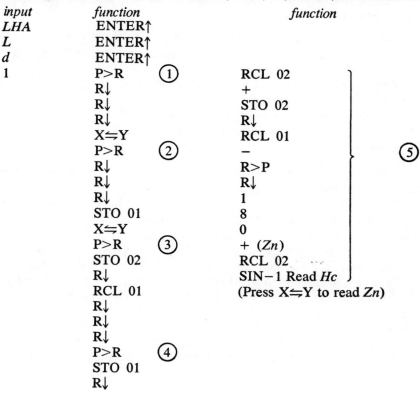

input	function		function	
LHA	ENTER↑		RCL 02	
L	ENTER↑		+	
d	ENTER↑		STO 02	
1	P>R	①	R↓	
	R↓		RCL 01	
	R↓		−	
	R↓		R>P	⑤
	X⇋Y		R↓	
	P>R	②	1	
	R↓		8	
	R↓		0	
	R↓		+ (*Zn*)	
	STO 01		RCL 02	
	X⇋Y		SIN−1 Read *Hc*	
	P>R	③	(Press X⇋Y to read *Zn*)	
	STO 02			
	R↓			
	RCL 01			
	R↓			
	R↓			
	R↓			
	P>R	④		
	STO 01			
	R↓			

Introducing the notation

$$R > P[b, a] = (a^2 + b^2)^{1/2} \angle \text{ atan} \left(\frac{a}{b}\right)$$

and

$$P > R[r, \theta] = b: r \cos \theta \quad a: r \sin \theta$$

and remembering that in RPN calculators

b and r are in the x-register (the display)
a and θ are in the y-register

and in AOS calculators

b and r are in R00
a and θ are in the display

we can write the above equation as

$Zn = R > P[\cos d \sin L \cos LHA - \cos L \sin d, \quad \sin LHA \cos d]$
$Hc = \text{asin}(\sin d \sin L + \cos d \cos LHA \cos L)$

We see that we can compute some of the five terms in the above equations simultaneously:

1. First we compute $\cos d$ and $\sin d$, and we save the latter.
2. Then we compute $\cos d \cos LHA$ and $\cos d \sin LHA$, and again save the latter.
3. Then we compute $\cos d \cos LHA \cos L$ and $\cos d \cos LHA \sin L$, and yet again save the latter.
4. We now recover $\sin d$ and L, and compute $\sin d \cos L$ and $\sin d \sin L$.
5. All five terms are now computed, and we can combine them appropriately to get Zn and Hc.

The routines given above may also be used to solve star identification and great-circle sailing problems.

To identify a star, first enter its true azimuth, Zn, then the best estimate of the ship's latitude, and finally the observed altitude, Ho; all values must be expressed in degrees and decimals.

The above routines will then provide the star's declination, in lieu of the computed altitude, and the star's LHA in lieu of the Zn. Frequently the star may be identified by its declination alone. The star's SHA may be found by first applying the vessel's estimated longitude to the LHA in order to obtain the star's GHA, and then by applying the GHA of Aries to the star's GHA in order to obtain its SHA.

To compute the great-circle distance between two points, and the initial heading, first enter the difference of longitude between the point of departure and the destination, then the latitude of the point of departure, and finally the latitude of the destination. The complement of the

ad-out is then multiplied by 60 to give the great-circle distance; the initial

heading may then be found by pressing $\boxed{x \leftrightarrows y}$.

Finding the Longitude by the Time Sight Formula

Given an accurate latitude, as obtained by an observation of Polaris, or the Sun, or some other body at transit, and carrying it forward until another observation is obtained of a body well to the East or West, the longitude can be computed.

This method of determining position was in wide use in the merchant fleets of the world at the time of World War II, and is probably still in use. Many ship owners did not buy reduction tables, charts, almanacs, and so forth, for their ships, and it was therefore desirable to have a method of fixing position that did not involve wear and tear on expensive charts or plotting sheets purchased by the captain or navigator. The latitude was carried forward by plane sailing, with allowance for current, if deemed necessary, to the time of the second observation. This second observation should, for the sake of accuracy, be made with the body as near the prime vertical, that is, bearing as nearly due East or due West, as possible.

The formula is

$$\cos t = \frac{\sin Ho - \sin L \times \sin d}{\cos L \times \cos d}$$

The meridian angle, t, will be named East or West according to the body's azimuth. Having found the meridian angle, we apply it to the GHA of the body at the time of the observation to find the longitude.

Example: Approximately 5 hours after LAN, in DR L 9°15.2' N, λ 151°17.8' W, the Sun bearing about 265°T was observed to have an Ho of 13°56.4'. At the time of the observation, the Sun's GHA was 226°36.1', and its declination was South 3°02.0'. We require the longitude.

The formula given above becomes:

$$\cos t = \frac{.24091 + .00851}{.98560} = .25306$$
$$t = 75.34148° = 75°20.5'$$

The Sun's meridian angle at the time of the observation was therefore 75°20.5' W.

In this case we subtract the meridian angle West from the Sun's *GHA* to obtain the longitude; if there is doubt as to how to apply *t* to the *GHA*, it can be resolved easily by sketching a time diagram.

$$
\begin{array}{ll}
GHA & 226°36.1' \\
t & - \ \ 75°20.5' \ W \\
\hline
\lambda & 151°15.6' \ W, \text{ which is the longitude}
\end{array}
$$

The longitude may be determined with considerable accuracy if a body is observed on or near the prime vertical. For determining the altitude of a body when it is on the prime vertical, or its meridian angle at that instant, see the section titled "Time and Altitude on the Prime Vertical" under the heading "Miscellaneous Celestial Computations."

Horizon Sights

A horizon sight is an observation of a celestial body obtained when the body is in contact with the sea horizon. The Sun is the body usually used for such observations, for which no sextant is required. The sine *H* formula, which has already been discussed in connection with computing altitude, lends itself well to the reduction of horizon sights by calculator. All that is needed is to obtain Greenwich mean time at the moment the Sun's limb is in contact with the horizon and to correct most carefully for dip, refraction, and semidiameter, the resulting altitude of 0°.

It must be borne in mind that the resulting corrected altitude, *Ho*, will be negative in value, and that, unless the DR position is greatly in error, the computed altitude, *Hc*, also will be negative. For negative altitudes, if *Ho* is greater than *Hc*, the intercept will be *away*, and will be plotted in the direction of the supplement of the azimuths.

Usually, the best way to find the azimuth is to convert it from an amplitude. Alternatively, it may be calculated by means of one of the azimuth formulae discussed in this text.

Low-altitude sights have been considered unreliable, mainly because of the presumed vagaries of refraction at altitudes below 5°. However, the refraction tables available today almost invariably give good results. In a number of horizon observations of the Sun, the average error was found to be 1.95 miles. This average would undoubtedly have been smaller, had the altitudes been computed to the nearest tenth of a minute, rather than to the nearest minute.

From positions at sea that could be accurately established, the writer made 378 observations of the Sun at altitudes ranging downward from 5° to the horizon. Of these sights, 336 yielded a line-of-position plotting within one mile of the actual position, 38 fell between 1.1 and 2.0 miles

We write the sine–cosine formula:

$$\sin Hc = \sin 35°02.1' \times \sin 13°58.1' + \cos 35°02.1' \times$$
$$\cos 13°58.1' \times \cos 101°14.5'$$
$$= 0.1386 - 0.1549 = -0.0163$$
$$Hc = -0°56.1'$$

The computed altitude, therefore, is $-0°56.1'$.
We now find the Sun's azimuth angle, Z, using the sine formula

$$\sin Z = \frac{\cos 13°58.1' \times \sin 101°14.5'}{\cos (-0°56.1')}$$
$$= \frac{0.9704 \times 0.9808}{0.9999}$$
$$Z = 72.1640°$$

The azimuth angle, therefore, is N 72°2'W, Zn is 287.8° (360° − 72.2°), and, since the negative value of Ho is less than the negative value of Hc, the intercept, a, is:

$$Ho - 0°52.6'$$
$$Hc - 0°56.1'$$
$$(-) \quad 3.5' \text{ Toward}$$

Noon Sights

For centuries the day afloat was reckoned to start as the Sun crossed the ship's meridian. The ship's clocks were set to 1200, and the navigator started the day by logging a latitude obtained by observing the Sun at transit. Our Navy continues this tradition at least in part; the officer of the deck sends his messenger to the captain with a request for permission to strike eight bells on time; the eight bells are now struck at 1200 zone time, however, rather than at local apparent noon.

The noon sight remains important; it is always desirable to know one's latitude, and this sight is usually the most accurate that can be obtained, as the Sun is stationary in altitude, and the horizon is sharply defined.

Latitude may be obtained from this observation by the regular formula used for sight reduction. The altitude is computed, and Zn is assumed to be 000° or 180°, as the case may be, without computation. The computed altitude, Hc, is compared with the observed altitude, Ho, and the difference establishes the value of the intercept, a. If the Ho is the greater, the intercept will be labeled "Toward" and the latitude used in reducing the sight will be moved in the direction of

Miscellaneous Celestial Computations, page 149:
Formula (2) should read:

$$\lambda = \lambda e + \frac{a_2 \times \cos Zn_1 - a_1 \times \cos Zn_2}{\sin (Zn_1 - Zn_2) \times \cos L}$$

Miscellaneous Celestial Computations, page 150:
Formula (2) should read:

$$\lambda = 60.0983° + \frac{0.0667 \times \cos 185° - (-0.050 \times \cos 281°)}{\sin (185° - 281°) \times \cos 41.0819°}$$
$$= 60.0983° + \frac{-0.0569}{-0.7496} = 60.1742°$$

Next example, 4th line should read:

$(Zn_1)[\uparrow](Zn_2)[-][\sin][\div]$ $[P \rightarrow R]$ $(Le)[\cos][\div] \rightarrow$ Read $\Delta\lambda$
$[x \leftrightarrows y]$ $\rightarrow$ Read ΔL

Miscellaneous Celestial Computations, page 155:
Second paragraph should read,

"Finally, P' is applied according to its sign to obtain the fully cleared lunar distance:

$$\text{Cleared LD} = D_o + P' \qquad (5)"$$

Miscellaneous Celestial Computations, page 156:
Formula (1) should read:

$x = 0.5 (\sin 34°29.7'/\sin 59°19.7') + 0.5 (\sin 59°19.7'/\sin 34°29.7')$
$= \qquad 0.32922 \qquad + \qquad 0.75936$

p. 162 line 12
Change 45.016667° N to read 45.061667° N

p. 163 last line
Change N 18.397458° to read N 18.379458°

Miscellaneous Computations, page 186:
Last example, add subscript:

$$D = \frac{HE}{\tan H_o}$$

Miscellaneous Computations, page 200:

Table 6-4. Change specific gravity of salt water to 1.025

of the position, and the remaining 4 fell between 2.0 and 2.2 miles of the position.

Horizon sights can be expected to yield good results in the great majority of cases, and they will yield useful information on position, in the event that no sextant is available. On a clear day in the tropics, it is easy to determine the instant the Sun's upper limb touches the horizon by observing a quite bright greenish-blue flash, known as the "green flash." This flash is caused by the greater refraction of the blue-violet end of the light spectrum, and consequently it remains visible slightly longer than does the red-yellow light.

Example: At sunset, when our DR position was L 35°02.1′ N, λ66°51.2′ W W, we observed the Sun's upper limb to have an altitude of 0°. Greenwich hour angle and declination were 168°05.7′ and N 13°58.1′, respectively, and the semidiameter was 15.8′.

The observer's height of eye was 12 feet, the barometric pressure was 30.27 inches, the sea temperature was 82°F, and the air temperature was 71°F.

We wish to find the computed altitude, *Hc,* using the sine–cosine formula, and to plot a line of position.

We first correct the altitude, in this instance using the tables in the *Nautical Almanac* and the sea–air temperature formula:

h_s ☉			0°00.0′
Dip, 12′	−3.4′		
R	−34.5′		
Additional R,			
Nautical Almanac, p. A4		+2.3′	
SD ☉	−15.8′		
Sea–Air Temp. Corr.	−1.2′		
	−54.9′ + 2.3′	Net. Corr.	−52.6′
Ho			−0°52.6′

where h_s ☉ represents altitude of the Sun's upper limb, *R* represents refraction, *SD* ☉ represents semidiameter of the Sun, and *Ho* represents corrected altitude.

We next obtain the *LHA:*

Greenwich hour angle	168°05.7′
λ	66°51.2′ W
LHA	101°14.5′

We write the sine–cosine formula:

$$\sin Hc = \sin 35°02.1' \times \sin 13°58.1' + \cos 35°02.1'$$
$$\times \cos 13°58.1' \times \cos 98°51.0'$$
$$= 0.1386 - 0.1222 = 0.0163$$

$$Hc = 0°56.1'$$

The computed altitude, therefore, is $-0°56.1'$.
We now find the Sun's azimuth angle, Z, using the sine formula

$$\sin Z = \frac{\cos 13°58.1' \times \sin 98°51.0'}{\cos 0°56.1'}$$
$$= \frac{0.9704 \times 0.9881}{0.9999}$$

$$Z = 73.54°$$

The azimuth angle, therefore, is N 73.5° W, Zn is 286.5° (360° − 73.5°), and, since the negative value of Ho is less than the negative value of Hc, the intercept, a, is:

$$Ho \ -0°52.6'$$
$$Hc \ -\underline{0°56.1'}$$
$$3.5' \ \text{Toward}$$

Noon Sights

For centuries the day afloat was reckoned to start as the Sun crossed the ship's meridian. The ship's clocks were set to 1200, and the navigator started the day by logging a latitude obtained by observing the Sun at transit. Our Navy continues this tradition at least in part; the officer of the deck sends his messenger to the captain with a request for permission to strike eight bells on time; the eight bells are now struck at 1200 zone time, however, rather than at local apparent noon.

The noon sight remains important; it is always desirable to know one's latitude, and this sight is usually the most accurate that can be obtained, as the Sun is stationary in altitude, and the horizon is sharply defined.

Latitude may be obtained from this observation by the regular formula used for sight reduction. The altitude is computed, and Zn is assumed to be 000° or 180°, as the case may be, without computation. The computed altitude, Hc, is compared with the observed altitude, Ho, and the difference establishes the value of the intercept, a. If the Ho is the greater, the intercept will be labeled "Toward" and the latitude used in reducing the sight will be moved in the direction of the Sun by the amount of the intercept; if Hc is the greater, the converse holds true.

However, the latitude at local apparent noon, LAN, may be accurately determined, without calculating an altitude, by one of three formulae which hinge on the relationship between the Sun's declination, d, and the latitude, L.

The first formula, for use when the latitude and declination are of the same name but the latitude is greater than the declination, is:

$$L = 90° + d - Ho \tag{1}$$

in which Ho represents the completely corrected sextant altitude.

When the declination and latitude are of opposite names, the formula is:

$$L = 90° - (d + Ho) \tag{2}$$

When latitude and declination are of the same name, but the declination is greater than the latitude, the formula is:

$$L = d + Ho - 90° \tag{3}$$

A fourth formula, which lends itself particularly well to use with the calculator, as a substitute for the above formulae, is:

$$\sin L = \cos (Ho \pm d) \tag{4}$$

in which the sign is $-$ if L and d are of the same name, and $+$ if they are of contrary name. The exception to this rule occurs when L and d are of the same name but d is greater than L; in this case, the sign is $+$, and a $-$ sign, which should be ignored, will appear to the left of the latitude.

Example 1: Our DR latitude is 37°45.0' N, and the Sun's declination at LAN is N 21°36.4'; the Ho was 73°50.2'. To find our latitude, we write formula (1) as:

$$L = 90° + 21°36.4' - 73°50.2' = 37°46.2'$$

Our latitude at LAN, therefore, is 37°46.2' N.

Example 2: At LAN we were in DR L 18°12.8' S, the declination was N 14°51.2', and the Ho was 56°55.6'. Latitude and declination being of opposite name, we here use formula (2), which becomes:

$$\begin{aligned} L &= 90° - (14°51.2' + 56°55.6') \\ &= 90° - 71°46.8' \\ &= 18°13.2' \end{aligned}$$

Our latitude, therefore, was 18°13.2' S.

Example 3: Our DR latitude at LAN was 12°14.5′ N, at which time the Sun's declination was N 21°29.7′; the *Ho* was 80°46.5′. As latitude and declination are of the same name, we select formula (3), and write:

$$L = 21°29.7′ + 80°46.5′ - 90° = 12°16.2′$$

At LAN our latitude, therefore, was 12°16.2′ N.

Example 4: In southern latitude we observed the Sun at transit to have an *Ho* of 63°51.7′; its declination at the time was S 14°12.6′. We desire to determine our latitude, using formula (4), which we write, using the − sign as *L* and *d* are of the same name:

$$\sin L = \cos (63°51.7′ - 14°12.6′) = 0.6474$$

Our latitude, therefore, is 40°20.9′ S.

Example 5: Our DR latitude is 12°15.0′ N, when we observed the Sun's *Ho* at LAN to be 80°30.5′; the declination was N 19°42.7′. We require our latitude, using formula (4). As the declination in this case is of the same name but greater than the latitude, we write formula (4) using a + sign, as *L* and *d* are of the same name, but *d* is greater than *L*:

$$\sin L = \cos(80°30.5′ + 19°42.7′) = -0.1774$$

which converts to − 10.2200°. Converting the decimals to minutes, and ignoring the −sign, we find we are in 10°13.2′ North latitude.

Hang of Sun at Local Apparent Noon

To determine the length of time the Sun will be within a given angle, say 1′, of its altitude at LAN, the formula is:

$$\cos t = \frac{\sin(Ho \ \text{LAN} - \dot{1}.0′) \times \sin L \times \sin d}{\cos L \times \cos d}$$

where *t* is the meridian angle; *t* is then multiplied by 4 to convert to minutes of time, and then by 2 to get the sum of the time periods before and after noon.

Time of Local Apparent Noon

A vessel under way can quite accurately determine the time of local apparent noon, LAN, by means of a calculator, provided that the DR longitude is known reasonably closely and that a *Nautical Almanac* or an *Air Almanac* is available. The *Long-Term Sun Almanac,* included in this text, may also be used. However, for this purpose, an *Air Almanac,* which gives ephemeristic data for every 10 minutes of time, rather than for every hour, is slightly more convenient than a *Nautical Almanac,* and both are much more convenient than the *Long-Term Sun Almanac.*

In the forenoon, while the Sun is still well to the East, enter the *Nautical Almanac,* and extract the tabulated Greenwich hour angle, *GHA,* of the Sun which is *nearest to, but East of,* your DR longitude, together with the Greenwich mean time, GMT, of this entry. Next, from the DR plot on the chart, determine the longitude for this GMT. Having obtained this longitude, find the difference between it and the Sun's *GHA,* as taken from the *Almanac.* This difference is meridian angle East, *t*E, which for this purpose is expressed in minutes of arc.

Next, in order to establish the time of LAN, it is necessary to determine the instant of time when the Sun's hour circle will coincide with the ship's longitude. This is done by combining the rate of change of longitude of the ship with that of the Sun. The former can be determined from the chart, or by working it as a mid-latitude sailing problem. The latter is an almost uniform 15°, or 900 minutes of arc per hour, toward the West.

If the ship is moving toward the East, the hourly rate of change of longitude is added to that of the Sun; if she is sailing toward the West, it is subtracted from that of the Sun. The result of this combination is then divided into *t*E, expressed in minutes of arc, as shown in the following formula:

$$\text{Interval to LAN} = \frac{t\text{E in minutes of arc}}{900' \pm \text{ship's change of longitude per hour}}$$

The answer to this equation will be in decimals of an hour, and should be determined to three significant places. If the answer is multiplied by 60, minutes and decimals of minutes are obtained; the decimals of minutes, multiplied by 60, will in turn yield seconds. The answer, which will be mathematically correct to within about 4 seconds, added to the hour of GMT obtained from the *Nautical Almanac,* will give the GMT of LAN at the ship. The ship's time zone description may be applied to the GMT to give the ship's time of LAN.

Example: On 23 March, we are steaming on course 064°, speed 20.0 knots, and we desire to observe the Sun at LAN. At 1140, zone + 4 time, we note that our 1200 DR position will be L 43°15.5' N, λ 66°27.6' W. Our zone description being plus 4, the GMT of our 1200 position will be 1600.

Turning to the *Nautical Almanac* for 23 March, we find that the Sun's *GHA* at 1600 GMT will be 58°20.1'. Subtracting this from our DR longitude for that time, we obtain a difference of 8°07.5', or 487.5'; this is the Sun's meridian angle East at 1200.

We elect to find our rate of change of longitude per hour by mid-latitude sailing. Using our 1200 DR position, course 064°, and speed 20.0 knots, we find that the mid-latitude at 1230 will be L 43°19.9' N, and that the departure is 17.98 miles per hour. This gives us a rate of change of longitude of 24.7′ per hour to the eastward. The formula, therefore, becomes:

$$\text{Interval to LAN} = \frac{487.5'}{(900' - 24.7')} = 0.557 \text{ hour}$$

0.557 hour multiplied by 60 equals 33.4 minutes; 0.4 minute multiplied by 60 equals 24 seconds. This, added to 1200, gives us the time of LAN.

The ship's time of LAN will, therefore, be 12 33 25 (+4).

Bear in mind that for a vessel moving on a near northerly or southerly course, the time of LAN must be computed because the Sun's maximum altitude, when reduced, will then yield a false latitude. This is particularly true if the vessel is moving at speed.

Obtaining Latitude at LAN by Plotting

When the latitude and the Sun's declination nearly coincide, it is often difficult to get a satisfactory observation at LAN because the Sun is almost directly overhead, its change of altitude is very rapid, and the hang is very brief. Under such conditions, the morning sights have yielded an excellent idea of longitude, but have not helped in determining latitude.

Under such conditions, the best way to find the latitude often is by plotting. The first step is to draw a line on the chart in a latitude to coincide with the Sun's declination; the Sun's *GHA*, converted to time, can be marked along this line as is convenient. When the Sun is about 12 minutes or 3 degrees to your East, start a series of timed observations, continuing until the Sun has passed about an equal distance to the West.

Each sextant altitude is corrected in the usual manner to obtain *Ho*, which is then subtracted from 90°. Using the resulting angle as a radius, strike in an arc centered at the appropriate time or longitude on this line to correspond to the Sun's *GHA* at the time of the observation. Repeat this process for each sight; if your vessel is moving at high speed, each arc may be advanced in the usual manner for the run. The intersection of the arcs will establish both latitude and longitude at the time of LAN.

Fixes in Conjunction with Noon Sight

Excellent running fixes may be obtained in conjunction with the noon sight when the Sun's declination is within about 30° of the ship's latitude.

If we desire a change of azimuth of about 45° between sights for a running fix obtained before and after noon, the time to make the observations can be approximated. All that is necessary is to find the numerical difference between the latitude and the declination; this will approximate the meridian angle when the sun will be 45° in azimuth angle from the meridian. The meridian angle thus found, multiplied by 4, will give the time in minutes relative to the time of LAN at which the observation is to be made.

Example 1: Our expected latitude at LAN will be 33°16′ N, and the Sun's declination, *d,* at that time will be N 20°37.0′.

Now 33°16′ − 20°37′ = 12°39′, or 12.65°, and 12.65 × 4 = 50.6.

The Sun, therefore, will bear about 135°, 51 minutes before LAN, and about 225°, 51 minutes after LAN.

Example 2: L 10°07′ S, *d* N 11°12′. Here, since *L* and *d* are of opposite name, we add them to find the numerical difference. 10°07′ + 11°12′ = 21°19′; for our purpose, we will call it 21.3°, and 21.3 × 4 = 85.2 minutes.

The Sun, therefore, will bear 45° from our meridian 85 minutes before and after LAN.

Example 3: L 8°53′ N, *d* N 21°16′. The difference 21°16′ − 8°53′ = 12°23′; call it 12.4°. 12.4 × 4 = 49.6.

The Sun, therefore, will bear about 045° some 50 minutes before LAN, and about 315°, 50 minutes after.

Longitude at Local Apparent Noon by Equal Altitudes

If the day is clear, and an almanac and the correct time are available, the ship's longitude at local apparent noon, LAN, can be approximated by what is generally called the "equal morning and afternoon altitude method." This, as we shall see, is a misnomer, because the afternoon altitude, which we will call the PM-H, is equal to the morning altitude, AM-H, only when a vessel is proceeding due East or due West, and the Sun's declination does not change between the AM-H and PM-H. The latitude at LAN can, of course, also be determined, thus yielding a close approximation of the true position at that time.

The best results are obtained when the AM-H is obtained while the Sun is still changing altitude fairly rapidly; that is, when its azimuth is not more than 140° True. In summer, in lower and mid-latitudes, the change in azimuth is very rapid, and the AM-H may be obtained only a short time before LAN. However, when the latitude and declination are, for example, 50° apart, the AM-H may have to be obtained more than 2 hours before LAN.

The technique in the equal-altitude method was to obtain an AM-H, noting the sextant angle and the time of observation. After the Sun was observed at LAN, the sextant was reset to the AM-H, and the time was taken when the Sun again reached the same altitude. However, for the new equivalent-altitude method, which yields far better results than the old, it is best to graph both the AM and PM altitudes, plotting altitudes against Greenwich mean time, GMT; a line of "best fit" is then drawn through, or as close as possible to, the plotted altitudes. An altitude from the AM graph is selected, and its GMT is noted.

As stated above, the PM-H will differ from the AM-H if the ship is changing latitude, or if the Sun is changing in declination between these two observations. Allowance can be made for each of these two factors.

The approximate effect of the ship's change of latitude on the PM-H can be determined by use of a correction factor, the cosine of the azimuth angle, Z, at the time the AM-H was obtained. Since it is usually difficult to obtain good azimuths at sea at altitudes higher than a few degrees, this may be approximated by means of the formula

$$\sin Z = \frac{\cos d \times \sin t}{\cos Ho} \qquad (1)$$

in which d is the Sun's declination, t the Sun's meridian angle found by using the best estimate of the longitude at the time of AM-H, and Ho the corrected sextant angle.

Having thus found the value of Z, at LAN we find the difference in latitude since our best estimate of our latitude at the time of AM-H, double it, and multiply it by the cosine of Z. The result, in minutes of arc, is applied to AM-H, the sign being + if the change in latitude has brought us nearer the Sun, and − if away from the Sun.

The effect of the change in declination may similarly be determined by means of the cosine of M, the angle at the Sun's geographic position in the navigational triangle PZM, in which P is the elevated pole, and Z the ship's position. The angle M is found by the formula

$$\sin M = \frac{\cos L \times \sin t}{\cos Ho} \qquad (2)$$

in which t and Ho are determined as in formula (1), and L is the latitude obtained at LAN.

Having found the value of M, we determine its cosine. Incidentally, in H.O. 214, the factor "Δd," used for correcting the tabulated altitude for minutes of declination over the tabulated declination, is the cosine of M stated to two decimal places.

We estimate the time of LAN, that is, the mid-time of the period during which the maximum altitudes were obtained, and find the difference between this time and the time of AM-H. This difference is doubled, and then multiplied by cosine M; the result in minutes is applied to AM-H, the sign being + if the change in declination is bringing the Sun nearer the ship, and − if away from the ship.

When both corrections have been applied to AM-H, we have the value of PM-H. For this sight, we commence observing the Sun when it is somewhat higher than the value of PM-H, and again make a string of observations, the final one being when the altitude is below PM-H. These sights are again plotted against time, and a line of "best fit" is drawn in. The altitude of PM-H is next found on this line, and the corresponding GMT is noted.

We now proceed to determine the GMT of LAN, that is, when the Sun was on our meridian, which establishes our longitude at LAN. We find this time by finding the difference in time between that of AM-H and PM-H, and halving it. This value is then added to the GMT of AM-H to find the GMT of LAN.

The Sun's Greenwich hour angle, *GHA*, is then determined for the time of LAN; in West longitude, this coincides with the vessel's longitude at LAN; in East longitude, it is subtracted from 360° to give the longitude.

It may be noted here that a given error in determining the correct GMT of PM-H is halved in finding the longitude at LAN. Thus, if the error in the time of PM-H were exactly one minute, the error in the longitude at LAN would be 30 seconds, or 7.5'.

The following extreme case was prepared to illustrate the marked effect that changes in the latitude and declination can have on the PM-H. It may be of interest to note that in this example the error in the longitude determined for the time of LAN did not exceed 0.5'; in other words, the difference between the AM-H and PM-H meridian angles was less than 1.0'. Ideally, they should have been equal.

Example: On 23 September we are in the Eastern Atlantic, bound for Galway, Ireland. We are on course 045°T, at speed 21.24 knots. All times are GMT.

We propose to determine our position at LAN using equivalent AM and PM altitudes, and the Sun's altitude at LAN. We commence observing the Sun's altitude about 1045, and plot the sights. We decide to use an altitude of 33°03.4' for AM-H, obtained at 10:50:00, at which time our DR position was L 50°05.8' N, λ 16°20.1' W, the Sun's azimuth was about 141° True, its *GHA* was 344°21.6', and the declination was N 0°05.8'.

We note from the *Nautical Almanac* that the Sun's declination is declining at the rate of 1.0' per hour, and realize therefore that the altitude of the PM sight will have to be adjusted for this change, as well as for our change of latitude, which is considerable on this course and speed. However, we will not calculate these corrections until we have obtained our latitude at LAN.

To determine the correction to be applied to AM-H for the change in latitude, we must determine Z as accurately as possible for the time of AM-H.

By applying our 1050 longitude to the Sun's *GHA* at that time, we find that the value of t is 31°58.5′ E, and we can write formula (1):

$$\sin Z = \frac{\cos 0°05.8′ \times \sin 31°58.5′}{\cos 33°03.4′} = 0.6318$$

Z, therefore, is 39.1845°, and its cosine is 0.775; we note this for use later.

At 1250 we begin Sun observations for LAN. During the 2-minute period from 1254 to 1256 we obtain the highest altitudes, which, when reduced, give a latitude of 50°37.1′ N.

We note that, in somewhat over 2 hours, our latitude has increased by some 31.3′, and we can proceed to determine the corrections to be applied to the AM-H to get the equivalent PM-H.

To correct for the change of latitude, we assume that our latitude at the time of PM-H will have increased by twice the amount of the increase to LAN. This would make it 62.6′, and multiplying this by 0.775, the cosine of Z for the AM sight, we get 48.5′ as the correction for latitude. The sign will be − because we shall be farther from the Sun.

From the *Almanac,* we note that the declination decreases by 3.9′ in the 4 hours from GMT 1100 to 1500. To correct for this change, we write formula (2):

$$\sin M = \frac{\cos 50°37.1′ \times \sin 31°58.5′}{\cos 33°03.4′} = 0.4009 \text{ or } 0.401$$

M, therefore, is 23.6332°, and its cosine is 0.9161.

We multiply the estimated decrease in declination, 3.9′, by 0.916, and obtain the correction, 3.6′, for the change in declination. Here, also, the sign will be −, because the Sun is moving away from us.

We can now apply the two corrections to obtain the equivalent PM-H:

AM-H	*H* 33°03.4′
Corr. for ΔL −48.5′	
Corr. for Δd −3.6′	
Net corr.	−52.1′
PM-H	32°11.3′

At about 1454 we begin observing the Sun, continuing to take sights until its altitude is below 32°. These sights are plotted against time, and from the line of "best fit" we find that the Sun's PM-H was 32°11.3' at GMT 14:59:53.

We can now proceed to find the time the Sun was on our meridian at LAN as follows:

Time of PM-H	GMT	14:59:53
		−
Time of AM-H	GMT	10:50:00
Difference		4:09:53
One-half difference		2:04:56
	+	
Time of AM-H	GMT	10:50:00
Time of LAN	GMT	12:54:56
GHA Sun at	GMT	12:54:56 = 15°36.0'

Our longitude at LAN, at GMT 12:54:56 was therefore 15°36.0' W; this, with the latitude we obtained at that time, 50°37.1' N, gives us a good approximation of our GMT 1255 position.

Reduction to the Meridian

The nineteenth-century navigator was extremely anxious to obtain his latitude at LAN; he used it as a numerical value, and not as a line of position—charts were much too expensive to permit the drawing and erasing of lines. He carried his latitude forward by dead reckoning until the Sun was well to the westward, when he would calculate his longitude by means of a time sight.

His forefathers in the first part of the eighteenth century, before the chronometer became available, were limited in their celestial navigation to obtaining latitude; they expected to reach their destination by arriving at its latitude, or slightly to weather of it, and then running down their easting or westing.

Clouds, therefore, could, on occasion, make for an unhappy navigator; to assist him when the cloud cover was not solid and the Sun broke through occasionally, shortly before or after transit, two tables were designed that enabled him to obtain a latitude from his observation (these tables are included in the current *Bowditch*). However, for him to use these tables, the observation had to be made within a comparatively short period of LAN; under favorable conditions, the maximum period was 28 minutes.

Such an observation was called an ex-meridian altitude; the process of computing latitude by such a sight was called reduction to the meridian. Included at the end of this section are formulae that approximate the data obtained by use of these tables. Also included are formulae for a second method of obtaining latitude, which was widely used; however, it suffers from the same general restrictions.

We shall, however, first discuss a method of obtaining the latitude without any arbitrary time limit, provided the longitude is known. In using this method, two factors must be borne in mind: first, the less the difference is between the observer's latitude and the body's declination, the greater will be the error in the computed latitude caused by a given error in the observed altitude, and second, the farther the body is located from the observer's meridian at the time of observation, the greater will be the effect on the computed latitude caused by an error in the observation. Under most conditions, this error is not too serious; even if the latitude and declination are separated by only 10°, a one-minute error in the observed altitude, obtained 40 minutes before or after transit, should not cause the computed latitude to be more than 1.5' in error.

Two formulae are required to find latitude by this method, the first being

$$\tan P = \frac{\tan d}{\cos LHA}$$

where P is an auxiliary angle, d the declination, and LHA the local hour angle.

The second formula is

$$\cos Q = \frac{\sin P \times \sin Ho}{\sin d} \qquad (2)$$

where Q is a second auxiliary angle, and Ho the fully corrected sextant altitude.

P is then applied to Q to obtain the latitude, the sign being $\sim$ if L and d are of contrary name, or if they are of the same name and d is greater than L; in all other cases, P and Q are added to obtain the latitude.

Example 1: In North latitude, we observed the Sun's corrected altitude to be 74°05.5', at a time when its declination was N 18°43.7', and the *LHA* was 9°15.0'. We write formulae (1) and (2):

$$\tan P = \tan 18°43.7' \times 1/\cos 9°15.0' \qquad = 0.3435 = P \quad 18.9576°$$
$$\cos Q = \sin 18.9576° \times \sin 74°05.5' \qquad +$$
$$\times 1/\sin 18°43.7' \text{ N} = 0.9730 = \underline{Q \quad 13.3335°}$$
$$P + Q \quad 32.2911°$$

As L and d are of the same name, and L is greater than d, P and Q are here additive, making our latitude 32°17.5′ N.

Example 2: The Sun's corrected altitude was 63°45.0′ at a time when its declination was N 16°26.6′ and its *LHA* was 11°26.3′ W. We know that we are in South latitude. Then:

$$\tan P = \tan \text{N } 16°26.6′ \times 1/\cos 11°26.3′ \quad = 0.3011 = P \quad 16.7580°$$
$$\cos Q = \sin 16.7580° \times \sin 63°45.0′ \qquad\qquad\qquad\qquad \sim$$
$$\times 1/\sin \text{N } 16°26.6′ = 0.9135 = Q \quad 23.9994°$$
$$P \sim Q = \qquad 7.2414°$$

As the declination and latitude in this example are of contrary name, we take the absolute difference between P and Q, which makes our latitude 7°14.5′ S.

The Bowditch Method

The two formulae that approximate the Bowditch method are included primarily as a matter of historical interest. They should not be used when the body's altitude exceeds 86°, or when the time interval from transit exceeds 28 minutes of time. Both require that an assumed or estimated latitude be used, which, if in considerable error, can seriously affect the accuracy; and both suffer from the same time limitations.

In the Bowditch method of reduction to the meridian, the change of altitude in one minute from meridian transit, a, is first calculated, using the formula:

$$a = \frac{1.9635'' \times \cos L \times \cos d}{\sin (L \sim d)} \tag{3}$$

L being the latitude by estimate.

The second formula computes the correction, c, stated in minutes of arc, which is to be applied to Ho, before solving for L:

$$c = \frac{a \times t^2}{60} \tag{4}$$

where a is the value found in formula (3), and t is the time in minutes and decimals before or after LAN.

The latitude thus found is the latitude at the time of the observation.

The Third Method

The third method also requires two formulae, the first being:

$$A = 30.56 \times \tan L + 30.56 \times \tan d \tag{5}$$

where A is a value to be used in the second formula and L is the latitude by estimate. The sign is $+$ if L and d are of contrary name, and $\sim$ if they are of the same name.

The second formula is:

$$c = t^2/A \qquad (6)$$

where c is the correction, in minutes of arc, to be added to the observed altitude in calculating L, t is the meridian angle in minutes of time and decimals before or after transit, and A is the value found in formula (5).

Example: In latitude 23°33.0' N by estimate, we observed the Sun 11 minutes and 15 seconds after the computed time of transit to have an *Ho* of 80°15.5'. The Sun's declination at the instant of observation was N 14°12.0'. We require our latitude at the time of observation.

Using the Bowditch method, we write formula (3):

$$a = \frac{1.9635'' \times \cos 23°33.0' \times \cos 14°12.0'}{\sin (23°33.0' - 14°12.0')}$$

$$= \frac{1.7450}{0.1625} = 10.7406$$

Formula (4) then becomes:

$$c = \frac{10.7406 \times 126.5625}{60} = \frac{1359.3572}{60}$$

Therefore, c is 22.6560', which we note as $+22.7'$, making the altitude 80°38.2'.

In this case, our latitude equals 90° + declination $-$ altitude, or 23°33.8' N.

Using the same data to illustrate the second method, formula (5) becomes:

$$A = 30.56 \times \tan 23°33.0' \sim 30.56 \times \tan 14°12.0'$$

A, therefore, equals 13.3196 $-$ 7.7329, or 5.5867.

We can now write formula (6):

$$C = \frac{126.5625}{5.5867} = 22.6543$$

We therefore note that the correction, c, is $+$ 22.7', the same as that obtained by the Bowditch method, yielding the same latitude, 23°33.8' N.

Note: For the stated declination, meridian angle, and observed altitude, our latitude actually was 23°34.3' N, which is what we would have obtained if we had used the same data and the first method, given above.

5
Miscellaneous Celestial Computations

Latitude Approximated by Altitude of Polaris

Approximate latitude may be determined by applying two corrections to the corrected sextant altitude of Polaris.

The first, and major, correction hinges on the local hour angle of Aries, LHA ♈; this correction is given in Table 5-1 for every 10° of LHA ♈ for the year 1971. Stated next to each correction is its annual change, together with the sign of the change. Although the change in the value of the correction is not linear, an approximation of the correction for nontabulated values of LHA ♈ may be obtained by interpolating either by eye or by calculator.

The second correction is an arbitrary one of +1.0'; it combines the mean values of the a_1 and a_2 corrections for latitudes between 10° and 50° North, and the month of the observation given in the *Nautical Almanac*.

Example: On 1 December 1980 we observed Polaris to have a corrected sextant altitude, of *Ho,* of 43°43.7'. Applying our estimated longitude to the GHA Aries taken from the *Almanac,* we find the LHA ♈ to be 320°. We wish to determine our approximate latitude.

We set the problem up as follows:

For 1971, LHA ♈ 320°, the main correction is −17.6'. Annual Δ +0.3'. From 1 January 1971 to December 1980 is 9 years and 11 months; for our purposes we shall call it 10 years. Multiplying the annual Δ of 0.3' by 10 years, we get +3.0'.

Table 5-1. Main Corrections for 1971.0 to be Applied to Corrected Sextant Altitudes to Obtain Latitude, and Annual Change in this Correction

LHA ϒ	Main Corr.	Annual Δ	LHA ϒ	Main Corr.	Annual Δ	LHA ϒ	Main Corr.	Annual Δ	LHA ϒ	Main Corr.	Annual Δ
0°	−45.4'	+0.4'	90°	−27.6'	0	180°	+43.3'	−0.4'	270°	+25.9'	0
10°	−49.5'	+0.3'	100°	−19.4'	−0.1'	190°	+47.2'	−0.4'	280°	+17.8'	+0.1'
20°	−52.0'	+0.3'	110°	−10.7'	−0.1'	200°	+49.7'	−0.3'	290°	+ 9.2'	+0.2'
30°	−53.0'	+0.3'	120°	− 1.7'	−0.2'	210°	+50.6'	−0.3'	300°	+ 0.2'	+0.2'
40°	−52.4'	+0.2'	130°	+ 7.3'	−0.2'	220°	+50.0'	−0.3'	310°	− 8.8'	+0.2'
50°	−50.2'	+0.2'	140°	+16.0'	−0.3'	230°	+47.9'	−0.2'	320°	−17.6'	+0.3'
60°	−46.4'	+0.2'	150°	+24.2'	−0.3'	240°	+44.3'	−0.2'	330°	−25.9'	+0.3'
70°	−41.3'	+0.1'	160°	+31.6'	−0.3'	250°	+39.3'	−0.1'	340°	−33.5'	+0.3'
80°	−35.0'	+0.1'	170°	+38.0'	−0.4'	260°	+33.1'	−0.1'	350°	−40.0'	+0.3'
90°	−27.6'	0	180°	+43.3'	−0.4'	270°	+25.9'	0	360°	−45.4'	+0.4'

We can now write:

Correction for *LHA* ♈ 320.0°, 1971.1	−17.6′
Adjustment for 1980, 10 × 0.3′	+3.0′
Second correction	+1.0′
Net correction	−13.6′
Ho	43°43.7′
Latitude	43°30.1′ N

In this instance, the error in latitude is only +0.1′.

Times of Sunrise, Sunset, and Civil Twilight

Sunrise and sunset occur when the Sun's upper limb touches the horizon; under standard conditions of atmosphere and refraction, the apparent times of sunrise and sunset occur at sea level when the Sun's center is 50 minutes of arc, or 0.8333°, below the visible horizon; in other words, when its altitude, H, is −0.8333°. In determining the times of these phenomena with the aid of the formula given below, allowance can be made for the height of eye by numerically adding the correction for the dip of the horizon to the altitude, −0.8333°. Thus, if the time of sunrise or sunset were required for a height of 100 feet, for which height of eye the correction for dip is −9.7′, or −0.1617°, the value used for H would be −0°59.7′, or −0.9950°.

The times of these phenomena are usually computed to the nearest minute of time. Temperature inversions and other vagaries of refraction at altitudes near 0° can cause a considerable error in the times of these phenomena. A British freighter, off the East Coast of Africa, some years ago, reported that the Sun set at the calculated time and then suddenly reappeared, well above the horizon, and proceeded to set again.

For a vessel at sea, on a more or less easterly or westerly course, once the time of sunrise or sunset is established, its time for the following day can be closely approximated by applying the change in longitude, converted to time, to the time of the preceding phenomenon.

Otherwise, the first step is to determine the coordinates of the position for which the time is required, after which we determine the Sun's meridian angle, t, at the time of the phenomenon. For this, we use the formula

$$\cos t = \frac{\sin H - (\sin L \times \sin d)}{\cos L \times \cos d} \tag{1}$$

in which H is usually assumed to be −0.8333°, L is the latitude, and d is the declination at about the time of the desired phenomenon. The declination may be computed by means of the long-term Sun almanac included in this volume.

The Sun's *GHA* should be computed at the same time, and, for convenience, both should be calculated for the integral hour of GMT preceding the time of the phenomenon.

Having obtained the value of the meridian angle, named East for sunrise and West for sunset, we apply our longitude to it, subtracting if in West longitude, and adding if to the East. The value thus obtained gives the Sun's angular distance East of Greenwich at the time of the phenomenon at our position, which is subtracted from 360° to find the Sun's *GHA* for that time.

From this value, we subtract the *GHA* of the Sun at the selected hour of GMT; the difference is then divided by 15 to obtain the GMT of the phenomenon in decimals of an hour. This value is then converted to minutes and seconds, and the answer is added to the integral hour of GMT used in calculating the Sun's *GHA* and declination. To this time the zone time to which the ship's clocks are set is applied, with sign reversed, to obtain the ship's time of the phenomenon.

When it is desired to determine the time of the commencement or termination of civil twilight, the twilight of interest to the navigator, the procedure is exactly the same, but the altitude −6° is used in computing the value of *t*.

Example 1: We wish to determine the time of sunrise on 13 July for L 35° N, λ 60° W. Our clocks are set to zone +4 time. We know that the Sun will rise at some time after 0400 ship's time. We, therefore, calculate the *GHA* and declination of the Sun for GMT 0800 on 13 July, finding them to be 298.3606°, and N 21.8983°, respectively.

We write formula (1):

$$\cos t = \frac{\sin (-0.8333°) - \sin 35° \times \sin 21.8983°}{\cos 35° \times \cos 21.8983°}$$

$$= \frac{-0.2285}{0.7600} = -0.3006$$

$$t = 107.4932° \text{ E}$$

We next apply our longitude, 60° W, to the value of *t*, subtracting because we are in West longitude: *t* 107.4932° − λ 60° W = 47.4932°, which is the angular distance the Sun will be East of the meridian of Greenwich at the time of our sunrise.

To obtain the Sun's *GHA* at this time, we subtract 47.4932° from 360°, which makes the *GHA* 312.5068°. We next subtract the Sun's *GHA* for GMT 0800, 298.3606°, from this, and obtain the difference, 14.1462°. Dividing this quantity by 15, we obtain 0.9431 hour, or 56m 35s. Adding this value to GMT 0800, we find that the GMT of our sunrise will be 0857, to the nearest minute. All that remains to obtain the ship's time of sunrise is to apply our zone description, +4, with sign reversed, to this GMT. The ship's time of sunrise is, therefore, 0457.

Example 2: We require the ship's time of the commencement of civil twilight and of sunrise for L 29°48.7′ S, λ 148°36.7′ E on 4 December. Our clocks are set to zone −10 time. We know that civil twilight will commence at some time after 0400 ship's time.

The value 0400 −10 4 December makes the GMT 1800 (0400 + 24 − 10) 3 December, the previous day. We calculate the Sun's *GHA* and declination for this time and date, and find them to be 92.5667°, and South 22.0883°, respectively.

To find *t* for the commencement of civil twilight, we use −6° for *H*. Formula (1) becomes:

$$\cos t = \frac{-0.2915}{0.8040} = -0.3625$$

which makes the value of *t* 111.2562° East. Adding our longitude, 148.6117° E, to this quantity, we get 259.8679°. Next, subtracting this value from 360°, we get 100.1321°, the *GHA* of the Sun at the commencement of our civil twilight. From this *GHA* we subtract the Sun's *GHA* 92.5667° for the GMT 1800 on 3 December, found above; the difference is 7.5654°, which, when divided by 15, gives us 0.5044 hour, or 30m 16s. This we add to the GMT, 1800, for 3 December (used to obtain the *GHA*), to obtain the GMT of the start of civil twilight; the answer is 1830, to the nearest minute. All that remains is to apply our zone description, −10, with sign reversed, making the ship's time 2830 on the 3rd, or 0430 4 December.

To obtain the time of sunrise, we do not need to complete the entire sunrise calculation; we need only compute the Sun's meridian angle for our sunrise, and compare this value with the *t* for the start of civil twilight. The difference between these two angles, converted to time, gives us the time of sunrise.

To obtain *t* for the time of sunrise, we use formula 1, entering *H* as −0.8333°. Then:

$$\cos t = \frac{-0.2015}{0.8040} = -0.2506$$

Therefore, *t* is 104.5139° E.

We subtract the value of this *t* from the *t* found above for the commencement of civil twilight. We then have *t* 111.2562° E − *t* 104.5139° E = 6.7423°. This value we divide by 15 to convert it to time; the result is 0.4495 hour, or 26m 58s, which we shall call 27m. Adding 27m to the ship's time of the start of civil twilight, 0430, found above, we find the ship's sunrise to be 0457.

Amplitudes

True amplitude is angular distance, North or South, measured from the observer's prime vertical (true East or true West) to a body centered on the celestial horizon. Amplitude observations made at sunrise and sunset, are extremely useful for checking the compass, as the body's bearing can be obtained with maximum accuracy when on the horizon, and the formula for calculating the amplitude is extremely simple. As a general rule, amplitudes should be avoided in high latitudes.

An amplitude, being a direction measured from the prime vertical, is given the prefix E for East, if the body is rising, and W for West, if it is setting. It is also given a suffix, N for North or S for South, to agree with the name of the body's declination. Amplitudes are expressed to the nearest tenth of a degree.

The body most frequently observed for the purpose of obtaining an amplitude is the Sun, although planets and stars may also be used. When the Sun's lower limb is some two-thirds of a diameter, or about 21 minutes, above the visible horizon, its center is on the celestial horizon. A planet or star is on the celestial horizon when it is about 32 minutes, or the diameter of the Sun, above the visible horizon. The Moon does not lend itself well to amplitude observations because it is on the celestial horizon when its upper limb is on the visible horizon.

It has been the practice to convert the bearing or azimuth as observed by compass to an observed amplitude, and then to compare it with the calculated amplitude. However, many people find it simpler to obtain the deviation, or gyro error, if both amplitudes are converted to azimuths reckoned from the North, Zn, and this is the method we shall use: for example, E 10.5° S becomes Zn 100.5° (90 + 10.5°), and W 10.5° S becomes Zn 259.5° (270.°−10.5°).

The true amplitude, with the body centered on the celestial horizon, is found by the formula

$$\text{sin amplitude} = \frac{\text{sin declination}}{\text{cos latitude}}$$

Example 1: We are in DR latitude 26°14.0′ N, and observe the setting Sun when its lower limb is about 21 minutes above the visible horizon; the declination, d, is S 8°46.4′. The Sun's azimuth by magnetic compass is 273.0°, and the variation is 13.6° W. We need the deviation on the current heading.

First, we determine the true amplitude, and convert it to azimuth. Then, we apply the variation to the azimuth obtained by compass, and compare the result to the true azimuth:

$$\text{sin amplitude} = \frac{\sin d\,(8°46.4')}{\cos L\,(26°14.0')}$$

$$= 0.1700 = \text{W } 9.8° \text{ S} = Zn \text{ } 260.2° \text{ True}$$

True	Zn 260.2°
Variation	13.6° W
Magnetic	Zn 273.8°
Azimuth by compass	Zn 273.0°
Deviation	0.8° E

We, therefore, call the deviation 1° E.

If the observation is made when the body is centered on the visible horizon, a correction is required in order to refer it to the celestial horizon. A close approximation of this correction in latitudes between 0° and 50° and for declinations between 0° and 24° N or S, is given in Table 5-2. In no instance will the error in the correction obtained from this table be greater than 0.2°; in the great majority of cases, it will not exceed 0.1°. If greater accuracy is required, Table 28 in *Bowditch* should be used.

The correction is applied to the azimuth obtained by compass in the direction *away* from the elevated pole; that is, for an observer in North latitude, the correction is toward the South, and vice versa.

Example 2: Our DR latitude is 33°42.1′ S, and the Sun's declination, *d*, is S 18°23.6′ when you observe it at sunrise, centered on the visible horizon. The Sun's azimuth by gyro is 113.5°. We need the gyro error.

As in Example 1, the first step is to determine the true amplitude and convert it to azimuth. We then take the correction from the

Table 5-2. Correction of Amplitudes for Bodies Observed Centered on the Visible Horizon for Declinations 0° to 24°

Latitude	Correction	Latitude	Correction
0°	0°	38°	0.6°
10°	0.1°	42°	0.7°
15°	0.2°	46°	0.8°
20°	0.3°	48°	0.9°
30°	0.4°	50°	1.0°
34°	0.5°		

table, apply it to the azimuth obtained by gyro, and compare the result to the true azimuth to obtain the gyro error.

$$\text{sin amplitude} = \frac{\sin d(18°23.6')}{\cos L(33°42.1')} = 22.2892° = \text{true amplitude E } 22.3° \text{ S}$$

$$= Zn\ 112.3°$$

Bearing by gyro	Zn 113.5°	
Correction for L from table	$-Zn$ 0.5° N	
	Zn 113.0°	observed Zn 113.0°
		gyro error 0.7° W

Time and Altitude on the Prime Vertical

Sometimes, as when working a time sight or when it is necessary to know the longitude, it is desirable to obtain an observation on the prime vertical.

It must be borne in mind that a body with a declination having a name opposite to that of the latitude of the observer, will not cross the latter's prime vertical above the horizon: its nearest approaches while visible will be at times of rising and setting. A body having a declination of the same name as the latitude of the observer, but numerically greater, will not cross the prime vertical. However, a body having a declination of the same name as the observer's latitude, but smaller numerically, will cross his prime vertical above the horizon. At each crossing, the meridian angles and altitudes are equal; the meridian angles are always less than 90°.

The meridian angle, $t,$ of a body on the prime vertical may be found by means of the formula

$$\cos t = \tan d \times \cot L \qquad (1)$$

where d is the declination, and L the latitude. When working with the slide rule, if L is less than 45°, it may be simpler to write the formula as

$$\cos t = \frac{\tan d}{\tan L} \qquad (2)$$

The altitude of a body, $H,$ when it is on the prime vertical, may be found by means of the formula

$$\sin H = \frac{\sin d}{\sin L} \qquad (3)$$

With these formulae, it is possible to determine the approximate time when a body will be on the prime vertical, and its altitude at that moment.

Where a body's declination is of the same name as, but numerically greater than, the observer's latitude, its meridian angle at the moment of nearest approach to the prime vertical may be found by the formula

$$\cos t = \frac{1}{\tan d \cot L} \tag{4}$$

or, if more convenient,

$$\cos t = \frac{\tan L}{\tan d} \tag{5}$$

Its altitude at this moment is found by the formula

$$\sin H = \frac{\sin L}{\sin d} \tag{6}$$

Its approximate azimuth angle, Z, at this moment may be found by the formula

$$\sin Z = \frac{\cos d \sin t}{\cos H} \tag{7}$$

Example 1: We are in L 51°25.0′ N, λ 47°41.0′ W, and the Sun bears slightly North of East; its declination is N 21°49.8′. We wish to observe the Sun on the prime vertical, and to know the approximate time when it will be on the prime vertical and its approximate altitude at that moment.

We first solve for t, by writing formula (1):

$$\cos t = \tan 21°49.8′ \times \cot 51°25.0′ = 0.3196$$

The meridian angle, therefore, is 71°21.7′ E.

We then apply our longitude to find the Sun's angular position relative to the meridian of Greenwich when its t is 71°21.7′ E.

$$
\begin{array}{ll}
t\text{E} & 71°21.7′ \\
\lambda\text{W} & \underline{47°41.0′} \\
& 23°40.7′
\end{array}
$$

The Sun's angular distance East of Greenwich when it is on our prime vertical is, therefore, 23°40.7′, which converts to 1 hour 34 minutes, 43 seconds.

If we are willing to assume that the Sun transits Greenwich at noon GMT, the GMT of our prime vertical sight would be about 1025 (12:00 − 1:35). A closer approximation may be found by determining the Greenwich hour angle, *GHA,* of the Sun, 336°19′ (360°−23°41′), then noting from the *Nautical Almanac* the GMT of this *GHA.* If the ship's time is required, it is necessary only to apply, with sign reversed, the zone description to which the ship's clocks are set to the GMT.

To find the altitude of the Sun when it is on our prime vertical, we use formula (3), which, if the Sun's declination has not changed, becomes:

$$\sin H = \frac{\sin 21°49.8'}{\sin 51°25'} = 0.4757$$

When the Sun is on our prime vertical, its altitude will, therefore, be 28°24.3'.

Example 2: We are in L 10°09.6' N, and the Sun's declination is N 19°30.1'. We wish to determine the meridian angle, altitude, and azimuth of the Sun at its nearest morning approach to our prime vertical.

We first find the meridian angle by formula (5), which here will be:

$$\cos t = \frac{\tan 10°09.6'}{\tan 19°30.1'} = 0.5060$$

The meridian angle, therefore, is 59°36.1' and is named East.

We next find the altitude, using formula (6), which we write:

$$\sin H = \frac{\sin 10°09.6'}{\sin 19°30.1'} = 0.5284$$

The altitude at this moment is, therefore, 31°53.8'.

The approximate azimuth we find by using formula (7):

$$\sin Z = \frac{\cos 19°30.1' \times \sin 59°36.1'}{\cos 31°53.8'} = 0.9577$$

The azimuth angle is, therefore, N 73.2654° E, which makes the azimuth 073.3° for practical purposes.

Rate of Change of Altitude

It is at times desirable to determine a body's rate of change of altitude. If a sequence of sights of the same body has been taken, the rate of change provides a check on the consistency of the observations. Also, if a star finder has been used to predict altitudes and azimuths, and visibility has caused a considerable delay in obtaining sights, correction of the sextant setting will compensate for the delay.

The formula for calculating the rate of change of altitude, ΔH, in *minutes of time* is:

$$\Delta H = \Delta t \times \cos L \times \sin Z \tag{1}$$

where Δt is 15.0 for the Sun and planets, 15.04 for stars, and 14.3 for the Moon.

To obtain ΔH in *seconds of time,* the formula is:

$$\Delta H = \frac{\cos L \times \sin Z}{4} \tag{2}$$

Example: We are in L 30°, and the predicted azimuth of the Sun is 100°. We want to find the rate of change of altitude in minutes of time.

Since the body's predicted azimuth is 100°, Z is 80° (180°–100°) and formula (1) becomes:

$$\Delta H = 15 \times \cos 30° \times \sin 80° = 12.8' \text{ per minute of time}$$

The rate of change of altitude, as found above, applies to a stationary observer. However, it yields acceptable results on board vessels steaming at normal speeds.

Rate of Change of Azimuth

A stationary observer may find the rate of change of azimuth of a heavenly body by use of two formulae: the first determines the parallactic angle, $M;$ the second provides the actual rate of change of azimuth. In the celestial triangle, *PZM,* the parallactic angle, $M,$ is the one that lies at the body.

To find the angle, we use the formula

$$\sin M = \frac{\cos L \times \sin Z}{\cos d} \tag{1}$$

in which L is the latitude, Z the azimuth angle, and d the declination.

Having found the angle, $M,$ we proceed to find the rate of change of azimuth per minute of time. For this we use the formula

$$\Delta Z' = \frac{15 \times \cos d \times \cos M}{\cos H} \tag{2}$$

in which $\Delta Z'$ is the rate of change of azimuth in minutes of arc per minute of time, and H is the computed altitude or the corrected sextant altitude.

Although formula (2) gives the rate of change of azimuth in relation to a stationary observer, the results it provides in relation to ships traveling at normal speeds are, in most cases, acceptably accurate.

Example: Our latitude is 40° N, and the declination is N 27°30'. The azimuth, *Zn,* is 163.9°, which we shall write as azimuth angle, 16°06' (180°–163°54'); and the corrected altitude, *Ho,* is 77°04.2'. We wish to determine the rate of change of azimuth in minutes of arc in one minute of time.

We write formula (1):

$$\sin M = \frac{\cos 40° \times \sin 16°06'}{\cos 27°30'} = 0.2395$$

$$M = 13.8568°$$

We next write formula (2):

$$\Delta Z' = \frac{15 \times \cos 27°30' \times \cos 13.8568°}{\cos 77°04.2'} = 57.7311'$$

The azimuth, therefore, is changing at a rate of about 57.7' per minute of time.

Star and Planet Identification

At times, particularly when there is a broken cloud cover, an unknown star is observed. H.O. Publications No. 214 and 229 include tables that facilitate identification of stars and planets; however, such bodies may also be identified by computation. Given the body's altitude and true azimuth, obtained by observation, one may compute its declination, d, and meridian angle, t. As true azimuth must be obtained by observation, best results are achieved with bodies situated at fairly low altitudes. However, no difficulty should be encountered in identifying a major navigational star or planet even if its computed declination and meridian angle are in error by a degree or more.

Two methods of making these calculations are in general use, and both are included. The first was suggested by Rear Admiral Arthur A. Ageton, U.S.N., when a lieutenant, in H.O. Pub. No. 211, *Dead Reckoning Altitude and Azimuth Table,* first published in 1931. The Ageton formulae are here modified for use with a calculator by substituting natural sines and cosines for log secants and cosecants.

In these formulae, R and K are auxiliary angles introduced to facilitate solution; Ho is the corrected sextant altitude; Z is the true azimuth reckoned East or West from the elevated pole; L is the latitude; d is the declination; and t is the meridian angle.

$$\sin R = \sin Z \times \cos Ho \qquad (1)$$

$$\sin K = \frac{\sin Ho}{\cos R} \qquad (2)$$

$$\sin d = \cos R \times \cos (K \sim L) \qquad (3)$$

$$\sin t = \frac{\sin R}{\cos d} \qquad (4)$$

We solve for t by writing formula (4):

$$\sin tE = \frac{\sin 43.150°}{\cos 38.6428°} = 0.8756$$

t, therefore, is 118.8810° E or 118°52.9′ E. See Rule 3 above: t is greater than 90°.

Having computed the star's meridian angle, we turn to the *Almanac* to find its *SHA*.

GHA Aries, GMT 2300, 2 May	205°26.3′
Increment, 59m 56s	15 01.5
GHA Aries, at time of sight	220°27.8′
Longitude West	− 60 28.5
LHA Aries	159°59.3′
Star's t 118°52.9′ E = *LHA*	~ 241 07.1
SHA	= 81°07.8′

We have now obtained a declination of N 38°38.6′, and an *SHA* of 81°07.8′. By referring to the list of primary navigational stars given in the daily pages of the *Nautical Almanac,* we find that Vega has a declination of N 38°46.0′ and an *SHA* of 80°57.5′; our star must, therefore, be Vega.

We might, of course, have observed one of the additional navigational stars, in which case identification could be made by use of the star data tabulated on pp. 268–73 of the *Nautical Almanac.*

In the second method, declination and meridian angle are also computed in order to identify an unknown star or planet.

The declination may be found by the formula:

$$\sin d = \sin L \times \sin Ho + \cos L \times \cos Ho \times \cos Zn \qquad (5)$$

In this formula, latitude L is entered as positive or negative, according to its name. The true azimuth Zn is entered without conversion. The declination d as computed is named North if its value is positive, and South if its value is negative.

Frequently, the declination thus found will be sufficient to identify the body. However, the meridian angle, t, may be computed by the formula:

$$\cos t = \frac{\sin Ho - \sin L \times \sin d}{\cos L \times \cos d} \qquad (6)$$

The following rules apply:

1. K takes the same name as the latitude.
2. When Z is greater than 90°, K is greater than 90°.
3. d is same name as L, except when Z and $(K \sim L)$ are both greater than 90°.
4. $(K \sim L)$ represents the algebraic difference between K and L; that is, the smaller is subtracted from the larger.
5. t is less than 90° when K is greater than L; conversely, it is greater than 90° when L is greater than K.

In most instances, it will not be necessary to solve for t, since a bright star can usually be identified by its declination.

Given the value of t, the local hour angle of Aries, LHA Υ, must be determined for the time of the observation; this is done by extracting the Greenwich hour angle, GHA Aries, from the almanac, and then applying the ship's longitude. If the star is to the eastward, its t is converted to LHA and compared with the LHA Aries to obtain its sidereal hour angle, SHA, as shown in the example.

Example 1: At Greenwich mean time, GMT, 23h 59m 56s, 2 May, in L 45°02.0′ N, λ 60°28.5′ W, a bright star is observed to have a corrected altitude of 10°05.5′, and a true azimuth of 044°. We wish to identify the star. Formula (1) becomes:

$$\sin R = \sin 44° \times \cos 10.0917°$$
$$= 0.6839$$

R, therefore, equals 43.150°.

Formula (2) then becomes:

$$\sin K = \frac{\sin 10.0917°}{\cos 43.150°} = 0.2402$$

K, therefore, equals 13.8969°, which we name North.

Having computed the value of K, 13.8969°, we obtain $K \sim L$, by subtracting it from the latitude, 45.0333°; $K \sim L$ therefore equals 31.1364°. We now write formula (3):

$$\sin d = \cos 43.150° \times \cos 31.1364°$$
$$= 0.6245$$

Therefore, d equals N 38.6428°, or N 38°38.6′, involving Rule 3 above to determine the name of the declination.

This calculation should usually be sufficient to allow us to consult the *Almanac* and identify the star as Vega. However, to make sure of the identification, we shall proceed to compute the value of t.

We solve for t by writing formula (4):

$$\sin t\mathrm{E} = \frac{\sin 43.150°}{\cos 38.6428°} = 0.8756$$

t, therefore, is 118.8810° E or 118°52.9′ E. See Rule 3 above: t is greater than 90°.

Having computed the star's meridian angle, we turn to the *Almanac* to find its *SHA*.

GHA Aries, GMT 2300, 2 May	205°26.3′
Increment, 59m 56s	15 01.5
GHA Aries, at time of sight	220°27.8′
Longitude West	− 60 28.5
LHA Aries	159°59.3′
Star's t 118°52.9′ E = *LHA*	~ 241 07.1
SHA	= 81°07.8′

We have now obtained a declination of N 38°38.6′, and an *SHA* of 81°07.8′. By referring to the list of primary navigational stars given in the daily pages of the *Nautical Almanac*, we find that Vega has a declination of N 38°46.0′ and an *SHA* of 80°57.5′; our star must, therefore, be Vega.

We might, of course, have observed one of the additional navigational stars, in which case identification could be made by use of the star data tabulated on pp. 268–73 of the *Nautical Almanac*.

In the second method, declination and meridian angle are also computed in order to identify an unknown star or planet.

The declination may be found by the formula:

$$\sin d = \sin L \times \sin Ho + \cos L \times \cos Ho \times \cos Z \qquad (5)$$

In this formula, it is convenient to consider L as always being positive, regardless of its name; the sign is always additive. The body's observed true Zn is converted to azimuth angle, Z, which will always be less than 90°, and will be reckoned East or West from either pole. Thus Zn 130° becomes Z S 50° W, and Zn 315° becomes Z N 45° W. Z is always considered to be a positive value, even when reckoned from South. If the sin d has a positive value, it will be of the same name as the latitude; if sin d is negative, the declination will be of contrary name to the latitude.

Frequently, the declination thus found will be sufficient to identify the body. However, the meridian angle, t, may be computed by the formula

$$\cos t = \frac{\sin Ho \pm \sin L \times \sin d}{\cos L \times \cos d} \qquad (6)$$

This, of course, is the classic time sight formula. L and d are entered as positive (North) or negative (South) in accordance with their names.

Having computed the value of t, and knowing the value of the *GHA* Aries for the time of the observation, the star's *SHA* may be determined, as in the above example, to assist in its identification.

Example 2: In latitude 36°18.0′ S, we observed an unknown star to have an *Ho* of 37°14.0′; its *Zn* was 240.0°. We wish to identify it, using formulae (5) and (6).

Formula (5) becomes:

$$\sin d = -0.3582 + (-)0.3208 = -0.6790$$
$$d = -42.7684°$$

As this value is negative, the declination is southerly; it, therefore, is S 42°46.1′.

We remain in doubt as to the star's identity, so we proceed to compute the star's meridian angle, using formula (6), which becomes:

$$\cos t = \frac{0.6051 - 0.5920 \times 0.6790}{0.8059 \times 0.7341} = \frac{0.2031}{0.5916}$$
$$= 0.3432$$

t, therefore, is 69.9265° W, which makes the *LHA* 69°55.6′. After applying the *LHA* Aries for the time of the observation, we find the star's *SHA* to be 95°50.7′.

We run down the star data tabulated on the daily pages in the *Almanac* with *SHA* 95°50.7′ and d approaching these values; we, therefore, turn to the complete tabulation of navigational stars, in the back of the *Almanac*, with these values, and find that the star is θ Scorpii, *SHA* 96°04.4′, d S 42°58.9′.

Times of Moonrise and Moonset

In the Navy, the times of moonrise and moonset are of particular interest. Unlike the Sun's altitude, which is always considered to be −50′ at rise or set, the Moon's altitude at rise or set varies with both its semidiameter and the horizontal parallax (a situation discussed further at the end of this section).

Both the *Nautical Almanac* and the *Air Almanac* tabulate the local mean times, LMT, of moonrise and set for selected latitudes, and the meridian of Greenwich, 0° λ, for every day, and the *Nautical Almanac* includes tables to facilitate correction for both latitude and longitude. However, these interpolations can be made both more rapidly and more accurately with the calculator.

In this formula, again, L and d are entered as positive values, regardless of name. The sign in the dividend is + if L and d are of contrary name, and − if they are of the same name.

Having computed the value of t, and knowing the value of the GHA Aries for the time of the observation, the star's SHA may be determined, as in the above example, to assist in its identification.

Example 2: In latitude 36°18.0′ S, we observed an unknown star to have an Ho of 37°14.0′; its Zn was 240.0°, or Z S 60° W. We wish to identify it, using formulae (5) and (6).

Formula (5) becomes:

$$\sin d = 0.3582 + 0.3208 = 0.6790$$

$$d = 42.7684°$$

As this value is positive, the declination will carry the same name as the latitude; it, therefore, is S 42°46.1′.

We remain in doubt as to the star's identity, so we proceed to compute the star's meridian angle, using formula (6), which becomes:

$$\cos t = \frac{0.6051 - 0.5920 \times 0.6790}{0.8059 \times 0.7341} = \frac{0.2031}{0.5916}$$
$$= 0.3432$$

t, therefore, is 69.9265° W, which makes the LHA 69°55.6′. After applying the LHA Aries for the time of the observation, we find the star's SHA to be 95°50.7′.

We run down the star data tabulated on the daily pages in the *Almanac* with SHA 95°50.7′ and d approaching these values; we, therefore, turn to the complete tabulation of navigational stars, in the back of the *Almanac*, with these values, and find that the star is θ Scorpii, SHA 96°04.4′, d S 42°58.9′.

Times of Moonrise and Moonset

In the Navy, the times of moonrise and moonset are of particular interest. Unlike the Sun's altitude, which is always considered to be −50′ at rise or set, the Moon's altitude at rise or set varies with both its semidiameter and the horizontal parallax (a situation discussed further at the end of this section).

Both the *Nautical Almanac* and the *Air Almanac* tabulate the local mean times, LMT, of moonrise and set for selected latitudes, and the meridian of Greenwich, 0° λ, for every day, and the *Nautical Almanac* includes tables to facilitate correction for both latitude and longitude. However, these interpolations can be made both more rapidly and more accurately with the calculator.

The first step in calculating the time of moonrise or set is to find the time correction for latitude, *TCL;* for this we use the formula

$$TCL = \frac{\Delta TT}{\Delta TL} \times \Delta L \qquad (1)$$

in which ΔTT is the difference in the tabulated values of time, ΔTL is the difference in the tabulated values of latitude, and ΔL is the difference in value between the desired latitude and the lower tabulated latitude.

Thus, for example, if we desire the time of moonrise on 14 August, in L 43°24.5′ N, and the *Almanac* tabulates moonrise for the 14th as:

L 45° N   2303
L 40° N   2324

we note that the difference for L 5° is −21 minutes, and formula (1) becomes:

$$TCL = \frac{-21m}{5°} \times 3.4083° = -14.3150m$$

For L 43°24.5′ N and 0° λ, therefore, moonrise will occur at 23-09.6850 (23h 24m − 14.3150m) on the 14th.

The next step is to interpolate for the desired longitude. If the ship is in *West longitude,* we repeat the same process to find the time of the phenomenon for the *following day;* for *East longitude,* we find its time for the *preceding day.*

For 14 August, and L 43°24.5′ N, let us assume that our longitude is 63°27.5′ W. Being in West longitude, we turn to the *Almanac* for the following day, the 15th, and note that moonrise is tabulated as:

L 45° N   2357
L 40° N   2419

2419, of course, means that on that night the Moon rises at 0019 on the following day, the 16th. The difference for 5° of latitude in this case is −22 minutes.

We therefore write formula (1):

$$TCL = \frac{-22m}{5°} \times 3.4083° = -14.9965m$$

For L 43°24.5′ N, and 0° λ, for the following night, the 15th, moonrise occurs at 24-04.0035, which makes it 00-04.0035 on the 16th.

The difference in the time of moonrise at our latitude and 0° λ in 24 hours, or 360°, is therefore +54.3185 minutes (24-04.0035 − 23-09.6850).

Next, we find the correction in time, *TC*, for the phenomenon between the 2 days for our longitude, 63°27.5′ W, using the formula

$$TC = \frac{\lambda}{360°} \times \Delta T \qquad (2)$$

in which λ is our longitude, and ΔT is the difference in time of the phenomenon for the 2 days. Formula (2) is, therefore, written:

$$TC = \frac{63.4583°}{360°} \times +54.3185m = +9.5749m$$

Moonrise at our location will therefore occur on 14 August at LMT 23-19.2599 (23 + 09.6850m + 09.5749m). Note that this is local mean time; we need to convert it to the ship's time.

Let us assume that for daylight saving purposes, our clocks are set to zone +3 time. The central meridian for this zone is 45° W. Our longitude, 63.4583° W, is 18.4583° West of this meridian, and 18.4583° converted to time is 1.2306 hours, or 1h 13m 50s. As we are West of our time zone meridian, we add this value to the LMT, 23h 19m 15s, and obtain 24h 33m 05s. The ship's time of moonrise, rounded off to the nearest minute, will therefore be 0033.

For a ship under way, it is usually necessary to calculate a second estimate of the time of moonrise or moonset; sometimes a third estimate is required. The first estimate may be based on a rough mental solution, made after inspecting the tables; the ship's position at this time is used to calculate the second estimate. From this, if it appears necessary, a third estimate is developed.

Should it seem desirable to check the final estimate, this may be done by means of the time sight formula:

$$\cos t = \frac{\sin H - \sin L \times \sin d}{\cos L \times \cos d}$$

in which the altitude, *H*, is found by means of the formula

$$H = HP - (SD + 34')$$

in which *HP* is the horizontal parallax, and *SD* the semidiameter, both taken from the *Nautical Almanac*. The meridian angle, *t*, as thus computed, may then be compared with the Moon's meridian angle at the time of the final estimate.

Error Caused by Timing Error

An error in the timing of a celestial observation will obviously cause an error in the location of the line of position, LOP, developed from that observation. Let us first consider a single LOP, which will give a most probable position, MPP; the MPP is determined by the point at which a perpendicular, dropped from our estimated or DR position, intersects the LOP. For a given error in time of the observation, the distance of the MPP from the estimated position, EP, may be found by means of the formula

$$D = \frac{E}{4} \times \cos L \times \sin Z$$

where D is the distance in nautical miles caused by the error, E is the error in seconds of time, L is the latitude, and Z is the azimuth angle.

For a given error of one second in time, the maximum error, expressed as distance, will occur on the equator, with the body bearing due East or due West, in which case it will be 0.25 mile.

It must be borne in mind that, in this case, the error referred to involves an MPP derived from a single observation. Where a fix, obtained from two or more LOPs, is involved, the position of the fix itself is in error; the error in placement of the component LOPs need not be considered. In such a case the fix will be in error only in longitude, the error being 15 minutes of arc for 1 minute of time, or 0.25 minute of arc per second of time.

If the watch used for timing was fast, the error in position will be to the West, and MPP must be moved to the East; conversely, if it was slow, the error will be to the East.

Example: A single observation of the Sun has been reduced, our DR being L 27°43.5' N. It was subsequently found that the stopwatch used for timing the observation had been started on chronometer time, which was 23 seconds slow. What adjustment should we make to the MPP, if the azimuth was 263.2°?

Here Z will be S 83°12' W (263.2°−180°), and the above formula will be:

$$D = \frac{23}{4} \times \cos 27°43.5' \times \sin 83°12' = 5.05 \text{ miles}$$

The MPP, therefore, should be moved 5.05 miles to the West.

Alternatively, the sight could be replotted. The watch error was 23 seconds; this, converted to longitude, equals 5.75'. The assumed or DR position from which the sight was originally plotted would, therefore, be moved 5.75' to the West, the watch being slow on GMT.

Interpolating in H.O. Publications Nos. 214 and 229

Altitudes tabulated in H.O. Publications Nos. 214 and 229 must be corrected for the difference between the actual declination and the declination assumed when entering the tables. In H.O. 214 a correction factor, called Δd, is provided for this purpose, and at the back of each volume there is a two-part multiplication table that facilitates determination of the value of the correction. When the actual declination differs from the assumed declination by both whole minutes and tenths of minutes, it is necessary to enter the portion of the table that is devoted to whole minutes, and then the portion that covers tenths of minutes. The two products must then be added together to obtain the correction that must be applied to the tabulated altitude.

This correction may be obtained more expeditiously, and in some instances more accurately, by use of the calculator: multiply the difference between the actual number of minutes and the number used in entering the tables by the Δd factor, then read off the correction factor to the nearest tenth of a minute.

Example 1: We have entered H.O. 214 with L 36° N, declination N 10°, and the meridian angle 19° E; the actual declination is N 10°14.4′. We find the tabulated altitude to be 58°48.2′, and the Δd factor to be .86.

We multiply 14.4′ (the difference between the true and assumed declination) by 0.86 by calculator, and obtain a correction of 12.4′ (to the nearest tenth) to apply to the tabulated altitude.

Now let us obtain the correction by means of the multiplication tables in the back of H.O. 214.

We find that	14′ × .86 = 12.0′
and that	0.4′ × .86 = 0.3′
giving a total correction of	12.3′

In this instance, the correction obtained by tables not only took longer to solve, but it was not as accurate as that obtained by calculator.

When H.O. 214 is to be used for reducing a sight from a DR, rather than an assumed, position, it is necessary to correct the tabulated altitude for the increment of meridian angle over the tabulated value, Δt, and for the increment of the DR latitude over the whole degree used for entering the tables, in addition to the usual Δd correction.

The Δt correction factor is tabulated, and the correction for the increment of meridian angle may easily and accurately be determined with the calculator in the same manner that the Δd correction is found.

However, H.O. 214 does not tabulate a correction for an increment of latitude over the tabulated degree. This correction, which we will call ΔL, is usually found by determining the difference in the tabulated altitude for the latitude used in entering the table, and the tabulated altitude for the next greater degree of latitude, using the same values of declination and meridian angle, and then interpolating.

Example 2: Our DR position is L 24°27.8′ N, λ 57°16.3′ W. We obtained an afternoon observation of the Sun, which had a corrected altitude of 48°02.6′. Its declination was S 12°17.8′ at the time of the observation. We wish to reduce the sight from our DR position, using H.O. 214. Having applied our DR λ to the Greenwich hour angle, *GHA*, of the Sun, we obtain a meridian angle, *t,* of 20°46.8′ W.

We enter H.O. 214 with L 24°, declination, *d,* 12° of contrary name, and *t* 20°, extract the tabulated altitude, *ht, Δd*, and Δ*t* corrections as noted below, and determine the values of the corrections by the calculator:

$$ht \quad 49°02.2′$$

Δ*d* 0.88 × −17.8′ =	−15.7′	
Δ*t* 0.48 × −46.8′ =	−22.5′	
Net. corr. for Δ*d* and Δ*t*	−38.2′	
ht for L 24°, corrected		−38.2′
computed altitude, *Hc* =		48°24.0′

We now find the difference in *ht* for our DR latitude:

L 24° N, *d* S 12°, *t* 20°	*ht* 49°02.2′
L 25° N, *d* S 12°, *t* 20°	*ht* 48°10.4′
Difference	−51.8′

The increment of latitude of our DR position over the base latitude of 24° is 27.8′. Then

$$-\frac{51.8′}{60′} \times 27.8′ = -24.0′$$

Therefore, our *Hc* of 48°24.0′ for L 24°, corrected for Δ*d* and Δ*t,* is decreased by this amount:

Hc	48°24.0′
Correction for *L*	−24.0′
Hc	48°00.0′
Ho	48°02.6′
Intercept, *a*	2.6′ Toward

Having found the intercept, we interpolate by eye to determine the azimuth.

For L 24° N, *d* (about) S 12°15′, and *t* (about) 20°45′, we see the azimuth will be 148.5°. The tabulated azimuth for L 24° N, *d* S 12°, and *t*

20° is 149.3°, and for L 25°, with the same values of d and t, it is 149.9°. Since for 1° of latitude the azimuth increases 1.6°, for 27.6′ it will increase 0.3°.

The azimuth therefore is N 148.8° W (148.5° + 0.3°), making the Zn 211.2° (360° − 148.8°).

Obtaining a Fix by Two Celestial Observations Without Plotting

The latitude and longitude of a fix, obtained from observations of two celestial bodies, may be computed, thus obviating the need for plotting. Each sight is reduced in the conventional manner, using the best estimate of the vessel's position, in order to obtain the intercepts, a_1 and a_2, and the two true azimuths, Zn_1 and Zn_2. Intercepts are treated as decimals of a degree; where an intercept is *away* it is treated as a negative value.

The latitude of the fix is then computed using the formula

$$L = Le + \frac{a_2 \times \sin Zn_1 - a_1 \times \sin Zn_2}{\sin (Zn_1 - Zn_2)} \tag{1}$$

where Le is the estimated latitude used in reducing the sights, a_1 and a_2 are the first and second intercepts, and Zn_1 and Zn_2 are the first and second computed true azimuths.

Longitude is computed by means of the formula

$$\lambda = \lambda e + \frac{a_2 \times \cos Zn_1 - a_1 \times \cos Zn_2}{\sin (Zn_1 - Zn_2) \times \cos L} \tag{2}$$

where λe is the estimated longitude used in reducing the sights.

For a vessel under way the same procedure is used, and each sight is reduced for the time at which it was obtained. In solving formula (1) for latitude, the best practice calls for using the ship's estimated latitude, Le, determined for the time of the second observation; similarly, λe in formula (2) should be the ship's estimated longitude at the time of the second observation. The result is equivalent to advancing the first LOP on the chart to the time the second LOP was obtained.

Example: We are on course 290°, speed 20 knots. At GMT 19h 20m 15s we observe Altair to have a corrected altitude of 57°40.0′; Hc proves to be 57°43.0′ and Zn is 185°. At GMT 19h 44m 15s we observe Alpheratz to have an Ho of 24°53.0′; its Hc is 24°49.0′, and its Zn is 281°. The ship's EP at GMT 19h 44m 15s is L 41°01.6′ N, 60°05.9′ W. We require the ship's position at GMT 19h 44m 15s. Comparing the observed with the computed altitudes, we note the first intercept, a_1, is Away 3.0′ or −0.050° and a_2 is Toward 4.0′, or +0.0667°.

Formula (1) becomes:

$$L = 41.0267° + \frac{0.0667 \times \sin 185° - (-0.050 \times \sin 281°)}{\sin(185° - 281°)}$$

$$= 41.0267° + \frac{-0.0549}{-0.9945} = 41.0819°$$

Our latitude at the time of the second observation, therefore, is 41°04.9′ N.

To obtain the longitude, we write formula (2):

$$\lambda = 60.0983° + \frac{0.0667 \times \cos 185° - (-0.050 \times \cos 281°)}{\sin(185° - 281°) \times \cos 41.0819°}$$

$$= 60.0983° + \frac{-0.0569}{-0.7496} = 60.1742°$$

which makes our longitude at GMT 19h 44m 15s 60°10.5′ W.

Above, we gave formulae for determining the latitude and longitude of a position by computation in lieu of plotting. For calculators using the Reverse Polish Notation, and programmed to make polar to rectangular conversions, and vice versa, the computation of the coordinates is extremely rapid.

The keying procedure to obtain the correction to the estimated longitude, $\Delta\lambda$, and the correction to the estimated latitude, ΔL, is as follows:

$(Zn_1)[\uparrow](a_2)[P \to R]$
$(Zn_2)[\uparrow](a_1)[P \to R]$
$[x \leftrightharpoons y][R\downarrow][-][R\downarrow][-][CHS][R\uparrow][R \to P]$
$(Zn_1)[\uparrow](Zn_2)[-][\sin][\div]\ [P \to R]\ (Le)[\cos][\div] \to$ Read $\Delta\lambda$
$[x \leftrightharpoons y] \to$ Read ΔL

The round brackets indicate data that are to be entered into the calculator; the square brackets indicate keystrokes (or functions).

Line-Of-Position Bisectors

A constant, but unknown, error may affect all celestial observations. When such an error, which may be caused by abnormal refraction, exists and the observed bodies are not well distributed in azimuth, the fix may not lie at the center of the polygon formed by the plotted lines of position, as one would ordinarily assume; it may be an *exterior fix,* that is, a fix lying outside the polygon.

When three or more bodies are observed lying within 180° of azimuth of each other, it is wise to use bisectors to determine the fix. The angle formed by each pair of lines of position is bisected by a line drawn in the direction of the *mean of the azimuths* of the two bodies.

For example, let us assume that because of partial cloud cover, we were able to observe only three stars at twilight. The azimuth of star #1 was 030°, that of star #2 was 060°, and of #3 it was 090°. Figure 5-1 shows the resulting lines of position as solid lines, and the bisectors for each pair of lines of position as dashed lines.

Note that the resulting fix at the intersection of the three bisectors lies well outside the triangle formed by the three position lines.

Lunar Distance

Regaining GMT and Longitude

In celestial navigation, if we do not know the Greenwich mean time, we cannot determine our longitude. True, our latitude can be obtained by observing the altitude of the Sun, or of some other body, as it transits our meridian, or by plotting the lines of position derived from observations of two or more stars, and reduced by means of an assumed GMT. Knowing only our latitude, we are reduced to bringing the ship to the latitude of our destination, or just to weather of it, and then running down the easting or westing until we reach port. This was the standard operational procedure for centuries, but it does, as a rule, cause unnecessarily long passages.

Time and longitude can, however, be regained by measuring the lunar distance—the distance between the Moon and a star or the Sun—and then comparing this carefully "cleared" or corrected lunar distance with a lunar distance computed from data in the almanac. This technique is made possible by the difference between the Moon's apparent speed of travel across the heavens and that of the other celestial bodies—a difference on the average of about 12 degrees a day, or about the Moon's diameter in an hour. Thus, at any instant, given an accurate measurement of the distance between the Moon and another celestial body, the GMT, and hence the longitude, may be determined.

This method served to check chronometer error before the day of the radio time tick, and an expert observer, such as the great explorer Captain Cook, could achieve excellent results, due both to the accuracy of his sextant observations and to the meticulous care used in the very lengthy mathematics of clearing the measured lunar distance. Today, the time required for the mathematics is reduced to a very few minutes by means of the calculator.

A lunar distance measurement is most easily made with the sextant when the angular distance between the Moon and the other body is not great. This usually implies a nighttime measurement between the Moon and one of the 57 selected stars listed in the daily pages of the *Nautical Almanac*. Incidentally, the *Nautical Almanac* rather than the *Air Al-*

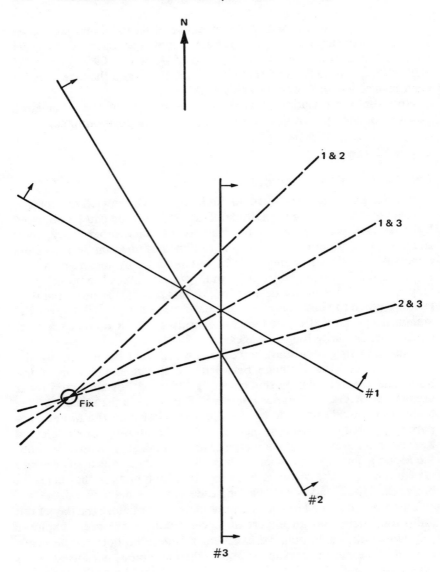

Figure 5-1. Line-of-position bisectors to determine the position of the fix

manac should always be used in working lunar distances. Jupiter or
Saturn may also be used if either is advantageously located; Venus and
Mars should not be used because of the problems introduced by the
parallax and phase corrections. In daytime, the Sun may be used as the
second body. For best results, the body selected should lie near the

path traced by the Moon across the sky, as this yields a more rapid change of lunar distance; the body may lie either ahead of or behind the Moon.

In addition to the lunar distance, the altitudes of the Moon and of the second body are also required; however, these measurements are not as critical as that of the lunar distance, as they are required only for the purpose of determining the corrections for refraction. Probably the most satisfactory procedure is first to measure the altitude of the Moon and of the second body, noting the time of each by pocket watch. A series of lunar distances are then measured against watch time. Finally, the two altitudes are again measured against time. If possible, the lunar distance measurements should be graphed against time, and a line of best fit should be drawn in, in order that an accurate lunar distance may be selected from the graph. The altitudes of the Moon and of the other body at the time of the selected lunar distance measurement may then be obtained by linear interpolation between the two sets of altitude measurements.

It will also be necessary to compute the true lunar distance for the whole hour of GMT before the distance is measured with the sextant, and again for the whole hour after, using data taken from the *Nautical Almanac;* this we shall discuss later.

Before going on to clearing the measured lunar distance, let us consider the correction for semidiameter. If a star is observed with the Moon, only the Moon's semidiameter need be allowed for; the correction for semidiameter, which is found in the daily pages of the *Nautical Almanac,* may be either additive or subtractive, depending upon the position of the star relative to the Moon. When the Sun is used as the second body, its semidiameter must also be allowed for. (See Figure 5-2.)

Clearing the Lunar Distance

The following formulae for clearing the lunar distance were developed by John S. Letcher, Jr., and published in his book *Self-Contained*

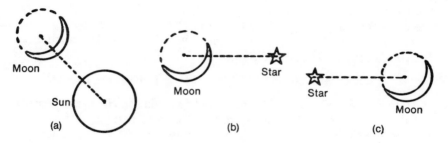

Figure 5-2.

Celestial Navigation; we are indebted to him for his permission to use them. They represent a great simplification of the systems used by our forefathers; this simplification may, on occasion, cause a loss of 0.3 minute of arc in accuracy. However, this is a maximum figure, and in the great majority of cases the answer will either be correct, or subject only to a very small error.

Apropos of accuracy, it must be borne in mind that to obtain satisfactory results with this or any other lunar distance method, far more care must be devoted both to the sextant measurements and to the necessary mathematics than is usually given to a routine altitude observation.

The altitude observations are corrected in the regular manner, instrumental error, index error, semidiameter, dip, and refraction being allowed for. The next step is to correct the lunar distance sight for refraction. For this, two formulae are required, the first being:

$$x = 0.5 \; (\sin Ho \; ⊂/\sin Ho^*) + 0.5 \; (\sin Ho^*/\sin Ho \; ⊂) \qquad (1)$$

where x is an auxiliary value, $Ho \; ⊂$ is the fully corrected altitude of the Moon, and Ho^* is the fully corrected altitude of the other body. The next formula is used to obtain the refraction correction to apply to the lunar distance, as measured with the sextant:

$$R' = 1.90' \; (x - \cos D)/\sin D \qquad (2)$$

in which R' is the correction for refraction; it is expressed in minutes of arc, and is always additive. The quantity x is the auxiliary value found by means of formula (1), and D is the measured lunar distance corrected for semidiameter. R' is next added to D to obtain Do, the measured lunar distance corrected for refraction.

The next step is to correct for the Moon's parallax. For this step two formulae are required. The first is:

$$y = \frac{(\cos Do \times \sin Ho \; ⊂) - \sin Ho^*}{\sin Do} \qquad (3)$$

in which y is an auxiliary value, Do the measured lunar distance, corrected by means of formula (2), and $Ho \; ⊂$ and Ho^* are, respectively, the corrected altitudes of the Moon and of the second body.

The final formula will determine the value of the parallax correction, P', which may be either additive or subtractive.

$$P' = HP \; \{y + .000145 \times HP \times \cot D \times [(\cos Ho \; ⊂)^2 - y^2]\} \quad (4)$$

Here y is the value found by means of formula (3), HP is the Moon's horizontal parallax expressed in minutes of arc, and found for every hour in the daily pages of the *Nautical Almanac, Do* is the lunar distance obtained by sextant and fully corrected, and Ho ☾ is the Moon's corrected altitude.

The refraction correction, R', found by formula (2), is next added to Do, and, finally, P' is applied according to its sign to obtain the fully cleared lunar distance:

$$\text{Cleared LD} = D_o + P' \qquad (5)$$

Having cleared the observed lunar distance, we must determine the GMT at which the observation was made. For this purpose we first compute the true LD for the integral hour of GMT before and the integral hour after we completed our observations, using data taken from the *Nautical Almanac*, and the formula

$$\cos LD = \sin d_1 \times \sin d_2 + \cos d_1 \times \cos d_2 \times \cos \Delta GHA \qquad (6)$$

where d_1 is the declination of the Moon, d_2 is the declination of the other celestial body, and ΔGHA is the difference between the GHAs of the two bodies.

Having obtained the two computed lunar distances, we find the difference between them, and then divide this difference by 60 to obtain the rate of change per minute of time. We then find the angular difference between the computed LD for the first hour, and the observed LD; dividing this difference by the rate of change per minute of time yields the number of minutes after the first integral hour of GMT at which the LD measurement was obtained.

It must be borne in mind that an error of one-tenth of a minute of arc, made in measuring the lunar distance, is greatly increased in the process of clearing the observation and can result in an error in the neighborhood of 12 seconds of time. Great care is therefore necessary in obtaining the measurement, as 0.1' is the smallest quantity that can be read on the verniers of most modern sextants.

If the manufacturer's certificate, furnished with the sextant, specifies fixed instrumental errors at various altitudes, the appropriate correction should be applied to the lunar distance, as read off the instrument. The index error existing at the time of the observation should also be allowed for.

The values of the corrections, R' and P', should be computed to several decimal places, in order that the algebraic sum of R' and P' may be correct to the nearest tenth of a minute of arc. In fact, this is true of all the computations involved—an "overkill" in accuracy is required in order to obtain satisfactory results.

In actual practice, a good observer should feel well satisfied if his cleared lunar distance is within 0.3' of the actual value, as many fine sextants are certified only to an accuracy of 10 seconds of arc, which amounts to almost two-tenths of a minute.

When the Sun is used as the second body, its altitude should be corrected by means of the star refraction tables in the *Almanac,* its semidiameter, as found in the daily pages should be applied, and 0.1′ should be added as the correction for parallax for all altitudes below 65°.

Example: On 27 May, near L 40.0° N, λ 135.0° W, at morning twilight, we decide to obtain a chronometer check by means of a lunar distance measurement, using the star Enif. We know that the chronometer error is less than one minute.

We graph the lunar distances and altitudes, and as of 13h 20m 05s we obtain the altitudes, fully corrected, and the lunar distance, D_1, corrected for the Moon's semidiameter, instrumental error, and index error, as listed below.

$$Ho \; ☾ \; 34°29.7', Ho \; Enif \; 59°19.7', D_1 \; 35°22.4'$$

The pertinent data from the *Nautical Almanac* are as follows:

GMT	1300	GHA ♈ 79°56.5′	Enif SHA 34°16.5′	
		GHA ☾ 79°32.3′	SD 15.8′	HP 58.1′
GMT	1400	GHA ♈ 94°58.9′	Enif dec N 9°45.1′	
		GHA ☾ 94°03.5′	SD 15.8′	HP 58.1′

Our first step is to correct the observed lunar distance, 35°22.4′, for refraction. We write formula (1):

$$x = 0.5 \,(\sin 34°29.7'/\sin 59°19.7') + 0.5 \,(\sin 59°19.7'/\sin 34°29.7')$$
$$= \qquad 0.32922 \qquad + \qquad 0.75936$$

$$\therefore x = 1.08859$$

We can now write formula (2):

$$R' = 1.90'(1.08859 - \cos 35°22.4')/\sin 35°22.4'$$

Therefore the correction for refraction, R', is +0.89662′.

We must next determine the correction for parallax, P', and write formula (3):

$$y = \frac{(\cos 35°22.4' \times \sin 34°29.7') - \sin 59°19.7'}{\sin 35°22.4'}$$
$$= \frac{0.46179 - 0.86010}{0.57890} = -0.68806$$

Having obtained the auxiliary value, y, we write formula (4):

$$P' = 58.1' \{-0.68806 + .000145 \times 58.1' \times \cot 35°22.4'$$
$$\times [(\cos 34°29.7')^2 - (0.68806)^2]\}$$
$$= 58.1' \{-0.68806 + 0.01187 \times [0.20584]\} = 39.83433'$$

The parallax correction, P', is, therefore, $-39.83433'$, and formula (5) becomes cleared.

$$LD = 35°22.4' + 0.89662' + -39.83433')$$
$$= 35°22.4' - 38.9' = 34°43.5'$$

The cleared lunar distance is, therefore, 34°43.5'.

We can now proceed to determine the GMT of the lunar distance observation. We start by computing the lunar distance at GMT 1300 and 1400, the integral hours before and after we made the measurement, using the data from the *Nautical Almanac,* and formula (6). First, however, we must determine the *GHA* of Enif for 1300 and 1400; the Moon's *GHA* we can take directly from the *Almanac.*

GMT 1300 ♈ *GHA*   79°56.5'
       Enif *SHA* +34°16.5' dec N 9°45.1'
  1300 Enif *GHA* 114°13.0'   Moon *GHA* 79°32.3', *d* N 5°50.3'

The difference in *GHA*, therefore, is 114°13.0' − 79°32.3' or 34°40.7'. We can now write formula (6):

cos Comp *LD* 1300 = sin 5°50.3' × sin 9°45.1' + cos 5°50.3'
                          × cos 9°45.1' × cos 34°40.7'

The computed lunar distance at GMT 1300 is, therefore, 34.56304°. For GMT 1400, we obtain the following data from the *Almanac:*

GMT 1400 ♈ *GHA*   94°58.9'
       Enif *SHA*   34°16.5'
  1400 Enif *GHA* 129°15.4' *d* N 9°45.1'
                    Moon *GHA* 94°03.5', *d* N 6°04.1'

To obtain ΔGHA we subtract the Moon's *GHA*, 94°03.5', from 129°15.4', and obtain 35°11.9', so that formula (6) becomes:

cos Comp *LD* 1400 = sin 6°04.1' × sin 9°45.1' + cos 6°04.1'
                          × cos 9°45.1' × cos 35°11.9'

which makes the GMT 1400 computed lunar distance 35.04039°.

Comparing the 1300 with the 1400 lunar distance, we find it has increased by 0.47735° in the hour, which divided by 60 makes the increase per minute 0.00796°. We next obtain the difference between the cleared lunar distance 34°43.5', or 34.7250°, and the lunar distance computed for GMT 1300, 34.56304°. The former is the greater by 0.16196°; the time of the distance observation was, therefore, after 1300. Dividing 0.16196° by the rate of change of computed hour angle per minute, 0.00796°, we get 20.34673 minutes, or 20m 20.482s. We would, therefore, call the true Greenwich time of our lunar observation 13h 20m 20s, thus indicating that the chronometer is 15 seconds slow (13h 20m 05s vs. 13h 20m 20s).

The following is a summary of the computations of this example:

27 May
Posit L 36 54.0 N, λ 135 06.0 W, GMT 13h 20m 20s

☾

GMT 1400 *GHA*	94 03.5	*d*N 6 04.1	
1300 *GHA*	79 32.3	*d* 5 50.3	
Δ *GHA* 1 hr	14.520°	*d* Δ 1 hr +0.230°	
Δ *GHA* 1 min.	0.2420°	Δ 1 min. 0.00383°	
Δ 20m 20s	4.92067°	Δ 20m 20s 0.07794°	
13h 20m 20s *GHA*	84.4590°	dec. N 5.91628	
True λ W	135.1000		
LHA	309.3590		
Hc	34.49464°		
Ho	34°29.7'		

✳ Enif

1400 ♈ *GHA*	94 58.9
1300 *GHA*	79 56.5
Δ *GHA* 1 hr	15.040°
Δ 1 min.	0.25067°
Δ 20m 20s	5.09689
GHA ♈ 13h 20m 20s	85.03856
Enif *SHA*	34.2750 *d* N 9°45.1'
Enif *GHA*	119.31356
λ W	135.10
Enif *LHA*	344.21356
Enif *Hc*	59.32802°
Enif *Ho*	59°19.7'

GMT 13h 20m 20s

For ☾ use *Ho* 34.4950° (34°29.7')
For Enif *Ho* = 59.32833° (59°19.7')

| Corr. sext. LD 35°22.4' | Computed LD at GMT 1300 27 May |

GHA ♈ 1300   79 56.5   ☾ *d* 1300 N 5.83833°
Enif *SHA*   34 16.5   *d* N 9.75167°
Enif *GHA*   114.216°
1300 *GHA* ☾   79°32.3'
                     Δ   34.67833° GMT 1300 Comp LD 34.56304° = 34°33.8'

Computed LD at GMT 1400

GHA ♈ 1400   94 58.9
Enif *SHA*   34 16.5   Enif *d* N 9.75167
Enif *GHA*   129.25667°
☾ *GHA*   94°03.5'   ☾ *d* N 6°04.1'
                     Δ   35.19833   GMT 1400 Comp LD 35.04039° = 35°02.4'

Comp. LD at GMT 13h 20m 20s
          Comp LD 1400   35.04039°
          Comp LD 1300   34.56304
          Δ 1 hr   0.47735/60 = 0.00796/min.

.00796 × 20m 20s =   0.16177°
Comp LD GMT 1300   34.56304
GMT 13h 20m 20s Comp LD   34.72481° = 34°43.5'

27 May GMT 13h 20m 20s True posit L 36°54.0' N

          135°06.0' W   Computed LD   34°43.5'
Ho ☾   34°29.7'   *Ho* Enif   59°19.7'
                        LD obsd. by sextant = 35°22.4'
R'   +0.89662'
P'   −39.83418
Net Corr.: −38.9'   −38.9'
                   Cleared LD   34°43.5' GMT 13h 20m 20s

          Cleared LD =   34.7250°
          Comp LD GMT 140000 =   35.0404
          Comp LD GMT 130000 =   34.5630
                        Δ   0.4774°/60 = 0.00796°/min.

          Cleared LD   =   34.7250°
          1300 Comp LD =   34.5630
                        Δ   .1620°/.00796 = 20m 21.3s

Working to tenths of minutes, we get:

Cleared LD	34°43.5′	ΔGHA 1 hr = 28.6′/60
1300 Comp LD	34 33.8	= 0.4767′/min.
Δ	9.7′	

9.7/0.4767 = 20.3482 min., or 20m 21s.

Second Method of Recovering Longitude

An alternative method of recovering the longitude by observation of the Moon and a second body was suggested almost four hundred years ago, long before instrumentation or ephemeristic data sufficiently accurate to implement it were available. The method has been independently "rediscovered," with minor improvements, at least twice since then. It was never widely used because any given error in angle, as read from the sextant, causes a greater error in the final answer than does a similar error in the use of the lunar distance method.

It is, however, of historic interest. It offers the advantage that a lunar distance need not be measured; and that is a measurement most observers find difficult to make without a good deal of practice.

In using this method, it is assumed that, while Greenwich time is not available, a good timepiece is on hand, showing time to within 30 minutes, or so, of GMT.

1. The first step is to determine the latitude, either by a transit observation or by obtaining a round of star sights. In making all observations, the greatest care should be used in correcting all sextant altitudes; all corrections, including that for sea–air temperature, should be applied to the sextant readings.

2. Next, a second body, a star, a planet, or the Sun, is selected, and a series of altitude observations, timed by watch, of the second body (which we shall call a star) and of the Moon, are obtained. By extrapolation, simultaneous altitudes of the two bodies are obtained, and the watch time of these altitudes, which we shall call To for future reference, is noted.

3. The GHA of the Moon and the star for the integral hours of GMT before and after the watch time of the simultaneous altitudes are extracted from the *Nautical Almanac,* and the difference in hour angle is divided by 60 to obtain the rate of change per minute of time.

4. The separation in hour angle between the star and the Moon for the watch time of the simultaneous altitudes is calculated and noted.

5. The next step is to compute the meridian angles, t, of the star and the Moon, using the formula:

$$\cos t = \frac{\sin Ho - \sin L \times \sin d}{\cos L \times \cos d} \tag{1}$$

In calculating the Moon's meridian angle, the watch time of the observation is used in obtaining its declination. The difference between the values of the two meridian angles is noted.

This difference in meridian angles is compared with the separation in hour angle at the second integral hour of GMT found in Step 3. If the star is East of the Moon, and the difference in meridian angle is less than the separation in hour angle at the second integral hour of GMT, the indication is that the simultaneous observations were obtained after the second integral hour of GMT. In this case, the separation in hour angle for a third integral hour of GMT must be determined, as must the rate of change in hour angle from the second to third integral hours, since the second has become the controlling hour.

6. The difference in meridian angle is next compared with the separation in hour angle found in Step 5, and the difference between the two is obtained. The difference in hour angle between the controlling hour of GMT and the previous integral hour is divided by 60, to obtain the rate of change per minute, R.

7. The difference between the separation in hour angle and the difference in meridian angle found in Step 6 is divided by R, found in Step 6. The time in minutes and decimals thus found is added to the controlling hour of GMT to give T_1. The Moon's declination for time, T_1, is next extracted from the *Almanac*.

8. The Moon's meridian angle is next computed, using the updated declination.

9. The Moon's revised meridian angle is now compared with the star's meridian angle, found in Step 5, to obtain the difference. This difference is next compared with the separation in hour angle, found in Step 3, and the difference is divided by R, found in Step 6, which gives us a correction in minutes and decimals to apply to the controlling integral hour of GMT. The time thus found constitutes T_2.

10. The GMT of the simultaneous observations may now be obtained by the formula:

$$\text{GMT} = \frac{To \times T_2 - T_1^2}{To + T_2 - 2T_1} \tag{2}$$

To we obtained in Step 2, T_1 in Step 7, and T_2 in Step 9.

11. Having obtained the GMT of the simultaneous sights, we reduce the observation of the body located nearer the prime vertical, either due East or West.

12. The departure, p, is now computed, using the formula:

$$p = \frac{a}{\sin Zn} \tag{3}$$

in which *a* is the intercept, and *Zn* is the true azimuth. The departure is then divided by the cosine of the latitude, found in Step 1, to obtain the difference in longitude. This is applied to the estimated longitude, in the direction East or West, as appropriate, to obtain the ship's actual longitude.

Example:

1. At morning twilight on 22 October, we are in L 45°10.0′ N, λ 60°30.0′ W by estimate. Our chronometer has run down, and the radio has failed. Fortunately, the visibility is excellent, and a good watch is available, which is known to be running within 30 minutes of GMT.

We proceed to observe a round of stars to establish our latitude, which we find to be 45°03.7′ N, or 45.061667° N

2. We select Aldebaran as the star we shall observe with the Moon, and make multiple observations of each body. By extrapolation, we obtain simultaneous altitudes of both, at 09h 45m 30s by watch; this time, less 9 hours, or 00h 45m 30s, we call *To,* and note for future reference.

The simultaneous altitudes are:

Aldebaran	*Ho* 37°56.9′ or 37.948333°	
Moon	*Ho* 26°39.2′ or 26.653333°	

3. Turning to the *Nautical Almanac,* we extract the *GHA* of Aries and of the Moon for GMT 0900. Adding the *SHA* of Aldebaran to the *GHA* of Aries, we obtain

GMT 0900 *GHA* Aldebaran	96°32.1′ or	96.535000°
	~	
GMT 0900 *GHA* Moon	115°11.2′ or	115.186666°
GMT 0900 Δ*HA*		18.651666°

We repeat this process for GMT 1000:

GMT 1000 *GHA* Aldebaran	111°34.5′ or	111.575000°
	~	
GMT 1000 *GHA* Moon	129°41.7′ or	129.695000°
GMT 1000 Δ*HA*		18.120000°

We next proceed to find the change in the difference in hour angle for the hour from GMT 0900 to 1000:

GMT 0900	ΔHA	18.651666°
	~	
GMT 1000	ΔHA	18.120000°
	Δ	0.531666°

We now divide this hourly difference in hour angle by 60 to obtain the rate of change per minute of time, which we call R; R proves to be 0.008861° and is decreasing with time.

4. The next step is to find the separation in HA between Aldebaran and the Moon at the watch time of the simultaneous observations:

Aldebaran	GMT 0900		*GHA*	96.535000°
			+	
ΔHA per minute, 0.25068447° × 45m 30s				11.406143
	GMT 09h 45m 30s		*GHA*	107.941143°

We repeat this process for the Moon:

Moon	GMT 0900	*GHA*	115.186667°
		~	
	1000	*GHA*	129.695000
	GMT 0900–1000	Δ*GHA*	14.508333°

This *GHA*, divided by 60, gives the Moon's rate of change of HA per minute, 0.241806°. Multiplying this quantity by 45m 30s, we get 11.002153°.

Moon	GMT 0900	*GHA*	115.186667°
		+	
	00h 45m 30s		11.002153
	09h 45m 30s		126.188819°

We now have:

Aldebaran	GMT 09h 45m 30s	*GHA*	107.941143°
		~	
Moon	GMT 09h 45m 30s	*GHA*	126.188819
Aldebaran–Moon	GMT 09h 45m 30s	Δ*GHA*	18.247676°

5. The next step is to compute the meridian angle, t, for both the star and the Moon. From the *Almanac*, we find that Aldebaran's declination, on the date of the observation, is N 16°27.7′, or N 16.461667°; its *Ho* was 37.948333°. We write formula (1):

$$\cos t = \frac{\sin 37.948333° - \sin 45.061667° \times \sin 16.461667°}{\cos 45.061667° \times \cos 16.461667°}$$

$$= \frac{0.414360}{0.677392} = 0.611698$$

Aldebaran's meridian angle, therefore, was 52.287589°.

Turning to the Moon, by interpolation we find that at GMT 09h 45m 30s its declination was N 18.379458° its *Ho* was 26.653333°. Therefore, for the Moon:

$$\cos t = \frac{\sin 26.653333° - \sin 45.061667° \times \sin 18.379458°}{\cos 45.061667° \times \cos 18.379458°}$$

$$= \frac{0.225394}{0.670314} = 0.336252$$

The Moon's meridian angle, therefore, was 70.351317°.

We next find the difference between the two meridian angles:

Aldebaran	t	52.287589°
		~
Moon	t	70.351316
	t	Δ 18.063727°

6. We now compare this difference in meridian angle with the separation in hour angle, obtained above:

HA Δ	18.247676°
	~
t Δ	18.063727
$HA\ t$ Δ	0.183949°

We note that the difference in meridian angle is less than the difference in hour angle for GMT 1000, found above. As Aldebaran is closing the Moon, this indicates that the time of the simultaneous observations was after GMT 1000.

We, therefore, turn to the *Nautical Almanac,* to obtain the *GHA* of Aldebaran and of the Moon for GMT 1100. Adding the *SHA* of Aldebaran to the *GHA* of Aries for GMT 1100, and then extracting the Moon's *GHA* for that time, we obtain:

Aldebaran	GMT 1100	*GHA*	126.616667°
			~
Moon	GMT 1100	*GHA*	144.201667
	GMT 1100		Δ 17.585000°

To this quantity, we apply the difference in *HA* for GMT 1000, found above:

GMT 1000	Δ*HA*	18.120000°
		~
GMT 1100	Δ*HA*	17.585000
Change in *HA* GMT 1000 to 1100	Δ	0.535000°

Dividing this value by 60, to obtain the rate of change in *HA* per minute of time, R_1, we get 0.008917° for the hour 1000–1100.

Above, using the *Almanac,* we found that the separation in *HA* between the two bodies at GMT 1000 was 18.120000°. To this quantity we apply the separation in meridian angle, Δt, 18.063727°:

$$
\begin{array}{llll}
\text{GMT 1000} & \Delta HA & 18.120000° \\
& & \sim \\
& \Delta t & \underline{18.063727} \\
& \Delta & 0.056273°
\end{array}
$$

7. We divide this difference, 0.056273°, by the value of R, obtained above:

$$\Delta\ 0.056273°/R\ 0.008917° = 6.310755 \text{ minutes}$$

which is added to GMT 1000 to give us T_1, 10h 06.310755m. We next obtain the Moon's declination for this GMT by interpolation in the *Almanac;* we find it to be N 18.408951°.

8. The next step is to recompute the Moon's meridian angle, using this new declination:

$$
\cos t = \frac{\sin 26.653333° - \sin 45.061667° \times \sin 18.408951°}{\cos 45.061667° \times \cos 18.408951°}
$$
$$
= \frac{0.225051}{0.670199} = 0.335794
$$

9. The Moon's meridian angle, using the revised declination, is, therefore, 70.379199°; we compare this value with that of the meridian angle of Aldebaran, previously computed:

$$
\begin{array}{llll}
\text{Aldebaran} & t & 52.287589° \\
& & \sim \\
\text{Moon} & \text{new } t & \underline{70.379199} \\
& \Delta t & 18.091610°
\end{array}
$$

The next step is to find the difference between this and the separation in *HA* for GMT 1000, obtained in Step 6:

$$
\begin{array}{llll}
& \Delta t & 18.091610° \\
& & \sim \\
\text{GMT 1000} & \Delta HA & \underline{18.120000} \\
& \Delta & 0.028390°
\end{array}
$$

We now divide this difference by the value of R, 0.008917°:

$$0.028390°/0.008917° = 3.183806 \text{ minutes}$$

To obtain T_2, we add 60 minutes to this value, as we are now dealing with GMT 1000, one hour later than the original time base, GMT 0900. T_2, therefore, is 63.183806 minutes.

We now have To 45.500000m (Step 2), T_1 66.310755m (Step 7), and T_2 63.183806m.

10. We can now write formula (2):

$$GMT = \frac{45.50\text{m} \times 63.183806\text{m} - 4397.116229}{45.50\text{m} + 63.183806\text{m} - 132.621510}$$

$$= \frac{-1522.253046}{-23.937704} = 63.592275\text{m} = 63\text{m } 35.3\text{s}$$

Adding 63m 35s to our base hour, GMT 0900, makes the GMT of the simultaneous altitudes 10h 03m 35s.

11. We now proceed to reduce the Aldebaran sight, using this GMT, L 45°03.7′ N or 45.061667°, d N 16°27.7′ or N 16.461667°, and LHA 51.975538°. The last value we obtained by adding the SHA of Aldebaran to the GHA of Aries for GMT 10h 03m 35s, and subtracting our estimated longitude, 60°30.0′ W. We find:

Hc 38.160249° and Zn 253.902820°

~

Ho 37.948333

a 0.211916° Away

12. We now compute the departure, p, which is − or East, using formula (3):

$$p = \frac{0.211916}{\sin 253.902820°} = -0.220564$$

The departure, p, in turn, is divided by the cosine of our latitude, 45.061667° N, to give the difference in longitude, − or East 0.312261°, which is 18.7′ E. Subtracting this from our estimated longitude, 60°30.0′ W, our longitude at the time of the simultaneous sights was 60°11.3′ W.

Note: The actual time of the observations was GMT 10h 03m 45s; the difference of 10s between this and the "recovered" GMT of 10h 03m 35s is due to the fact that the sextant can be read only to the nearest 0.1′ (0.001667°). The error in longitude is, therefore, 2.5′.

Fix by Observations of a Single Body

Willis Method

Another method of obtaining a fix by observation of a single body was suggested by Edward J. Willis. This method hinges on the rate of change of altitude of a body and its actual altitude at a point midway in time between the first and third observations. For best results, the time span for the three observations should be about 4 seconds (1 minute of meridian angle), and the altitudes should be obtained to an accuracy of better than a thousandth of a minute of arc. However, fair results can be obtained if the interval of time between the first and third observations is 8 minutes, or 120 minutes of arc, and the altitudes are obtained to the nearest tenth of a minute of arc.

The Willis method does not lend itself well to solution by slide rule; however, it is a good method for solution by calculator.

The first step in this method is to find the rate of change of altitude of the body, ΔH. The quantity ΔH divided by the difference in time between the first and third observations, expressed in minutes of arc, Δt, gives the sine of an auxiliary angle, N, as shown in the following formula:

$$\sin N = \frac{\Delta H}{\Delta t} \tag{1}$$

Having found the angle N, we proceed to find our latitude by means of the formula:

$$\sin L = \cos N \times \cos \left[Ho \pm \sin^{-1} \left(\frac{\sin d}{\cos N} \right) \right] \tag{2}$$

In this formula, Ho is the corrected sextant altitude of the body, obtained exactly halfway between the first and third observations; $\sin^{-1}$ indicates that $\sin d$ divided by $\cos N$ represents the sine of an angle; and d is the declination of the body. The sign following Ho is $-$ when L is of the same name and greater than the declination. When d is of the same name, and considerably greater than L, the angle represented by $\sin^{-1} (\sin d/\cos N)$ may be greater than 90°.

Having found our latitude, we can proceed to find the body's meridian angle, t, by the formula:

$$\sin t = \frac{\sin N \times \cos Ho}{\cos d \times \cos L} \tag{3}$$

The meridian angle is then converted to local hour angle, LHA, and the longitude is found by subtracting the LHA from the Greenwich hour angle, GHA, of the body at the instant of the second sight, Ho.

This method should not be used when the body is near the observer's meridian, and it must be borne in mind that the second observation, termed Ho above, must be a separate observation, and not half the sum of the first and third altitude observations.

Example: To illustrate this method, three altitudes, H_1, Ho, and H_3, have been extracted from Volume III of H.O. Pub. No. 214 for L 26° and a d of 16°, d having the same name as L, which we will assume is

North. These altitudes are for three successive degrees of meridian angle, 14°, 13°, and 12°; in other words, we assume that we have obtained them exactly 4 minutes apart, and that they were morning Sun sights. In actual practice, all three sextant altitudes would have been corrected.

$$H_1 \quad 73°33.9' \qquad\qquad Ho \; 74°17.6'$$
$$H_3 \quad 75°00.0'$$
$$\Delta H \quad 1°26.1' \; = 86.1'$$

We can now find the value of the angle N by writing formula (1):

$$\sin N = \frac{86.1'}{120'} = 0.71750$$
$$N = 45.84846°$$

Having obtained the value of N, we can proceed to find the latitude, using formula (2), which becomes:

$$\sin L = \cos 45.84846° \times \cos \left[74.29333° - \sin^{-1}\left(\frac{\sin 16°}{\cos 45.84846°}\right) \right]$$
$$= 0.69656 \times \cos [74.29333° - 23.31046°]$$
$$= 0.69656 \times 0.62955 = 0.43852$$
$$L = 26.00957°$$

Our latitude is, therefore, 26°00.6′ N, and we can proceed to find the meridian angle, using formula (3):

$$\sin t = \frac{\sin 45.84846° \times \cos 74.29333°}{\cos 16° \times \cos 26.00957°} = 0.22483$$
$$t = 12.99317°$$

The meridian angle is therefore 12°59.6′ E, which we would convert to LHA, and then apply to the Sun's GHA to obtain our longitude.

The error in meridian angle in this example is 0.4′, and the error in latitude is 0.6′; the primary cause for both errors is the rounding off of the altitude to the nearest 0.1′.

Aquino Method

When and if there is available instrumentation that will permit azimuth to be obtained to the same degree of accuracy with which altitude can be measured by means of the sextant, we shall be able to calculate both our latitude and longitude by means of simultaneous altitude and azimuth observations of a celestial body.

A simple method of obtaining a fix in this manner was suggested in the 1930s by Radler de Aquino, a Brazilian naval officer and mathematician. Solution is by three simple formulae, given below. Meridian angle is found first, and converted to longitude; then latitude is found by two additional formulae.

The first formula is:

$$\sin t = \frac{\cos Ho \times \sin Z}{\cos d} \tag{1}$$

where t is the meridian angle, Ho is the corrected sextant altitude, Z is the observed azimuth angle, and d is the declination. The meridian angle is then converted to local hour angle, LHA, and the longitude will equal the body's Greenwich hour angle, GHA, less the LHA.

The first formula for the latitude solution is:

$$\cot A = \frac{\tan Ho}{\cos Z} \tag{2}$$

In this and the following formula, A and B represent auxiliary angles. In connection with formula (3), remember that the cotangent of an angle equals the tangent of the complement of that angle.

The second latitude formula is:

$$\tan B = \frac{\tan d}{\cos t} \tag{3}$$

If latitude and declination are of the same name, A and B are added together; if they are of opposite name, the smaller is subtracted from the larger.

Example: In DR latitude 50° N we obtain a simultaneous altitude and azimuth of the star Deneb, Ho being 83°07.4', and Zn being 133°49.9'. Deneb's GHA was 39°27.3', and the declination N 45°10.3'. We require our position.

The body's azimuth angle, Z, is 46°10.1' (180° − 133°49.9'), so formula (1) becomes:

$$\sin t = \frac{\cos 83°07.4' \times \sin 46°10.1'}{\cos 45°10.3'} = 0.1225$$

The meridian angle is, therefore, 7.0374° E, which makes the LHA 352.9626°.

$$
\begin{array}{lcc}
 & D & M \\
GHA & 39 & 27.3 \\
+ & & \\
 & 360 & 00.0 \\
\hline
 & 399 & 27.3 \\
- & & \\
LHA & 352 & 57.8 \\
\hline
\lambda & 46 & 29.5 \ \text{W}
\end{array}
$$

To find the latitude, we write formula (2) with formula (3) below it:

$$\cot A = \frac{\tan 83°07.4'}{\cos 46°10.1'} = 11.9731 = A \quad 4°46.5'$$

$$+$$

$$\tan B = \frac{\tan 45°10.3'}{\cos 7°02.2'} = 1.0136 = \begin{array}{l} B \ 45°23.2' \\ L \ 50°09.7' \end{array}$$

Our latitude, therefore, is 50°09.7' N and our longitude is 46°29.3' W. In this case, B was added to A, since latitude and declination were of the same name.

Almanacs

Background

For the navigator practicing celestial navigation, an almanac in some form is essential, as observations cannot be reduced without the ephemeristic data contained in an almanac.

The word "almanac" is derived from the Arabic *al-manakh,* a list of geographic or climatic data. It gradually acquired its present meaning as a compendium of celestial data and came into general use in Europe. The early almanacs were handwritten on parchment; those intended for marine use included only data on the Sun's declination. Abraham Zacuto published the printed *Almanach Perpetuum* in 1474, which presented the Sun's declination in a convenient format for the mariner. At about the same time, Regiomontanus, at Nuremberg, published the first of a series of more inclusive almanacs, which established a new standard of accuracy. The *Tabulae Prutenicae,* computed on Copernican principles, were published by Erasmus Reinhold in 1551, and clarified for the reader the motion of the celestial bodies. However, these data were primarily of interest only to the astronomer; the navigator relied chiefly on the Sun. The *Rudolphine Tables,* published in 1627, included the advances in astronomy made by Tycho Brahe and Johannes Kepler.

In 1696, the French National Observatory published the first official almanac, the *Connaissance des Temps.* This was followed in 1767 by the

British *Nautical Almanac,* primarily designed, as its name indicates, for use afloat. The British Almanac was used on board American vessels until 1855, when our Navy published the first American *Nautical Almanac.* By today's standards, using these almanacs entailed a great deal of work; the astronomical day began at noon of the civil day of the same date. Greenwhich hour angle was not used; instead, angular distance was expressed as right ascension, that is, angle East of the First Point of Aries stated in hours, minutes, and seconds.

P. V. H. Weems, then a lieutenant commander, U.S.N., designed an *Air Almanac* in 1933, in which Greenwich hour angle was used for all bodies; the manifest advantages of this system were so obvious that the same presentation was adopted for the *Nautical Almanac* in the following year. This latter publication was further improved in 1950; since 1958 the production of the *Nautical Almanac* has been a joint British and United States venture.

The latest publication in this field is the *Almanac for Computers,* published annually by the U.S. Naval Observatory. The *American Ephemeris and Nautical Almanac,* also published annually by the U. S. Naval Observatory, gives data to a high degree of precision, on a large number of celestial objects. It is intended primarily for the use of astronomers, and is arranged to suit their convenience.

Interpolation in the *Nautical Almanac*

When the utmost accuracy is desired in extracting the Greenwich hour angle of the Moon or planets from the *Nautical Almanac,* increments of GHA for minutes and seconds of time should be computed, rather than extracted from the "Increments and Corrections" pages, as the latter practice can lead to errors of about 0.2'. Errors of such magnitude can seriously affect results in some computations, as when time or longitude is to be recovered by means of a lunar distance observation.

For example, for 19 December the *Nautical Almanac* tabulated *GHA* for the Moon as follows:

GMT	1500	*GHA*	291°32.7'	v	13.7'
GMT	1600	*GHA*	306°05.4'		

We require the Moon's *GHA* for GMT 15h 30m 04s, and we shall first use the "Increments and Corrections" pages:

GMT	1500	*GHA* 291°32.7'
	30-04	7 10.5
·	v 13.7'	7.0
GMT 15h 30m 04s		*GHA* 298°50.2' or 298.83667°

To compute the Moon's *GHA* for GMT 15h 30m 04s we proceed as follows:

GMT   1500   *GHA* 291°32.7′ =   291.54500°

                              ~

GMT   1600   *GHA* 306°05.4′ =   306.09000

                      Δ   14.54500°

This value, divided by 60, gives us an increase in *GHA* per minute of 0.24242°. We require the increase for 30m 04s, or 30.06 minutes. Multiplying 0.24242° by 30.06, we get the increase in *GHA* for 30m 04s, which, when added to the *GHA* for GMT 1500, gives us the required *GHA*.

                GMT   1500   *GHA*   291.54500°
                Increment for 30.06   7.28866
Computed *GHA* for GMT 15h 30m 04s   298.83366°

                                              ~

N.A. *GHA* for GMT 15h 30m 04s   298.83667
                      Difference   0.00301°

This difference of 0.00301° equals 10.8″, or almost 0.2′, a difference that could adversely affect some calculations.

Long-Term Sun Almanac

The Sun's Greenwich hour angle and declination for any instant in time for the years 1979 to 1999 may be calculated by means of the four formulae given below. The error in *GHA* and declination should, in no case, exceed 0.3′; in most cases, the error may be expected to be considerably smaller.

To understand what we are doing, it will be necessary to consider the situation from the astronomer's point of view.

The Earth orbits the Sun in an elliptical path, making a complete circuit of the ellipse from perihelion to perihelion in 365.2596 days. (See Figure 5-3). Perihelion is the point of the Earth's nearest approach to the Sun; it occurs 10 to 12 days after the winter solstice, when the Sun reaches its maximum southerly declination.

A fictitious Sun, traveling (Figure 5-4) at a constant angular velocity, would move 360°/365.2596, or 0.9856° per day. The angular position of the fictitious Sun, measured from the point of perihelion, is called the Sun's mean anomaly, *M; M* may be calculated by means of the formula:

$$M = 0.9856 \times \left(DOY + \frac{GMT}{24}\right) + Mo \qquad (1)$$

in which GMT is the Greenwich mean time, Mo is the mean anomaly on day 0 of the required year, found in Table 5-3, and DOY is the numerical value of the day of the year; a table for the ready determination of this value is given below as Table 5-4. Because the Earth does not complete its circuit of the Sun in a year of precisely 365 days, the value of Mo changes from year to year.

After we compute the value of M, the next step is to determine the Sun's longitude, λ, using formula (2); astronomers call this formula "the equation of the center." The Sun's longitude is measured westward to 360° from the First Point of Aries, Υ, rather than from the point of perihelion. The longitude is found by using the formula:

$$\lambda = M + (1.9160° \times \sin M) + (0.02° \times \sin 2M) - \Pi_E \qquad (2)$$

in which Π_E is the longitude of perihelion; its value for each year is also given in Table 5-3.

Next, the Greenwich hour angle of the Sun is determined by the formula:

GHA =
$$M + (15 \times GMT) - \tan^{-1}(0.9175 \times \tan \lambda) - (\Pi_E + 180°) \qquad (3)$$

When this latter formula is used, $\tan^{-1}(0.9175 \times \tan \lambda)$ must be placed in the same quadrant as λ; this may be achieved by adding 180° if the result is in the wrong quadrant.

Finally, the Sun's declination, d, may be found by the formula:

$$\sin d = 0.3978 \times \sin \lambda \qquad (4)$$

Example: We require the Sun's *GHA* and declination for GMT 12h 47m 23s on 27 November 1980.

We turn to Table 5-4 and find that 27 November in a leap year is the 332nd day of the year; from Table 5-3 we note that the value of Mo for 1980 is −3.7737. Formula (1), therefore, becomes:

$$M = 0.9856 \times \left(332 + \frac{12.7897}{24}\right) + (-3.7737°)$$
$$= 327.7444° - 3.7737° = 323.9707°$$

which is the value of M.

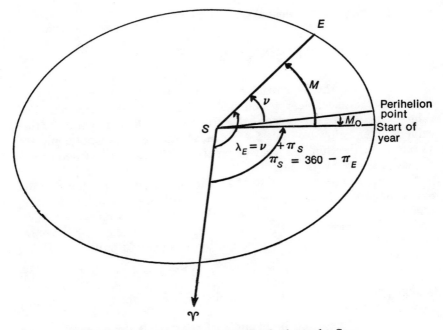

Figure 5-3. The orbit of the Earth about the Sun

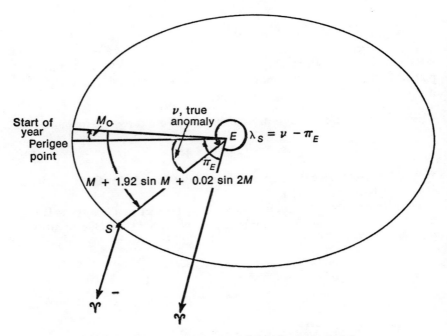

Figure 5-4. The orbit of the Sun about the Earth

Table 5-3

	Mo (Mean anomaly on day 0)	Π_E (Earth's longitude at perihelion)
1979	−3.5070	77.4120
80	−3.7737	77.4006
81	−3.0452	77.3835
82	−3.3020	77.3663
83	−3.5583	77.3491
84	−3.8140	77.3320
85	−3.0836	77.3148
86	−3.3383	77.2976
87	−3.5927	77.2805
88	−3.8470	77.2633
89	−3.1157	77.2461
90	−3.3702	77.2289
91	−3.6251	77.2118
92	−3.8804	77.1946
93	−3.1507	77.1774
94	−3.4071	77.1603
95	−3.6640	77.1431
96	−3.9212	77.1260
97	−3.1930	77.1087
98	−3.4505	77.0916
99	−3.7078	77.0744

We now extract the value of Π_E from Table 5-3, and write formula (2):

$$\lambda = 323.9707° + (-1.1270°) + (-0.0190°) - 77.4006° = 245.4241°$$

which is the Sun's longitude.

The next step is to calculate the Sun's Greenwich hour angle. Formula (3) becomes:

$$GHA = 323.9707° + 191.8458° - 63.5061° - 257.4006° = 194.9098°$$

From this value we subtract 180°, to bring the *GHA* into the proper quadrant, making it 14.9098°. The Sun's *GHA* is, therefore, 14°54.6′, which is correct, according to the *Nautical Almanac*.

To find the Sun's declination, formula (4) is written:

$$\sin d = 0.3978 \times -0.9094 = -0.3618$$

Table 5-4. Annual Number of the Last Day of Each Month

Non–Leap Year		Leap Year	
January	31	January	31
February	59	February	60
March	90	March	91
April	120	April	121
May	151	May	152
June	181	June	182
July	212	July	213
August	243	August	244
September	273	September	274
October	304	October	305
November	334	November	335
December	365	December	366

To find the numerical value of any day of a non–leap year, or of a leap year, enter the correct section of the table above, and extract the value of the last day of the preceding month. To this is added the current day of the month, using the Greenwich date. Thus, 17 September in a leap year would be the 261st day of the year (244 + 17).

Table 5-5. Sun's Semidiameter

Date	SD
1 January–2 February	16.3'
3 February–4 March	16.2'
5 March–28 March	16.1'
29 March–18 April	16.0'
19 April–15 May	15.9'
16 May–25 August	15.8'
26 August–18 September	15.9'
19 September–12 October	16.0'
13 October–2 November	16.1'
3 November–2 December	16.2'
3 December–31 December	16.3'

The correction for parallax in Sun observations is +0.1' to altitude 65°.

The Sun's declination is, therefore, −21.2086°, or South 21°12.5', which is also correct if careful interpolation is used in the *Nautical Almanac*.

Table 5-5 shows values for the Sun's semidiameter that must be used when reducing your sight.

Long-Term Aries and Star Ephemeris

To obtain the Greenwich hour angle and the declination of a star, for a given time and date, we require the *GHA* of Aries, ♈, the star's sidereal hour angle, *SHA,* and the declination, *d.* After computation of both *GHA* ♈ and *SHA*∗, the latter is added to *GHA* ♈, and 360° is subtracted if necessary; the vessel's longitude is then applied to the star's *GHA* to obtain the star's local hour angle, *LHA,* which, with the star's declination, *d,* is used to reduce the sight.

We shall first discuss computing *GHA* ♈ for any time and date.

Long-Term Aries Ephemeris

The *GHA* ♈ for any instant to the year 2000 may be computed by means of the formula:

$$GHA\ ♈ = C + [0.985647°(D)] + 15T \tag{1}$$

in which C is a constant for the specified year, found in Table 5-6, T is the specified GMT, and D is the numerical value of the specified day within the year, plus T divided by 24. Table 5-4, introduced in the preceding section, is designed to assist in determining the numerical value of the day. Use of these tables is illustrated in the following example.

Where a number of observations are made in series, it is necessary to compute *GHA* ♈ only for the first observation; subsequent values may be obtained if the time difference in minutes and decimals is multiplied by 0.250684°. The error in *GHA* ♈ obtained by this formula should not exceed 0.2′.

Example: We require the *GHA* ♈ for GMT 22h 17m 42s on 19 August 1989, and for 22h 33m 17s on the same day.

We extract the constant, C 99.6382°, for 1989 from Table 5-6. From Table 5-4 we note that in a non–leap year the last day of July is the 212th day of the year; 19 August will, therefore, be the 231st day of 1989. To this we add the first GMT, 22h 17m 42s, expressed as decimal hours, 22.2950.

We can now write formula (1):

GHA ♈ =
     99.6382° + [0.985647° × (231 + 22.2950°/24)] + (15 × 22.2950°)
     = 99.6382° + [228.60008°] + 334.4250°
     = 662.6633°

From 662.6633° we subtract 360°, and convert the answer to degrees and minutes, 302°39.8′, the *GHA* ♈ for GMT 22h 17m 42s.

Table 5-6. The Value of the Correction Factor C for the Years 1980 to 1999 (see text)

1980	98.8256
1981	99.5713
1982	99.3317
1983	99.0926
1984	98.8540
1985	99.6017
1986	99.3641
1987	99.1268
1988	98.8897
1989	99.6382
1990	99.4008
1991	99.1631
1992	98.9250
1993	99.6719
1994	99.4326
1995	99.1929
1996	98.9529
1997	99.6982
1998	99.4579
1999	99.2177

To obtain the *GHA* ♈ for 22h 33m 17s on the same day, we find the difference in minutes and decimals between this time, and the base GMT, 22h 17m 42s; this difference is 15.5833 minutes. Multiplying this difference by 0.250684°, the change in the *GHA* ♈ per minute of time, we get 3.9065°. Adding this to 302.6633°, the *GHA* ♈ for the base GMT, we get 306.5698°, which converts to 306°34.2′, the *GHA* ♈ for GMT 22h 33m 17s.

Long-Term Star Ephemeris

The sidereal hour angle of 57 major navigational stars, that is, their angular distance West of the First Point of Aries, and their declinations, may be determined for any time and date within this century with an accuracy in the great majority of cases of better than 0.5′, by the use of Tables 5-7 and 5-8.

Table 5-7 lists the *SHA* and *d* of each star for the epoch 1980.0, together with the annual corrections for each. Table 5-8 gives the deci-

Table 5-7. Long-Term Star Ephemeris, Epoch 1980.0

Star	SHA (degrees)	Annual change in SHA	Declination (degrees)	Annual change in dec.
Acamar	315.6232	−0.00942	−40.3847	0.004
Achernar	335.7575	−0.00917	−57.3374	0.005
Acrux	173.6225	−0.0138	−62.9899	−0.0055
Adhara	255.5374	−0.00983	−28.9463	−0.0014
Aldebaran	291.3032	−0.01425	16.4688	0.002
Alioth	166.7119	−0.0108	56.0672	−0.0053
Alkaid	153.3111	−0.0097	49.4103	−0.005
Al Na'ir	28.2531	−0.0156	−47.0563	0.0048
Alnilam	276.1968	−0.0126	−1.2157	0.0006
Alphard	218.3453	−0.0122	−8.5739	−0.004
Alphecca	126.5376	−0.0105	26.7818	−0.0033
Alpheratz	358.1578	−0.0128	28.9814	0.0055
Altair	62.5546	−0.01217	8.8171	0.00267
Ankaa	353.6739	−0.0123	−42.4132	0.0053
Antares	112.9507	−0.0153	−26.3876	−0.00217
Arcturus	146.3103	−0.0113	19.2857	−0.00517
Atria	108.3565	−0.026	−68.9915	−0.00175
Avior	234.4704	−0.0051	−59.4471	−0.0032
Bellatrix	278.9822	−0.0133	6.3307	0.0008
Betelgeuse	271.4740	−0.0134	7.4026	0.0002
Canopus	264.1210	−0.0056	−52.6869	−0.0006
Capella	281.1924	−0.0183	45.9774	0.0009
Deneb	49.8092	−0.0084	45.2110	0.0036
Denebola	182.9871	−0.0127	14.6819	−0.0055
Diphda	349.3257	−0.0125	−18.0951	0.0054
Dubhe	194.3736	−0.0153	61.8572	−0.0054
Elnath	278.7392	−0.0157	28.5900	0.0008
Eltanin	90.9631	−0.0058	51.4931	−0.0001
Enif	34.1954	−0.0122	9.7850	0.0045
Fomalhaut	15.8601	−0.0138	−29.7264	0.0053
Gacrux	172.4811	−0.0138	−57.0025	−0.0055
Gienah	176.3022	−0.0128	−17.4326	−0.0055
Hadar	149.3918	−0.0176	−60.2775	−0.0048
Hamal	328.4849	−0.014	23.3688	0.0047

Table 5-7. (*Continued*)

Star	SHA (degrees)	Annual change in SHA	Declination (degrees)	Annual change in dec.
Kaus Australis	84.2844	−0.0164	−34.3935	−0.0006
Kochab	137.3182	0.0007	74.2374	−0.0041
Markab	14.0554	−0.0124	15.0996	0.0053
Menkar	314.6885	−0.013	4.0117	0.0039
Menkent	148.6199	−0.0146	−36.2728	−0.0048
Miaplacidus	221.7482	−0.0028	−69.6374	−0.0041
Mirfak	309.2719	−0.0178	49.7907	0.0035
Nunki	76.4899	−0.0154	−26.3201	0.0013
Peacock	53.9778	−0.0196	−56.7979	0.0033
Polaris	Polaris precesses too rapidly for such a simple technique as this one.			
Pollux	243.9731	−0.0152	28.0732	−0.0024
Procyon	245.4326	−0.013	5.2746	−0.0026
Rasalhague	96.4954	−0.0115	12.5754	−0.0007
Regulus	208.1699	−0.0133	12.0632	−0.00492
Rigel	281.6028	−0.012	−8.2256	0.0011
Rigil Kentaurus	140.4333	−0.017	−60.7521	−0.004
Sabik	102.6886	−0.0143	−15.6999	−0.0012
Schedar	350.1526	−0.0142	56.4293	0.0054
Shaula	96.9326	−0.0169	−37.0886	−0.0008
Sirius	258.9308	−0.0109	−16.6907	−0.0014
Spica	158.9617	−0.0131	−11.0578	−0.0051
Suhail	223.1813	−0.009	−43.3539	−0.004
Vega	80.9324	−0.0084	38.7667	0.001
Zubenelgenubi	137.5535	−0.0138	−15.9592	−0.0041

mal part of a year represented by any month and day; this permits easy updating of the annual corrections to the tabulated *SHA* and *d*. The use of these tables is illustrated in the example.

To reduce an observation of one of the tabulated stars, it is recommended that the *GHA* ♈ for the time of the observation be first computed, and that the star's *SHA* and *d* be then determined by means of Tables 5-7 and 5-8. The star's *SHA* is then added to *GHA* ♈ to obtain the star's *GHA*.

Table 5-8. Decimal Parts of Year

Deci-mal	0.0	0.1	0.2	0.3	0.4	0.5
Day of year	1 Jan. to 18 Jan.	19 Jan. to 23 Feb.	24 Feb. to 1 Apr.	2 Apr. to 7 May	8 May to 13 June	14 June to 19 July

Deci-mal	0.6	0.7	0.8	0.9	1.0
Day of year	20 July to 25 Aug.	26 Aug. to 30 Sept.	1 Oct. to 6 Nov.	7 Nov. to 12 Dec.	13 Dec. to 31 Dec.

Example: We require the *GHA* and *d* of the star Acamar for GMT 22h 17m 42s on 19 August 1989. (Note: The *GHA* ♈ for that time and date is 302°39.8′; see the above example for finding the *GHA* ♈.)

We extract the *SHA* and *d* for epoch 1980.0 from Table 5-7, together with their annual corrections, and enter them as shown below. Using Table 5-8, we find that 19 August constitutes 0.6 year; 19 August 1989 will, therefore, be 9.6 years after epoch 1980.0.

Acamar

SHA 1980.0	315.6232°	*d* 1980.0	−40.3847°
Annual Corr.		Annual Corr.	
−0.00942° × 9.6	−0.0904°	0.004° × 9.6	0.0384°
SHA	315.5328°	*d*	−40.3463°
GHA ♈	302.6633°		
	618.1961°		
	− 360°		
Acamar *GHA*	258.1961° (258°11.8′)	*d*	−40.3463° (40°20.8′ S)

We would then apply our longitude to Acamar's *GHA* in the usual manner to obtain its *LHA,* and proceed to reduce the sight.

6

Miscellaneous Computations

Storm Avoidance

We are at sea when we receive a WWV report of a small low-pressure area, accompanied by strong winds and high seas. The disturbance is reported to be moving in the direction 035° at 22 knots. Allowing for the time that has elapsed since the storm's position was first reported, we plot its present position, and find that it bears 195°, distant 395 miles. From the plot, it is obvious that our avoidance course will lie somewhere toward the northwest.

We therefore bring the vessel to a heading of 315°, and find that we can make good a speed of 7 knots on this heading.

To determine the optimum avoidance course, given our speed of 7 knots, and the storm's present direction and speed of travel, we must next determine its speed and direction of advance relative to our vessel's eventual course and speed of 7 knots. To help in visualizing the problem, we start a rough sketch, which need not be to scale. We draw the line AB (see Figure 6-1) in the direction 035°; its length represents the storm's speed of travel, 22 knots. This sketch will end up as a triangle, the length of the side AC representing our speed of 7 knots, but as yet we do not know its exact direction.

If we were solving the problem by plotting, we would strike an arc, centered at A, with a radius of 7 units, in a northwesterly direction, and then drop a tangent to this line; by definition, a line tangent to a circle is perpendicular to a radius drawn to the point of tangency.

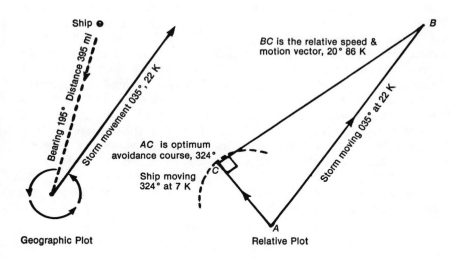

Figure 6-1.

We can now complete our triangle, knowing that C is a right angle, and the length of the sides AB and AC. What we need is the value of the angle A, which will enable us to compute the optimum course.

To find A, we first compute the value of B by the law of sines:

$$\frac{\sin 90°}{22} = \frac{\sin B}{7}$$

B therefore equals 18.55°, and subtracting this value from 90°, we find that A equals 71.45°. We can now find the avoidance course by subtracting 71.45° from the direction of the storm's advance, 035°. Our course will, therefore, be 323.55° (035° + 360° − 71.45°); we shall call it 324°.

We need to find one additional vector in this triangle—the length of the line BC, which represents the storm's speed of advance relative to our ship. Again, by the law of sines:

$$\frac{BC}{\sin 71.45°} = \frac{22}{\sin 90°}$$

BC, therefore, represents 20.86 knots, the storm's relative speed of advance. After bringing the ship to the avoidance course, 324°, we can go below, have a cup of coffee, and, at our leisure, calculate what our distance will be from the storm center at the closest point of approach, and the time required for the storm to reach that point, provided it does not change its direction of travel and/or its speed of advance. To visualize the problem, we put a penciled dot on a piece of paper, and label it *A;* this represents our present position. From *A* we draw a line in the direction 195°; the other end of this line, labeled *B,* represents the storm's present position, distant 395 miles. This drawing need not be accurate; it is merely intended as an aid in visualizing the problem.

We next draw a second line from *A* in the direction 144°, the reciprocal of our course line; this forms the second leg of our triangle. For the third leg, we drop a perpendicular from *B* to the reciprocal of our course line. In this triangle, we know that the angle *A* equals 51° (195° − 144°), and that *C* is a right angle; *B* therefore equals 39° (90° − 51°).

We can now proceed to find the storm's distance at the CPA (point *C* in our triangle) by the law of sines:

$$\frac{395}{\sin 90°} = \frac{CPA}{\sin 39°}$$

The distance at the CPA is, therefore, 248.58 miles.

To find the time the storm will reach the CPA, we calculate the length of the side *BC,* which represents the relative distance the storm will travel to the CPA:

$$\frac{395}{\sin 90°} = \frac{BC}{\sin 51°}$$

The relative distance is, therefore, 307 miles. From the first triangle we found the storm's relative speed of advance to be 20.86 knots, which we will call 21 knots. Dividing the relative distance, 307 miles, by the relative speed, 21 knots, we find the storm, if it maintains its present advance, will reach the CPA in about 14 hours 40 minutes.

At this point, it is appropriate to add a cautionary note.

Storms frequently change both the direction and the speed of their advance. Every opportunity of updating all available weather data should be seized, and a new avoidance course should be calculated if necessary.

Finally, it goes without saying that the avoidance course should not take the ship into shoal water, or, save under exceptional circumstances, into the dangerous semicircle of a circular tropical storm, such as a hurricane.

Temperature Conversion

Three methods of expressing temperature are in general use today—Fahrenheit, Celsius (Centigrade), and Kelvin. They may readily be interconverted by the formulae given below, in which F stands for degrees Fahrenheit, C for degrees Celsius, and K for degrees Kelvin.

To convert degrees F to degrees C, the formula is:

$$C = 0.556 \ (F - 32°) \tag{1}$$

The formula for converting degrees Celsius to degrees Fahrenheit is:

$$F = (1.8 \times C) + 32° \tag{2}$$

To convert degrees Celsius to degrees Kelvin the formula is:

$$K = C + 273.16° \tag{3}$$

For converting degrees K to degrees C we use the formula:

$$C = K - 273.16° \tag{4}$$

Example 1: We wish to convert 63°F to degrees C. We write formula (1):

$$C = 0.556 \times (63° - 32°) = 0.556 \times 31° = 17.2°C$$

Example 2: We wish to convert −23.8°C to degrees F. We write formula (2):

$$F = (1.8 \times -23.8°) + 32° = -42.8° + 32° = -10.8°F$$

Example 3: We wish to convert 26°F to degrees C. Formula (1) becomes:

$$C = 0.556 \times (26° - 32°) = 0.556 \times -6° = -3.3°C$$

Example 4: We wish to convert 60°C to degrees K. We write formula (3):

$$K = 60° + 273.16° = 333.16 \ K$$

Example 5: We wish to convert 320 K to degrees C. Formula (4) becomes:

$$C = 320° - 273.16° = 46.84°C$$

Barometric-Pressure Conversion

Inches of mercury, millimeters of mercury, and millibars may be interconverted with sufficient accuracy for all ordinary purposes by means of the calculator and the following formulae.

To find the atmospheric pressure in inches of mercury, when it is stated in millibars, the formula is:

$$IM = 0.02953 \times Mbs \tag{1}$$

where *IM* is pressure in inches of mercury, and *Mbs* represents the number of millibars.

To convert inches of mercury to millibars, the formula is:

$$Mbs = \frac{IM}{0.02953} \tag{2}$$

When atmospheric pressure is stated in millimeters of mercury, the equivalent value in millibars may be found by the formula:

$$Mbs = \frac{Mm}{0.75} \tag{3}$$

in which *Mm* represents the atmospheric pressure stated in millimeters.

Example 1: The atmospheric pressure is given as 998 millibars; we wish to convert this value to inches of mercury. Formula (1) becomes:

$$IM = 0.02953 \times 998 = 29.47$$

The atmospheric pressure is, therefore, 29.47 inches.

Example 2: The barometer reads 30.56 inches; we wish to state it in millibars. We use formula (2), which we write:

$$Mbs = \frac{30.56}{0.02953} = 1035$$

Therefore, 1035 millibars are the equivalent of 30.56 inches of mercury.

Example 3: The atmospheric pressure is given as 764 millimeters of mercury, which we wish to convert to millibars. We write formula (3):

$$Mbs = \frac{764}{0.75} = 1019$$

The pressure expressed in millibars is, therefore, 1019.

Finding the Diameter of the Turning Circle

To find the diameter of the turning circle by the method given below, it is necessary that a clear horizon be available. The rudder is set to the required angle, and after the ship has turned through more than 180°, the angle between the horizon and the center of the wake abeam of the vessel is measured with the sextant. To this angle, the sextant's index correction and the correction for dip, *with sign reversed,* are applied to give the angle *Ho.*

The diameter of the turning circle, *D,* may then be found by means of the formula

$$D = \frac{HE}{\tan H_o} \tag{1}$$

where *HE* is the observer's height of eye in feet.

To find the diameter of the turning circle in yards, it is only necessary to divide the answer thus found by 3. If *HE* is entered in meters, the diameter of the turning circle will be in meters.

For merchantmen, the diameter of the turning circle, without backing one engine on a twin screw ship, will usually lie between six and nine times the vessel's length. However, for any given ship, the diameter will usually vary with any change in trim.

Example: We wish to determine the diameter of our turning circle, in yards, using standard rudder. Our height of eye is 66 feet; when the ship has turned through more than 180°, we measure the angle between the center of the wake abeam and the horizon beyond it and find the angle to be 0°57.5′. The index error is −2.0′; the corrected angle is, therefore, 0°59.5′.

We write formula (1):

$$D = \frac{66}{\tan 0°59.5′ \times 3} = \frac{66}{0.0519} = 1270.97$$

The diameter of our turning circle is, therefore, 1271 yards.

Area and Volume

In these formulae, *D*, represents diameter, *H* represents height, *L* represents length, *r* represents radius, *S* represents the length of a side, and *W* represents width.

$$\text{Surface area of a triangle} = H/2 \times L \tag{1}$$

$$\text{Surface area of a square} = L \times L \tag{2}$$

$$\text{Surface area of a rectangle} = H \times L \tag{2}$$

$$\text{Surface area of a parallelogram} = H \times L \tag{2}$$

$$\text{Surface area of a cube} = 6 \times H^2 \tag{3}$$

Surface area of a rectangular solid
$$= (2 \times L \times H) + (2 \times L \times W) + (2 \times H \times W) \tag{4}$$

$$\text{Surface of a circle} = \pi \times r^2 \tag{5}$$

$$\text{Surface area of a sphere} = \pi \times r^2 \times 4 \tag{6}$$

$$\text{Surface area of a cylinder} = \pi \times D \times L + 2 \times \pi \times r^2 \tag{7}$$

$$\text{Surface area of a cone} = \pi \times r^2 + \pi \times r \times \text{length of side} \tag{8}$$

$$\text{Volume of a cube} = H \times L \times W \tag{9}$$

$$\text{Volume of a rectangular solid} = H \times L \times W \tag{10}$$

$$\text{Volume of a sphere} = \pi \times D^3/6 \tag{11}$$

$$\text{Volume of a cone} = \frac{\pi \times H \times r^2}{3} \tag{12}$$

Fuel Consumption

For large ships steaming at economical speeds, that is, well below hull speed, *fuel consumption varies as the cube of the speed for a given time, and as the square of the speed for a given distance.*

For *time,* the formula is:

$$\frac{S_2^3}{S_1^3} \times F_1 = F_2 \tag{1}$$

where S_1 is the speed for which the fuel consumption in known, S_2 is the speed for which the fuel consumption is desired, F_1 is the fuel in units consumed per hour or per day at S_1, and F_2 is fuel consumed at the new speed.

For *distance,* the formula is:

$$\frac{S_2^2}{S_1^2} \times F_1 = F_2 \tag{2}$$

using the same notation as in formula (1).

Example 1: At 14 knots we burn 40 tons of fuel a day. What will be our fuel consumption per day at 12 knots?

The cube of 14 is 2744, and the cube of 12 is 1728, so we write formula (1):

$$F_2 = \frac{1728}{2744} \times 40 = 25.1895$$

Fuel consumption at 12 knots will, therefore, be 25.1895 tons per day.

Example 2: At 13 knots we burn 2.65 tons of fuel per hour, and we wish to determine our hourly fuel consumption at 15 knots.

The cube of 13 is 2197, and the cube of 15 is 3375. We, therefore, write formula (1):

$$F_2 = \frac{3375}{2197} \times 2.65 = 4.0709$$

At 15 knots our hourly fuel consumption will, therefore, be 4.1 tons.

Example 3: At 13 knots we require 323 tons of fuel to steam 2,085 miles. How much fuel will we require to steam the same distance at 15 knots?

In this case, we use formula (2), which we write:

$$F_2 = \frac{225}{169} \times 323 = 430.0296$$

We shall, therefore, require 430 tons of fuel to cover 2,085 miles at 15 knots.

By rearranging or transposing factors as required, formulae (1) and (2), above, can be used to solve variations of these fuel-consumption problems.

Example 4: We know that we require 323 tons of fuel to make a run of 2,085 miles at 13 knots. What speed must we use to make the same run using only 260 tons of fuel?

In this case, S_2 is not known, but F_2 is, so we transpose formula (2) to read:

$$S_2{}^2 = \frac{F_2 \times S_1{}^2}{F_1}$$

which becomes:

$$S_2{}^2 = \frac{260 \times 169}{323} = 136.0372$$

The square of the speed we must use to cover the required distance on 260 tons of fuel is 136.

Therefore, the required speed is the square root of 136, or 11.66 knots.

Example 5: We know that our ship burns 232 tons of fuel to travel 2,085 miles at 13 knots. We wish to determine how much fuel we would require to travel 1,850 miles at 16 knots.

We first determine how much fuel she would consume steaming the first distance, 2,085 miles, at 16 knots. Formula (2) becomes:

$$F_2 = \frac{256}{169} \times 323 = 489.2781$$

which we shall call 490 tons. For 2,085 miles at 16 knots, we would require 490 tons of fuel.

We can now find the amount of fuel required to steam 1,850 miles at 16 knots:

$$F_3 = \frac{D_2}{D_1} \times F_2 = \frac{1,850}{2,085} \times 490 = 434.7722$$

We would, therefore, require 435 tons to steam 1,850 miles at 16 knots.

Some fuel problems are best solved by ratios. The following example is a case in point.

Example 6: We know that our ship requires 323 tons of fuel to travel 2,085 miles at 13 knots. At what speed must we steam to travel 3,450 miles on 400 tons of fuel?

We first determine how many miles we would cover at 13 knots on 400 tons of fuel. For this purpose, we use the ratio

$$F_1 : F_2 :: D_1 : D_2$$

in which D_1 is the known distance and D_2 is the distance to be found, and we write:

$$323:400::2,085:2,582$$

At 13 knots, therefore, we would cover 2,582 miles on 400 tons. Next, using the ratio

$$D_2:D_3::F_2:F_3$$

we find how many tons of fuel would be required to steam 3,450 miles at 13 knots:

$$2,582:3,450::400:534$$

We would, therefore, require 534 tons of fuel for 3,450 miles at 13 knots. Now, using a third ratio,

$$F_3:F_2::S_1{}^2:S_2{}^2$$

we can determine the speed required to traverse 3,450 miles on 400 tons of fuel:

$$534:400::169:126.5$$

The square of the required speed is, therefore, 126.5, and its square root is 11.25.

Therefore, we must steam at 11.25 knots to cover 3,450 miles on 400 tons of fuel.

Propeller Slip

Apparent propeller slip is the difference between the pitch of a propeller multiplied by the number of revolutions it makes and the vessel's advance. Slip is expressed as a percentage. Thus, a steamer turning a propeller having a 20-foot pitch at 152 revolutions per minute (rpm) would move 3,040 feet in one minute, or would be steaming at almost exactly 30.0 knots (actually, 30.02):

$$\frac{3,040 \text{ feet} \times 60 \text{ minutes}}{6,076 \text{ feet}}$$

If she made 27.0 knots, the slip would be 10% (27:30::90:100).

For most use, the length of the nautical mile is generally considered to be 6,080 feet; in fact, its length is 6,076.11548556 feet.

Slip varies tremendously with vessel type. Under fine weather conditions, the slip for a large freighter driven at an economical speed by a slow-turning propeller may approach a highly favorable 5%. On the other hand, for a heavy auxiliary sailboat turning a small propeller at a high number of revolutions, it may approach 50% in smooth water, and on a windless day. Head winds and head seas, of course, greatly increase the slip, and high speeds have the same effect on many vessels.

For small craft of various types, average slip is approximately as listed below:

Fast open motor boats	20%
Light cruisers	25%
Heavy cruisers	28%
Auxiliary sailboats	33% to 50%

A graph or table showing the number of engine or propeller turns per minute required to achieve any given speed in still water is most helpful. For large cargo carriers, graphs or tables for various loadings are required. The diameter and pitch of propellers for small craft are stamped on the wheel, and are usually given in inches.

To find the speed in knots a propeller would give a boat if there were no slip, we could use the formula:

$$\text{Speed in knots} = \frac{\text{propeller rpm} \times \text{pitch in inches} \times 60 \text{ minutes}}{6{,}080 \text{ feet} \times 12 \text{ inches}}$$

However, this formula can be more simply written:

$$\text{Speed in knots} = \text{propeller rpm} \times \text{pitch in inches} \times 0.000822 \quad (1)$$

because $60/(6{,}080 \times 12) = 0.000822$.

To find speed in miles per hour, we would substitute 0.000947 as the constant, since $60/(5{,}280 \times 12) = 0.000947$.

Example 1: Our propeller has a pitch of 22 inches. If there were no slip, what would be our speed in knots, if the propeller were turning at 1,800 rpm?

Here, we use formula (1) and the constant 0.000822, and write:

$$\text{Speed in knots} = 1{,}800 \times 22 \times 0.000822 = 32.55$$

In the absence of slip, we would, therefore, make 32.55 knots.

Now let us assume that when our propeller is turning at 1,800 rpm, we are actually making 22.5 knots, and we wish to determine the slip. We use the ratio

$$\frac{22.5}{32.55} = 0.6912 \times 100$$

The slip, therefore, is 30.9% (100 − 69.1). Remember that the slip percentage is based on the propeller pitch and its rpm and *not* on the speed made good.

For ships, propeller pitch is stated in feet and inches or feet and decimals of feet. If it is stated in feet and inches, the inches should be converted to decimals. Thus, for a pitch of 18 feet 3 inches, we would use 18.25 feet. To find the ship's speed if there were no slip, the formula would be:

$$\text{Speed in knots} = \frac{\text{propeller rpm} \times \text{pitch in feet} \times 60 \text{ minutes}}{6,080}$$

However, this also can be simplified:

$$\text{Speed in knots} = \text{propeller rpm} \times \text{pitch in feet} \times 0.00987 \quad (2)$$

because 60 divided by 6076 gives the constant 0.00987.

Example 2: Our propeller pitch is 11 feet 6 inches, and we wish to know what speed we would obtain at 170 rpm if there were no slip. We write formula (2):

$$\text{Speed in knots} = 170 \times 11.5 \times 0.00987 = 19.2959$$

Our speed, therefore, would be 19.3 knots.

Suppose that we wanted to allow for 11% slip, and still obtain a speed of 19.3 knots. How many shaft rpm should we call for?

We arrive at the required number of rpm by using the ratio

$$\frac{170}{89\%} = \frac{\text{rpm}}{100\%}$$

To make 19.3 knots we should, therefore, call for 191 rpm.

The engine rooms of large vessels have revolution counters, which record the number of turns the shaft has made in a given period. If the value of the slip is known, such counters are most useful in determining the distance run over a given period: all that is required is to calculate how far the ship would have advanced for the given pitch and number of turns, and apply the slip to the result of that calculation.

Example 3: Our propeller pitch is 11 feet 6 inches, and the shaft counters show that we have made 28,300 propeller revolutions in a given period. We wish to determine how far we have steamed, allowing for an 11% slip.

The slip being 11%, we multiply the advance by 0.89 (1 − 0.11). We then have:

Miles steamed

$$= \frac{\text{pitch 11.5 feet} \times 28,300 \text{ shaft revolutions} \times 0.89 \text{ slip factor}}{6,080 \text{ feet}}$$

$$= 47.6399$$

Allowing for an 11% slip, we have, therefore, steamed 47.6 miles.

Review of Alterations in Ship Stability and Trim

This brief section on stability and trim is intended as an aide-mémoire for the mariner who, at some time in the past, has studied that portion of naval architecture dealing with ship stability, and is suddenly faced with a stability problem, without access to the usual textbooks dealing with this subject.

Table 6-1 presents hydrostatic and intact stability nomenclature.

Figure 6-2 shows a ship with positive stability at an angle of heel ϕ, which in this case is less than or equal to 7°.

Figure 6-3 illustrates trim, showing a ship attempting to return to waterline WL.

The following sections on ship hydrostatics and intact stability contain several sample problems. For consistency, these examples will

Table 6-1. Hydrostatic and Intact Stability Nomenclature

Symbol	Definition	Units
L	Length of waterline	ft
BEAM	Max. beam of waterline	ft
T	Mean draft to waterline	ft
Δ	Displacement at T	Long tons
∇	Volumetric displacement at T	ft³
C_B	Block coefficient at T	—
C_{wp}	Waterplane coefficient at T	—
$\overline{KG}$	Height of the vertical center of gravity above the keel	ft
$\overline{KM}$	Height of the transverse metacenter above the keel	ft
$\overline{GM}$	Transverse metacentric height	ft
$\overline{KB}$	Height of the vertical center of buoyancy above the keel	ft
$\overline{BM}$	Transverse metacentric radius	ft
$MT\,1''$	Moment to alter trim one inch	ft-tons/in.
A_{wp}	Area of the waterplane at T	ft²
KM_L	Longitudinal metacentric height above the keel	ft
BM_L	Longitudinal metacentric radius	ft

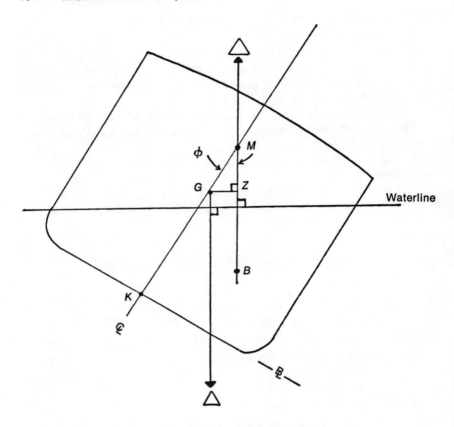

K	Intersection of baseline (B̲L̲) and centerline (C̲L̲)
G	Center of gravity
B	Center of bouyancy
M	Metacenter (G must be below M for positive stability)
ϕ	Angle of heel, deg
$\overline{GZ}$	Righting arm, ft
$\overline{GZ} \times \Delta$	Righting moment, ft - tons

Figure 6-2. A ship with positive stability will attempt to return to the upright. As drawn (for $\phi \le 7°$) this ship has positive stability.

refer to a single ship having the following characteristics:

$$L = 150 \text{ feet}$$
$$\text{BEAM} = 25 \text{ feet}$$
$$T = 10 \text{ feet}$$
$$\text{TRIM} = 0 \text{ feet}$$
$$C_{wp} = 0.75$$
$$C_B = 0.65$$

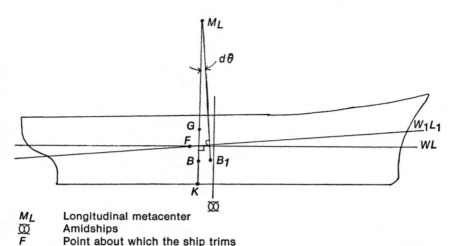

M_L	Longitudinal metacenter
⋈	Amidships
F	Point about which the ship trims

Figure 6-3. As drawn, this ship is attempting to return to waterline WL.

I. To find displacement (Δ) in long tons (1 long ton = 2240 pounds):

A. $\Delta = \displaystyle\sum_{i=1}^{N} W_i = W_1 + W_2 + W_3 + \cdots + W_N$

where W_i = weight of the ith item in long tons, N = total number of weight items.

B. $\Delta = (C_B \times L \times \text{BEAM} \times T)/k_1$

where $k_1 \simeq 35$ ft^3/ton for salt water and $k_1 \simeq 36$ ft^3/ton for fresh water. (See Table 6-2 for C_B values.)

Example 1: Estimate the example ship's displacement when she is floating in salt water.

Equation:

$$\Delta = (C_B \times L \times \text{BEAM} \times T)/k_1$$

Table 6-2. Representative Values for C_B

Ship type	Approximate range of C_B	
Barge	0.85–0.98	
Tanker	0.75–0.88	
Fast cargo ship	0.60–0.75	finer ↕ hull form
Trawler	0.50–0.65	
Power cruiser	0.50–0.60	
Yacht	0.45–0.65	

Table 6-3. Representative Values for C_{wp}

Ship type	Approximate value of C_{wp}
Barge	1.0
Tanker	0.90
Fast cargo ship	0.80
Trawler	0.75
Power cruiser	0.72
Yacht	0.70

Assume: $k_1 \simeq 35$ ft³/ton

Since: $C_B = 0.65$
              $L = 150$ feet
  BEAM $= 25$ feet
              $T = 10$ feet

Then: $\Delta = $ 700 long tons.

II. To find the vertical center of gravity (KG) in feet:
  A. Inclining experiment

$$\overline{KG} = \overline{KM} - \overline{GM}$$

1. $\overline{KM} = \overline{KB} + \overline{BM}$
   $\overline{KB} \simeq T - 0.33[(0.5 \times T) + (\nabla/A_{wp})]$
   $\nabla = \Delta \times k_1$ (See I.B.)
   $A_{wp} = C_{wp} \times L \times$ BEAM (See Table 6-3 for C_{wp} values.)
   $BM \simeq$ BEAM²$/(k_2 T)$

   where k_2 varies from about 10 for a fuller waterplane form to about 15 for a finer waterplane form.
2. $GM = (w \times d)/(\Delta \times \tan \phi)$
   where $w = $ amount of onboard weight that is shifted (long tons), $d = $ distance w is moved across the ship (feet), and $\phi = $ the angle of heel that results from this weight shift. The induced heeling moment ($w \times d$) should be selected to produce an angle of heel of less than 5°.

Example 2: If a 1-long-ton weight is moved 13 feet off the centerline, the example ship heels 0.75°. Estimate the ship's *KG*.
Equations:

$$\overline{KG} = \overline{KM} - \overline{GM}$$
$$\overline{KM} = \overline{KB} + \overline{BM}$$

$$\overline{KB} \approx T - 0.33[(0.5 \times T) + (\nabla/A_{wp})]$$
$$\nabla = \Delta \times k_1$$
$$A_{wp} = C_{wp} \times L \times \text{BEAM}$$

Since: $C_{wp} = 0.75$
          $L = 150$ feet
   BEAM $= 25$ feet
          $\Delta = 700$ tons (using Example 1)
          $T = 10$ feet

Then: $A_{wp} = 2{,}812.5$ ft^2
   $\nabla = 24{,}500.$ ft^3
$\overline{KB} = 5.48$ feet

$$\overline{BM} \approx \text{BEAM}^2/(k_2 \times T)$$

Assume: $k_2 \approx 13$ for this ship
Then: $\overline{BM} = 4.81$ feet
And: $\overline{KM} = 10.29$ feet

$$\overline{GM} = (w \times d)/(\Delta \times \tan \phi)$$

Since: $w = 1$ long ton
       $d = 13$ feet
       $\phi = 0.75°$

Then: $\overline{GM} = 1.42$ feet
Therefore: $\overline{KG} = 10.29 - 1.42 = \underline{8.87 \text{ feet}}$.

   B. Using the ship's period of roll

$$\overline{KG} = \overline{KM} - \overline{GM}$$

   1. $\overline{KM}$ (See II.A.1.)
   2. $\overline{GM} = (k_3 \times \text{BEAM/PERIOD})^2$
      where PERIOD = period of roll for one complete oscillation
      (seconds), and k_3 varies between 0.4 and 0.5 for surface
      ships. A value of 0.44 is a good approximation.

Example 3: The example ship's complete period of roll (port to starboard and back to port) is measured to be 9 seconds. Estimate the
vessel's $\overline{KG}$.
Equations:

$$\overline{KG} = \overline{KM} - \overline{GM}$$

$$\overline{GM} = (k_3 \times \text{BEAM/PERIOD})^2$$

Since: $\overline{KM} = 10.29$ feet (using Example 2)
   BEAM $= 25$ feet
   PERIOD $= 9$ seconds

Assume: $k_3 \approx 0.44$
Then: $\overline{GM} = 1.49$ feet
Therefore: $\overline{KG} = 10.29 - 1.49 = \underline{8.80 \text{ feet}}$.

III. To find the influence of weight changes on displacement (Δ), draft (T), and the vertical center of gravity ($\overline{KG}$):

A. $\Delta_{\text{new}} = \Delta_{\text{old}} + \sum\limits_{i=1}^{N} W_i$

B. $T_{\text{new}} = T_{\text{old}} + \left(\sum\limits_{i=1}^{N} W_i/TPI \right)/12$

C. $\overline{KG}_{\text{new}} = \left\{ (\overline{KG}_{\text{old}})(\Delta_{\text{old}}) + \sum\limits_{i=1}^{N} (W_i)(\overline{KG}_i) \right\} \Big/ \left(\Delta_{\text{old}} + \sum\limits_{i=1}^{N} W_i \right)$

where W_i = the ith weight (long tons), + if added and − if removed; N = the total number of items added or removed; TPI = tons per inch immersion (tons/in.); $TPI = A_{wp}/(12 \times k_1)$ (see I.B. and II.A.1); $\overline{KG}_i$ = the location of the vertical center of gravity of the ith weight above the keel (feet).

Example 4: The example ship is subjected to the following weight changes: (1) 30 long tons are added 16 feet above the baseline, and (2) 21 long tons are removed from a position 7 feet above the baseline. Calculate the ship's new Δ, T, and $\overline{KG}$.
Equation:

$$\Delta_{\text{new}} = \Delta_{\text{old}} + \sum\limits_{i=1}^{N} W_i$$

Since: $\Delta_{\text{old}} = 700$ tons (using Example 1)

$$N = 2 \text{ with } W_1 = +30 \text{ tons}, W_2 = -21 \text{ tons}$$

Then: $\sum\limits_{i=1}^{N} W_i = +9$ tons
And: $\Delta_{\text{new}} = 700 + 9 = \underline{709 \text{ long tons}}$.

$$T_{\text{new}} = T_{\text{old}} + \left(\sum\limits_{i=1}^{N} W_i/TPI \right)/12 \text{ with } TPI = A_{wp}/(12 \times k_1)$$

Since: $T_{\text{old}} = 10$ feet
$A_{wp} = 2812.5$ ft^2 (using Example 2)
$k_1 \cong 35$ ft^3/ton (salt water)
Then: $TPI = 6.70$ tons/in.
And: $T_{\text{new}} = 10.11$ feet.

$$\overline{KG}_{\text{new}} = \left\{ (\overline{KG}_{\text{old}})(\Delta_{\text{old}}) + \sum\limits_{i=1}^{N} (W_i)(\overline{KG}_i) \right\} \Big/ \left(\Delta_{\text{old}} + \sum\limits_{i=1}^{N} W_i \right)$$

Since: $\overline{KG}_{old} \simeq 8.87$ feet (using Example 2)

Then: $\displaystyle\sum_{i=1}^{N} (W_i)(\overline{KG}_i) = (+30)(16) + (-21)(7)$

$\left(\Delta_{old} + \displaystyle\sum_{i=1}^{N} W_i\right) = 700 + 30 + (-21)$

And: $\overline{KG}_{new} = 9.23$ feet.

IV. To find the influence of an onboard weight shift on the position of the ship's vertical center of gravity ($\overline{KG}$):

    A. $\overline{KG}_{new} = \overline{KG}_{old} \pm \overline{GG}'$

       $\overline{GG}' = (w \times d)/\Delta$

       where $\overline{GG}'$ = the distance the center of gravity shifts as a result of weight (w) moving a distance (d). The ship's center of gravity will shift in the same direction that the weight moves (feet). (For w and d, see II.A.2.)

Example 5: A 50-long-ton weight is shifted downward a distance of 11.5 feet. What is the example ship's new $\overline{KG}$?

Equations:

$$\overline{KG}_{new} = \overline{KG}_{old} \pm \overline{GG}'$$
$$\overline{GG}' = (w \times d)/\Delta$$

Since: $w = 50$ long tons

      $d = 11.5$ feet downward

      $\Delta = 700$ long tons (using Example 1)

Then: $\overline{GG}' = 0.82$ foot

Note: Since the onboard weight was moved downward, the ship's $\overline{KG}$ will decrease.

Since: $\overline{KG}_{old} = 8.87$ feet (using Example 2)

Then: $\overline{KG}_{new} = 8.87 - 0.82 = \underline{8.05 \text{ feet}}$.

Note: A new longitudinal center of gravity (LCG_{new}) or a new transverse center of gravity (TCG_{new}) may be found by using equations similar to (III.C) and (IV.A). To do this, a reference axis for moments and a sign convention must first be established.

V. To find changes in the vertical center of gravity ($\overline{KG}$) or the transverse metacentric height ($\overline{GM}$) because of a free surface:

    A. $\overline{KG}_{new} = \overline{KG}_{old} + \overline{GG}_v$

    B. $\overline{GM}_{new} = \overline{GM}_{old} - \overline{GG}_v$

    C. $\overline{GG}_v = \gamma' k_4 \, lb^3 / \gamma \nabla$

       where $\overline{GG}_v$ = virtual change in the position of G due to the existence of a free surface (feet), γ' = specific gravity of the liquid in the tank, γ = specific gravity of the water in which

Table 6-4. Some Specific Gravities

Substance	Approximate specific gravity
Fresh water	1.0
Salt water	1.025
Lube oil	0.90
Oil	0.85
Gasoline	0.75

the ship is floating, l = length of the free surface (feet), b = width of the free surface (feet), and $k_4 = 0.083$ is an acceptable value for a rectangular free surface. (See Table 6-4 for some specific gravities.)

Example 6: The example ship has a partially full fuel tank with a length of 20 feet and a width of 6 feet. The fuel oil has a specific gravity of 0.88. Compute the virtual change in G because of this free surface.

Equations:

$$\overline{GG}_v = \gamma' k_4\, lb^3/\gamma \nabla$$
$$\nabla = \Delta \times k_1$$

Since: Δ = 700 long tons (using Example 1)

k_1 = 35 ft³/ton (salt water)

γ = 0.98 (salt water)

γ' = 0.88

l = 20 feet

b = 6 feet

Assume: $k_4 = 0.083$

Then: ∇ = 24,500 ft³

And: $\overline{GG}_v$ = 0.013 foot.

VI. To predict changes in trim:

A. When shifting an onboard weight

$\delta \text{trim} = (w \times a)/MT1''$ (inches)

$MT1'' = (\Delta \times \overline{GM}_L)/(12 \times L)$

$\overline{GM}_L = \overline{KM}_L - \overline{KG}$

$\overline{KM}_L = \overline{KB} + \overline{BM}_L$

$\overline{BM}_L \simeq (3 \times A_{wp}{}^2 \times L)/(40 \times \text{BEAM} \times \nabla)$

or:

$MT1'' = (k_5 \times C_{wp}{}^2 \times L^2 \times \text{BEAM})/(144 \times k_1{}^2)$

where k_5 = function (C_B) (see Table 6-5).

Table 6-5. C_B vs. k_5

C_B	k_5
0.50	32.6
0.60	31.8
0.70	31.0
0.80	30.2

w = amount of onboard weight that is shifted (long tons)
a = distance w is moved along the ship and parallel to the keel (feet)

Example 7: A 14-long-ton weight is moved 39 feet aft on the example ship. Estimate the change in trim (δtrim).
Equations:

$$\delta\text{trim} = (w \times a)/MT1''$$
$$MT1'' = (\Delta \times \overline{GM_L})/(12 \times L)$$
$$\overline{GM_L} = \overline{KM_L} - \overline{KG}$$
$$\overline{KM_L} = \overline{KB} + \overline{BM_L}$$
$$\overline{BM_L} \simeq (3 \times A_{wp}^2 \times L)/(40 \times \text{BEAM} \times \nabla)$$

Since: L = 150 feet
        BEAM = 25 feet
        ∇ = 24,500 ft^3 (using Example 2)
        A_{wp} = 2,812.5 ft^2 (using Example 2)
Then: $\overline{BM_L} \simeq$ 145.3 feet
Since: $\overline{KB}$ = 5.48 feet (using Example 2)
     $\overline{KG}$ = 8.87 feet (using Example 2)
Then: $\overline{GM_L}$ = 141.91 feet
And: $MT1''$ = 55.19 ft-tons/in.
Therefore: δtrim = 9.89 inches.
Note: Since the weight was moved aft, the ship will trim by the stern (draft aft will increase).

   B. When adding or removing a weight
      1. First, determine how this weight change will affect displacement (Δ), draft (T), and the vertical center of gravity ($\overline{KG}$) (see III).
      2. Second, using the results from the above step, compute the change in trim (see VI.A).
   C. Probable direction of trim (refer to Table 6-6)

Table 6-6. Probable Direction of Trim

If the weight causing the trim ends up:	Aft of Amidships			Forward of Amidships		
And if the weight is:	Onboard	Added	Removed	Onboard	Added	Removed
Then the draft at the bow will:	Decrease	Decrease	Increase	Increase	Increase	Decrease

Note: This table is only an approximation, since the ship, in general, will not trim about amidships.

Rigging Loads

The load on masts, booms, derricks, and shear legs, as well as on their rigging, can be determined by means of the calculator considerably more rapidly and accurately than by construction. Essentially, the process involves solving the triangles in a parallelogram of forces by trigonometry rather than by construction and careful linear measurement.

Let us assume that a naval architect has specified that the headstay to the bowsprit on a sailboat must have a tensile strength of 12,000 lb, which allows for a factor of safety of 4 to 1. We wish to determine what the tensile strength of the bobstay should be, allowing for the same safety factor, and what the compression load would be on the bowsprit at the stays' tensile limit.

We first determine that the angles made by the headstay and the bobstay with the bowsprit are 70° and 24°, respectively; see Figure 6-4a. The resulting parallelogram of forces is shown in Figure 6-4b, but we do not need to draw it. To help visualize the solution, which we obtain by the law of sines, we can sketch the triangle forming the upper half of the parallelogram; see Figure 6-4c. In this triangle, the side AB represents the headstay; its length represents the tensile strength of the wire, 12,000 lb. The length of the side AC will then represent the required tensile strength of the bobstay, and the length of BC the compression load on the bowsprit, when the headstay is loaded to 12,000 lb. Now:

$$\frac{12,000 \text{ lb}}{\sin 24°} = \frac{BC}{\sin 86°}$$

$$BC = 29,431 \text{ lb}$$

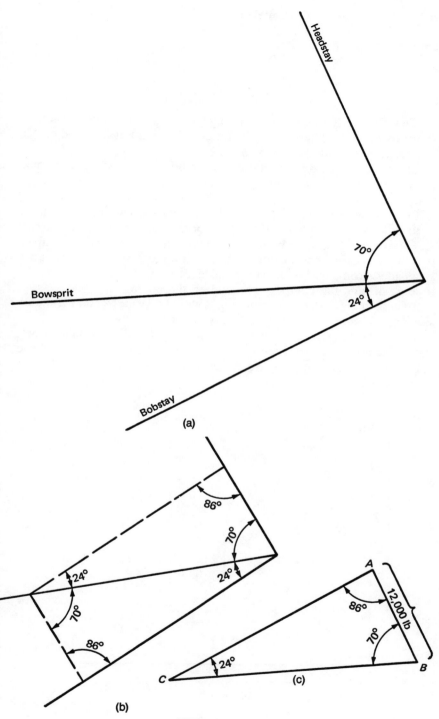

Figure 6-4.

and:

$$\frac{12,000 \text{ lb}}{\sin 24°} = \frac{AC}{\sin 70°}$$

$$AC = 27,724 \text{ lb}$$

Therefore, if the headstay were loaded to 12,000 lb, the tension on the bobstay, AC, would be 27,724 lb, and the compression load on the bowsprit, BC, would be 29,431 lb.

Other and more complex problems can be similarly solved. In some instances, drawing a rough diagram may assist in visualizing the problem.

Let us consider such a problem. A cargo boom is attached to a mast at deck level; the topping lift for the boom is attached to the mast 60 feet above the deck. The boom is 40 feet in length, and is topped up so that the falls hang 30 feet from the mast; see Figure 6-5. A 10-ton load is suspended from the boom. We wish to determine the tension on the topping lift and the compression load on the boom.

To help in visualizing the problem, it would be wise to make a sketch similar to Figure 6-6; it does not have to be carefully drawn.

The first step is to determine the angle the falls make with the boom; this is the angle ABD in Figure 6-6. The boom is 40 feet long, and the falls, which hang vertically, are centered 30 feet from the mast. By the

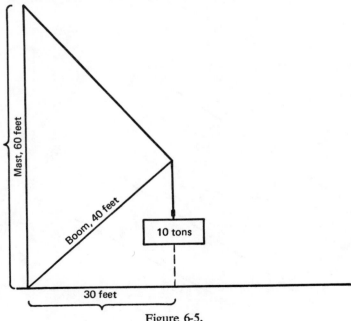

Figure 6-5.

law of sines, we therefore find the required angle, *ABD:*

$$\frac{\sin 90°}{40 \text{ feet}} = \frac{\sin \angle ABD}{30 \text{ feet}}$$

$$\sin \angle ABD = 0.7500$$

$$\angle ABD = 48.5904°$$

The falls, therefore, hang at an angle of 48.59° relative to the boom. We also know that the boom makes an angle, *CAB,* of 48.59° with the mast, because the latter and the falls are parallel; and we know that the boom makes an angle, *BAD,* of 41.41° with the deck (90° − 48.59°).

On the sketch, we draw a horizontal line, *BX,* from the top of the boom to the mast; this line will be the same length, 30 feet, as the distance from the mast to the point plumbed by the falls, *AD.* We now determine the height of the boom relative to the mast, *AX,* again by the law of sines, using the right triangle, *AXB.* Since the boom is 40 feet long, we write:

$$\frac{AX}{\sin 41.41°} = \frac{40 \text{ feet}}{\sin 90°}$$

AX, therefore, equals 26.4577 feet, which we shall call 26.5 feet.

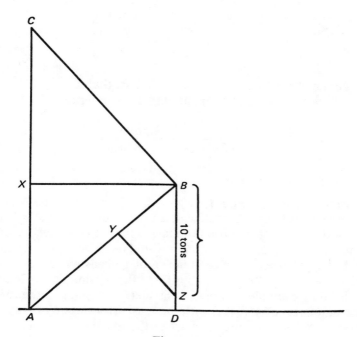

Figure 6-6.

The horizontal line, *BX*, from the top of the boom therefore meets the mast 26.5 feet above the deck, and as the head of the mast is 60 feet above the deck, the head, *C*, is 33.5 feet above *X* (60' − 26.5').

Next we find the angle made by the topping lift with the mast, in the triangle *XCB*. As horizontal *XB* is 30 feet in length, and the head is 33.5 feet above where this line reaches the mast, the tangent of the angle *BCX* formed by the lift and the mast is 30 ft/33.5 ft, or 0.8955, which makes the angle 41.8452°.

By drawing a line, *YZ*, from the boom to the falls parallel to the topping lift *CB*, we have the triangle *BZY*, which enables us to determine the compression load on the boom, and the tension on the topping lift. If the length of the line *BZ* represents the 10-ton load, by the law of sines, the length *BY* represents the compression load on the boom, and the length *YZ* the tension on the lift. Since we have found the angle made by the mast and boom, *CAB*, to be 48.5904°, and as the falls and mast are parallel, the angle *YBZ* also is 48.5904°. Furthermore, the angle *YBZ* must equal the angle *ACB* formed by the mast and lift, which is 41.8452°. In the triangle *BYZ*, *B* is 48.5904°, and *Z* is 41.8452°; the angle, *Y*, therefore, must equal 89.5644° (180° − 48.5904° − 41.8452°). Using the law of sines, we now write:

$$\frac{BY}{\sin 41.8452° \ (\angle Z)} = \frac{10 \text{ tons}}{\sin 89.5644°}$$

$$BY = 6.6714 \text{ tons}$$

The compression load on the boom, *BY*, is, therefore, 6.6714 tons. To find the tension on the topping lift, *YZ*, we write:

$$\frac{YZ}{\sin 48.5904°} = \frac{10 \text{ tons}}{\sin 89.5644°}$$

$$YZ = 7.50 \text{ tons}$$

The tension on the topping lift, *YZ*, is, therefore, 7.50 tons.

By the same process, we could calculate the compression load on the mast, and the strain on a shroud or stay supporting the masthead, and opposite the topping lift. The solution would be as in the first example, in which, having been given the tension of a headstay, we calculated the compression load on the bowsprit and the tension on the bobstay.

In this latter example, the mast is 60 feet in length, and the topping lift forms an angle of 41.8452° with the mast. If a shroud or stay leads from the deck 30 feet from the mast to the masthead, and is directly opposite the lift, the compression load on the mast is 15.59 tons, and the tensile load on the shroud is 11.19 tons.

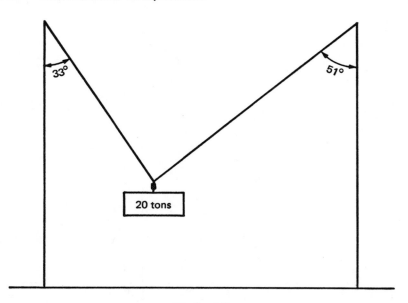

Figure 6-7.

Span Loads

If the two parts of a span form equal angles with the vertical, each leg will carry an equal load. In many cases, however, the angles will not be equal, and the loads on the legs will differ.

The load on each leg of a span can be readily calculated by means of the calculator. The angle each part of the span forms with the vertical can usually be determined by eye with sufficient accuracy for practical purposes; in critical cases it should be determined by solution of right triangles.

Let us suppose that a weight of 20 tons is suspended from a span, one part of which forms an angle of 33° with the vertical, while the other part forms an angle of 51° (see Figure 6-7), and we wish to determine the tension on each part of the span.

To assist in visualizing the problem you can sketch a triangle; see Figure 6-8. Side c is vertical, and its length represents the load of 20 tons. Side a represents the more nearly horizontal leg of the span; angle B is 51°. Side b represents the other leg of the span, and angle A is 33°. Angle C, therefore, must equal 96° [180° − (51° + 33°)]. Solution is by the law of sines, using 84° (180° − 96°) for angle C:

$$\frac{a}{\sin 33°(\angle A)} = \frac{20 \text{ tons}(c)}{\sin 96°(\angle C)}$$

$$a = 10.9528 \text{ tons}$$

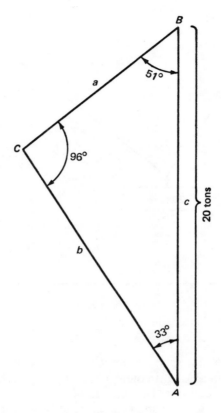

Figure 6-8.

Bear in mind that the more nearly horizontal the legs of a span are, the greater will be the tension on each leg. Thus, in the span we considered, if the angle each leg formed with the vertical were increased by 10°, so that the angles were 61° and 43°, the solution to the ratio would be that the tensile loads on the legs would increase to 18.03 tons and 14.06 tons, respectively.

Wind-Generated Pressure on a Ship

Much study has been devoted to determining the force that winds exert on a vessel. Some findings have been contradictory, probably because of the great fluctuations in wind speed over a very brief period of time. However, it is believed that, under most conditions, the following formula will give acceptable results:

$$P = 0.004 \times v^2$$

where P is the pressure in pounds per square foot of frontal area, and v is the wind velocity in knots.

For a vessel at anchor, P will be increased owing to surge and yaw. With fresh winds, this factor may be considered to have a value of about 33%; under highly adverse conditions it may be much greater, if the vessel is yawing considerably. Excessive yawing may, of course, be reduced if two anchors, with considerable spread between them, are laid out.

Example: A vessel has a total frontal area of 2,500 square feet. What would be the approximate wind pressure on her if she were lying to a single anchor in a protected anchorage with a 30-knot wind blowing?

We would write the formula:

$$P = 0.004 \times 2,500 \times 900 = 9,000$$

If she were lying true to the wind, the pressure generated by the wind would, therefore, be in the neighborhood of 9,000 lb. If she were yawing somewhat, the pressure might approach 12,000 lb.

Draft of a Steamer When Heeled

Ships that have more or less rectangular midships sections increase their draft when heeled. That increase may be approximated by the formula:

$$\text{Increase in draft} = \text{sine angle of heel} \times \frac{\text{ship's beam}}{2}$$

Example: Our steamer has a beam of 64 feet 6 inches, and is drawing 24 feet 9 inches. We wish to determine her approximate draft when she is inclined 9°. The formula becomes:

$$\text{Increase in draft} = \sin 9° \times \frac{64.5 \text{ feet}}{2} = 5.05$$

The increase in draft, therefore, is 5.05 feet, or 5 feet 0.6 inch. When the ship is heeled 9°, her approximate draft to the nearest inch will, therefore, be 29 feet 10 inches (24'9" + 5'1").

Sailing to Weather

It is axiomatic that success in the majority of sailing races hinges on the boat's performance to weather. With the mark dead to weather, if the boat can harden her wind slightly, the distance to the mark is somewhat reduced. Conversely, if she must bear off, as in a steep head sea, in order to maintain speed, the distance to the mark is considerably increased.

The calculator can be used to advantage to determine the increase or decrease in the distance to be sailed as the heading relative to the wind is changed. If the boat has a good speed log, the optimum heading on the wind can readily be determined. All that is required is to weigh changes in speed, considered as percentages, against changes in distance, also considered as percentages.

Leeway enters into the problem, but it is imponderable; it varies with hull form, wind speed, and sea state. Allowance for leeway must therefore be made by the skipper, based on his own experience. The only safe generality here is that for any given wind and sea condition, a sailboat tends to make less leeway when moving rapidly than when moving slowly.

The distance a boat must sail to reach a mark dead to weather is best expressed as a percentage of the actual distance to the mark. This percentage may be found by the formula:

$$D = \frac{200}{\text{sine angle between boards}} \times \text{sine attack angle}$$

where D is the percentage of the distance to the mark, the angle between boards is the angle through which the boat tacks when on the wind, and the attack angle is the angle off the wind when sailing; that is, one half the angle between boards.

Example: We wish to determine the distance to be sailed to a mark 6.5 miles dead to weather if the boat tacks (1) through 84°, (2) through 90°, and (3) through 96°.

(1) In this case, the formula is written:

$$D = \frac{200}{\sin 84°} \times \sin 42° = 134.6\%$$

and

$$6.5 \times 134.6\% = 8.75$$

When tacking through 84°, therefore, we must sail 8.75 miles.

(2) Here, the formula is written:

$$D = \frac{200}{\sin 90°} \times \sin 45° = 141.4\%$$

and

$$6.5 \times 141.4\% = 9.19$$

When tacking through 90°, therefore, we must sail 9.19 miles.

(3) In this instance, the formula is written:

$$D = \frac{200}{\sin 96°} \times \sin 48° = 149.5\%$$

and

$$6.5 \times 149.5\% = 9.71$$

When tacking through 96°, therefore, we must sail 9.71 miles.

It is obvious from the above solutions that a considerable increase in speed is necessary to justify bearing off from the normal attack angle. We can see that if we ordinarily tack through 90°, but then change, and tack through 96°, we must increase our speed by about 6% to justify the additional distance we must sail: $\left(\dfrac{100}{9.19} \times 9.71 = 105.7\%\right)$.

Tacking Down Wind

When Lee Mark is Dead to Leeward

In light going, a sailboat running can ordinarily increase her speed if she hardens her wind. The problem then is to determine whether the increase in speed will more than offset the additional distance it will be necessary to sail to the mark after hardening up.

In considering this problem, vagaries of the weather must be ruled out, and, it must be assumed that the wind will remain steady in both direction and speed. When there is a shift in either wind force or direction, a new problem is created, and a new solution will be required. We shall start by considering the problem when the next mark is dead to leeward.

The first step is to determine the increased speed for a given angle of divergence from the base course: usually this angle is 10°. This process is repeated as often as seems desirable, again ordinarily using increments of 10°, and noting the speed on each divergence angle.

In the interests of simplicity, we shall assume that we shall make only two legs in running to the mark. In practice, this might not be a desirable procedure, as it might take us too far from the rhumb line. For any given angle of divergence from the rhumb line, the distance sailed will remain the same, regardless of the number of legs.

The total distance sailed for a given angle of divergence from the base line can be determined from the following formula, which is based on the law of sines:

$$\text{Total distance sailed} = \frac{2 \times \text{base distance} \times \text{sine divergence angle}}{\text{sine (divergence angle} \times 2)}$$

Knowing the speed for each divergence angle, and also the total distance to be sailed if that divergence is used, the divergence angle that will permit arrival at the lee mark in the least time can be readily determined.

Example: The lee mark is distant exactly 10 miles, and when we sail directly for it, our speedometer shows 5.0 knots. When we harden up 10°, our speed increases to 5.25 knots; hardened 20°, it is 5.65 knots, and at 30° it is 6.0 knots. What is the optimum divergence angle?

First we list the divergence angles, as shown in Table 6-7, and note the speed for each divergence angle. Next, we use the formula above to calculate the total distance sailed for each divergence angle, and note the results. Last, we determine how long it will take us to reach the mark for each divergence angle. The table shows that we shall get to the mark in the least time if we harden our wind 20°.

When Lee Mark is Not Dead to Leeward

Determining the best course to select for tacking down wind, when the lee mark is not dead to leeward, presents a slightly different problem, as the two legs will not be of equal length. As a general rule, it would be wisest to sail directly for the mark unless the divergence between the course and the true wind is fairly small, say in the neighborhood of 10°.

Let us assume that such a divergence exists and that the wind will remain steady. To determine the gain to be derived from hardening up, we proceed as in the previous example to obtain our increase in speed, but in smaller increments, say, 5° each.

We next calculate the distance to be sailed to the mark for each relative heading, bearing in mind that the headings relative to the wind must, in this case, be converted to headings relative to the base line to the lee mark, and that each heading relative to the wind must be solved for two headings relative to the base line. Thus, if the mark bears 000°, the wind is from 185° (or blowing in the direction 005°), and we propose to harden the wind 20°, the heading for the long leg would be 345° (005° − 20°), and that for the short leg would be 025° (005° + 20°). We have then, a triangle two of whose angles are 15° (360° − 345°) and

Table 6-7

Divergence angle in degrees	Speed in knots or mph	Distance to sail in miles	Time required in hours
0	5.0	10.0	2.0
10	5.25	10.15	1.935
20	5.65	10.64	1.88
30	6.00	11.54	1.923

025°, and whose third angle must, consequently, be 140° [180° − (15° + 25°)].

The distances on the two headings can be determined by the law of sines:

$$\sin \angle A : a :: \sin \angle B : b :: \sin \angle C : c$$

Set the sine of the angle between the two headings to the direct distance to the mark, and under the sine of the larger angle read the distance on the long leg, and under the sine of the smaller angle, read the distance on the short leg.

Enter these two distances, together with their sum, opposite the appropriate wind divergence angle on a form, as shown in the example below. The length of each leg, rather than only the sum of the two, should be entered, as it may be necessary to determine the time to gybe on the basis of the length of the first leg, or the time spent on the leg. Also enter the speed obtained on that divergence angle and the compass headings for the two legs.

Next, calculate the lengths of the legs when the wind is hardened an additional 5°, and enter them, together with their sum, the speed obtained on this divergence angle, and the compass headings for the two legs on the form. This process is repeated in 5° increments. The number of increments required will depend on the sailing characteristics of the boat, and can be determined only by experience.

The final step is to determine the time required to sail the two legs for each divergence angle at the speed obtained on that angle. This is done by means of the ratio

Speed : 1 hour, or 60 minutes :: Sum of distance on the two
legs : total time required   (1)

and these total times are entered in the form.

An inspection will then determine the wind divergence angle that will enable the boat to reach the lee mark in minimum time.

Example: The distance to the lee mark is 10.0 miles, and the direction is 090°. The true wind is from 260°; its divergence from the direction of the mark is therefore 10°. When sailing directly for the mark, our speed is 4.6 knots.

After hardening up 5°, heading 095°, our speed is 4.9 knots.
After hardening up 10°, heading 100°, our speed is 5.25 knots.
After hardening up 15°, heading 105°, our speed is 5.45 knots.

We require the optimum heading, to reach the mark in the least time.

As in the previous example, the first step is to determine the total distance we shall have to sail each time we harden the wind, as well as the distance on each leg. In each instance, one long and one short leg will be involved; however, if the distance is considerable, it will be wise to sail two or more long and two or more short legs, in order not to depart too far from the base line. In any case, the total distance to be sailed, as well as distance or distances to be sailed on the long and short legs may be obtained from a single solution for one long leg and one short leg.

We next determine what the compass headings will be for each divergence angle from the wind. In this example they will be 095° (080° + 15°) and 065° (080° − 15°), 100° and 060°, and 105° and 55°.

We enter these data in a form, as follows:

Headings	Divergence from wind in degrees	Speed in knots	Distance on long leg in miles	Distance on short leg in miles	Total distance in miles	Total time in minutes
090°	10	4.6			10	
095° and 065°	15	4.9				
100° and 060°	20	5.25				
105° and 055°	25	5.45				

We next calculate the lengths of the long and short legs for each divergence angle from the wind. Thus, when the wind divergence angle is 15°, our headings will be 095° and 065°; as the mark bears 090°, we shall first be 5° and then 25° away from its present bearing. We thus have two angles whose sines will supply the lengths of the two legs, when used in conjunction with the direct distance to the mark, and the angle between the first leg, 095°, and the second leg, 065°.

Using the law of sines and the ratio

$$\sin 30° : 10.00 \text{ miles} :: \sin 25° : \text{long leg, and } \sin 5° : \text{short leg} \quad (2)$$

we find the long leg will be 8.45 miles, and the short leg will be 1.74 miles, making the total distance to be sailed 10.19 miles when we harden the wind 15°.

We repeat the process for the next wind divergence angle, 20°. In this instance the headings sailed will be 100° and 060°, so we shall first sail 10° and then 30° away from the bearing of the mark. The difference between the two headings, 100° and 060°, is 40°. Using this, and the direct distance to the mark 10.00, by means of the law of sines, we find that the long leg will be 7.78 miles, and the short leg 2.70 miles, giving a total distance to sail of 10.48 miles.

The process is repeated a third time for a wind divergence angle of 25°. Here the headings sailed are 105° and 055°, and by the law of sines, we find the long leg to be 7.49 miles, and the short to be 3.38 miles, for a total distance sailed of 10.87 miles.

These data can now be entered in the appropriate columns in the form, and all that remains is to find the time required to reach the mark for the various wind divergence angles, using the ratio (1) above:

Speed : 60 minutes : : distance : required time

Thus, for the wind divergence angle 15°, we have:

4.9 knots : 60 minutes : : 10.19 miles : 124.75 minutes

For the wind divergence angle 20°, we have:

5.25 knots : 60 minutes : : 10.48 miles : 119.7 minutes

and, coincidentally, the wind divergence angle of 25° also yields a time of 119.7 minutes.

These data are now entered in the form, as shown below, and we note that a wind divergence angle of 20° is the most desirable, as it combines the best obtainable elapsed time with the most direct route to the mark.

Headings	Divergence from wind in degrees	Speed in knots	Distance on long leg in miles	Distance on short leg in miles	Total distance in miles	Total time in minutes
090°	10	4.6	—	—	10.00	130.4
095° and 065°	15	4.9	8.45	1.74	10.19	124.75
100° and 060°	20	5.25	7.78	2.70	10.48	119.7
105° and 055°	25	5.45	7.49	3.38	10.87	119.7

The fact that the last two times are the same shows that we need not try additional headings, because the increased distances will offset any expected gains in speed.

Further, if no change in wind speed or direction could be foreseen, with two divergence angles that would permit us to reach the mark at the same time, we would, as a matter of sound racing tactics, select the one that would keep us nearer to the base line to the mark.

This solution seems rather lengthy; however, with some practice, solutions to this type of problem may be obtained very rapidly.

A somewhat similar problem arises occasionally on a reach in light going, when the wind is a little too far forward to permit carrying a spinnaker. Under such conditions, it may pay to harden your wind somewhat and close reach above the direct course to the mark carrying a #1 Genoa, then bear off for the mark under a spinnaker when it will draw. If such a maneuver is adopted, the additional distance to be covered is determined as in the above problem.

Draft Variation of a Sailboat When Heeled

A deep-draft sailboat, when heeled, draws less than when she is upright. The exact reduction in draft depends on the shape of the cross section of the keel at its deepest point. However, the reduction can be closely approximated by the formula:

Inclined draft = cosine angle of inclination × draft when upright

Example: Let us assume that, when upright, our sloop draws 6 feet, and we wish to determine her approximate draft when she is heeled 30°. We write the formula:

$$\text{Inclined draft} = \cos 30° \times 6 \text{ feet} = 5.2$$

When our sloop is heeled 30°, her approximate draft is, therefore, 5.2 feet, or 5 feet 2.4 inches.

If the boat has a keel of rectangular cross section and of known thickness, further refinement in determining draft when heeled may be obtained. The depth to be added to the inclined draft, as previously determined, may be found by the ratio:

$$\sin 90° : \frac{\text{keel thickness}}{2} :: \sin \text{angle of inclination} : \text{additional depth}$$

Thus, if our sloop had such a keel 6 inches thick, for the above example we would write:

$$\sin 90° : 3 \text{ inches} :: \sin 30° : 1.5 \text{ inches}$$

The increase in draft due to the keel thickness, therefore, is 1.5 inches, and the total draft at an angle of inclination of 30° would be 5 feet 3.9 inches.

Small angles of inclination achieve very little reduction in draft. Our boat, which normally draws 6 feet, would draw only slightly less than 5 feet 11 inches if heeled 10°, and if heeled 20°, her draft would be about 5 feet 7¾ inches. If we have the misfortune of putting her aground, and if the point of greatest draft is pretty well aft, it would be best first to try getting her off by putting the crew all the way forward in the eyes.

Conversion Tables

The following conversion tables for length, mass, speed, and volume have been adapted from the Corrected Reprint, 1962, of U.S. Naval Oceanographic Office, H.O. Pub. No. 9 (Bowditch).

Length		*Equivalent Values to Five Decimal Places*
1 inch	=	25.4 millimeters*
1 inch	=	2.54 centimeters*
1 foot	=	0.3048 meter*
1 yard	=	0.9144 meter*
1 fathom	=	6 feet*
1 fathom	=	1.8288 meters*
1 cable (U. S.)	=	720 feet*
1 cable (British)	=	0.1 nautical mile*
1 cable (British)	=	607.6 feet
1 statute mile	=	5,280 feet*
1 statute mile	=	1,609.344 meters*
1 statute mile	=	0.86898 nautical mile
1 nautical mile	=	6,076.11549 feet
1 nautical mile	=	2,025.37183 yards
1 nautical mile	=	1,852.0 meters*
1 nautical mile	=	1.15078 statute miles
1 meter	=	39.37008 inches
1 meter	=	3.28084 feet
1 meter	=	1.09361 yards
1 meter	=	0.54681 fathom
1 kilometer	=	3,280.83990 feet
1 kilometer	=	1,093.61330 yards
1 kilometer	=	0.62137 statute mile
1 kilometer	=	0.53996 nautical mile

Mass		
1 ounce	=	437.5 grains*
1 ounce	=	28.34952 grams
1 ounce	=	0.0625 pound*
1 pound	=	7,000 grains*
1 pound	=	0.45359 kilogram
1 short ton	=	2,000 pounds*
1 short ton	=	907.18474 kilograms*
1 short ton	=	0.90718 metric ton
1 short ton	=	0.89286 long ton

* Exact relationship.

Mass (*cont.*)		*Equivalent Values to* *Five Decimal Places*
1 displacement ton	=	2,240 pounds*
1 long ton	=	2,240 pounds*
1 long ton	=	1.12 short tons*
1 long ton	=	1,016.04691 kilograms
1 long ton	=	1.01605 metric tons
1 kilogram	=	2.20462 pounds
1 kilogram	=	0.00110 short ton
1 kilogram	=	0.00098 long ton
1 metric ton	=	1,000 kilograms*
1 metric ton	=	2,204.62262 pounds
1 metric ton	=	1.10231 short tons
1 metric ton	=	0.98421 long ton

Speed

1 yard per minute	=	0.03409 statute mile per hour
1 yard per minute	=	0.02962 knot
1 yard per minute	=	0.01524 meter per second*
1 statute mile per hour	=	88 feet per minute*
1 statute mile per hour	=	29.33333 yards per minute
1 statute mile per hour	=	1.60934 kilometers per hour
1 statute mile per hour	=	1.46667 feet per second
1 statute mile per hour	=	0.86898 knot
1 statute mile per hour	=	0.44704 meter per second*
1 knot	=	1.68781 feet per second
1 knot	=	101.26859 feet per minute
1 knot	=	33.75620 yards per minute
1 knot	=	1.852 kilometers per hour*
1 knot	=	1.15078 statute miles per hour
1 knot	=	0.51444 meter per second
1 kilometer per hour	=	0.62137 statute mile per hour
1 kilometer per hour	=	0.53996 knot
1 meter per second	=	196.85039 feet per minute
1 meter per second	=	65.61680 yards per minute
1 meter per second	=	3.6 kilometers per hour*
1 meter per second	=	3.28084 feet per second
1 meter per second	=	2.23694 statute miles per hour
1 meter per second	=	1.94384 knots

Volume

1 cubic foot	=	1,728 cubic inches*
1 cubic foot	=	7.48052 U. S. gallons

* Exact relationship.

Volume (cont.)

Equivalent Values to Five Decimal Places

1 cubic foot	=	6.22884 British imperial gallons
1 cubic foot	=	0.02832 cubic meter
1 cubic foot	=	28.31606 liters
1 cubic yard	=	46,656 cubic inches*
1 cubic yard	=	201.97401 U. S. gallons
1 cubic yard	=	168.17859 British imperial gallons
1 cubic yard	=	0.76455 cubic meter
1 cubic yard	=	764.53368 liters
1 cubic meter (stere)	=	264.17203 U. S. gallons
1 cubic meter (stere)	=	219.96924 British imperial gallons
1 cubic meter (stere)	=	35.31467 cubic feet
1 cubic meter (stere)	=	1.30795 cubic yards
1 U. S. gallon	=	3,785.39848 cubic centimeters†
1 U. S. gallon	=	231 cubic inches*
1 U. S. gallon	=	0.13368 cubic foot
1 U. S. gallon	=	3.78531 liters†
1 U. S. gallon	=	0.83267 British imperial gallon
1 British imperial gallon	=	1.20095 U. S. gallons
1 liter	=	1,000.028 cubic centimeters
1 liter	=	1.05672 U. S. quarts
1 liter	=	0.26418 U. S. gallon
1 register ton	=	100 cubic feet*
1 register ton	=	2.83168 cubic meters*
1 measurement ton	=	40 cubic feet*
1 measurement ton	=	1 freight ton*
1 freight ton	=	40 cubic feet*
1 freight ton	=	1 measurement ton*

Speed of Sound

Sound in dry air at 60°F and standard sea-level pressure	=	1,116.99 feet per second
	=	761.59 statute miles per hour
	=	661.80 knots
	=	340.46 meters per second
Sound in 3.485% salt water at 60°F	=	4,945.37 feet per second
	=	1,648.46 yards per second

* Exact relationship.
† A better conversion is:
      1 U. S. gallon = 3,785.411784 cubic centimeters*
                      = 3.78541 liters

Speed of Sound (*cont.*)

Equivalent Values to
Five Decimal Places

= 3,371.85 statute miles per hour
= 2,930.05 knots
= 1,507.35 meters per second

Volume-Mass

1 cubic foot of seawater	=	64 pounds
1 cubic foot of fresh water	=	62.428 pounds at temperature of maximum density (4°C = 39.2°F)
1 cubic foot of ice	=	56 pounds
1 displacement ton	=	35 cubic feet of seawater
	=	1 long ton

Bibliography

Ball, John A., *Algorithms for RPN Calculators,* John Wiley & Sons, New York, 1978.

Bowditch, *American Practical Navigator,* H.O. Pub. No. 9, U. S. Naval Oceanographic Office, Washington, D.C., 1966.

Buchanek, J., and Bergin, E., *Piloting/Navigation with the Pocket Calculator,* Tab Books, Blue Ridge Summit, Pennsylvania, 1976.

Budlong, John P., *Sky and Sextant (Practical Celestial Navigation),* Van Nostrand Reinhold Company, New York, 1975.

Cotter, Charles H., *A History of Nautical Astronomy,* Hollis & Carter, London, 1968.

Dunlap, G. D., and Shufeldt, H. H., *Dutton's Navigation and Piloting,* Twelfth Edition, United States Naval Institute, Annapolis, 1969.

Hobbs, Richard R., *Marine Navigation 1, Piloting,* United States Naval Institute, Annapolis, 1974.

Hobbs, Richard R., *Marine Navigation 2, Celestial and Electronic,* United States Naval Institute, Annapolis, 1974.

Jones, Aubrey, *Mathematical Astronomy with a Pocket Calculator,* John Wiley & Sons, New York, 1978.

Letcher, John S., Jr., *Self-Contained Celestial Navigation with H.O. 208,* International Marine Publishing Company, Camden, Maine, 1977.

Mechtly, E. A., *The International System of Units,* NASA SP-7012, U. S. Government Printing Office, Washington, D.C., 1973.

Melluish, R. K., *An Introduction to the Mathematics of Map Projections,* Cambridge University Press, London, 1931.

Mills, H. R., *Positional Astronomy and Astro-Navigation Made Easy*, John Wiley & Sons, New York, 1978.

Mueller, Ivan I., *Spherical and Practical Astronomy as Applied to Geodesy*, Fredric Ungar Publishing Co., Inc., 1969.

Norton, A. P., and Inglis, J. G., *Norton's Star Atlas*, Fifteenth Edition, Gall and Inglis, Edinburgh, 1964.

O'Neil, W. M., *Time and the Calendars*, Sydney University Press, Australia, 1975.

Podmore, J. L., *The Slide Rule for Sea and Air Navigation*, Brown, Son & Ferguson, Ltd., Glasgow, 1974.

Rogoff, Mortimer, *Calculator Navigation*, W. W. Norton & Co., New York, 1979.

Shufeldt, H. H., *Slide Rule for the Mariner*, United States Naval Institute, Annapolis, 1972.

Smart, W. M., *Text-Book on Spherical Astronomy*, Fifth Edition, Cambridge University Press, Cambridge, 1971.

Almanac for Computers 1980, Nautical Almanac office, U. S. Naval Observatory, Washington, D.C. 20390 (published each year).

The Star Almanac for Land Surveyors for the Year 1980, H. M. Nautical Almanac Office, Her Majesty's Stationery Office, London (published each year).

Index

The text of this book is set in ten-point Times Roman with two points of leading by Bi-Comp Inc., York, Pennsylvania.

The book was printed and bound by Fairfield Graphics, Fairfield, Pennsylvania.